MELISSA EXPLAINS IT ALL

Melissa

EXPLAINS IT ALL

TALES FROM MY ABNORMALLY NORMAL LIFE

MELISSA JOAN HART

WITH KRISTINA GRISH

ST. MARTIN'S PRESS ☙ NEW YORK

www.stmartins.com

All photographs are courtesy of the author except where otherwise noted.

Library of Congress Cataloging-in-Publication Data

Hart, Melissa Joan, 1976–
    Melissa explains it all : tales from my abnormally normal life /
by Melissa Joan Hart. — First edition
        pages cm
    ISBN 978-1-250-03283-6 (hardcover)
    ISBN 978-1-250-03284-3 (e-book)
   1. Hart, Melissa Joan, 1976–   2. Television actors and actresses—United States—
Biography.   I. Title.
    PN2287.H29A3 2013
    791.45'028'092—dc23
    [B]

                                                               2013020800

10   9   8   7   6   5   4   3   2

For Mom, my guiding light and biggest fan.

For Mark, the love of my life.

For Mason, Brady, and Tucker:
you gave me my favorite role yet.

CONTENTS

MELISSA EXPLAINS IT ALL

INTRODUCTION

For years, people have been asking me why I haven't written a book, and my answer is always the same: Because I don't know how it ends yet. I was talking about my book and my life, because the most satisfying end to any book is when the main character dies. But then I thought about this and realized that I'm not sure how I'd make the two coincide in a memoir. Without getting too dark, my life could be snuffed out before I get to write a book or I could end up in a straitjacket that doesn't let me use my hands. So I decided to just do it. Better now than never.

So here it is finally. And I could kill Oprah for going off the air before she could have me on to promote it.

When people meet me, they want to know what it was like growing up a child star, if I keep in touch with old cast mates, what happened during my half-naked-photo-shoot phase, how I spend private time with my husband and kids, about my best "mom advice," what it was like to work with certain celebrities, and if I'm as "normal" as they think I am. The short answers are: cool, sometimes, drugs, snuggles, wing it, fun, sometimes. If you want to hear me dig a little deeper, you'll need to keep turning the pages.

You may have even bought this book hoping I'd tell you how to get your child into Hollywood, meet your dream guy, vote, or raise your kids. But I'm not big on lectures, and if you wanted an advice book written by a '90s teen star, you should've bought one by Jennifer Love Hewitt or Alicia Silverstone. I like to think of myself as more of a storyteller, so that's what I'll attempt to do throughout these stories—lie on my imaginary couch and tell tales from my life that I hope will explain me to you.

This doesn't mean I haven't learned *anything* from my past thirty-something years in this world. So I will now share with you my top twelve life lessons. They all relate to themes or stories you'll find in this book. I hope they're helpful. Follow them at your own risk.

1. Editors don't like when you overuse exclamation points, so don't do this when you write your own book. Save it for Twitter!!!!

It was also hard to write without smiley faces and LOLs to get my tone across. I hope you'll tell people that this made you LMFAO anyway. Oh, and by the way, this book totally MAGG (makes a great gift)!

2. Own a lucky dress.

It doesn't have to be fancy, expensive, or covered in pennies and rabbits' feet. You'll know it works when good stuff happens while wearing it. Owning lucky lingerie can be helpful too, but that's a whole other book.

3. If you want the world to see you as a "good girl," don't party hard or often, unless it's with my mom.

Preferably in a wig and go-go boots. Her, not you.

4. Tequila always leads to a memorable night, one way or another.

Best-case scenario: you'll make new friends. Worst case: those friends will encourage you to get into a hot tub with no water or ride the bull at a Mexican nightclub. Err on the side of caution and bring along some sober friends to save your ass if you need it.

5. If you ever find yourself in a situation where you're exhausted and miked, don't make crass jokes. People who bravely bash you while hiding behind their computer screens will care too much.

Other inconvenient times to forget you're miked: when you get the burps from soda, have "Gangnam Style" stuck in your head, or if you dish about a roll in the hay from the night before.

6. The best part of being the boss is that you get to be bossy.

People like to say there's no "I" in team, but I never understood why this matters if you're in charge. You can also transpose the letters in the word "team" to get "meat," and that has nothing to do with running an efficient business either.

7. Always eat a spoonful of lentil soup on New Year's Day.

It brings good fortune and is full of B vitamins. Counting your coins is so much more fun when you have lower stress and depression, less PMS, a sharper memory, and a lower risk of heart disease.

8. Never wear mascara.

I borrowed this one from Mom, but I tell everyone it'll make your lashes thinner than an Olsen twin by the time you're twenty-eight. Forget I said this if you want to offer me a contract to be the face of Maybelline.

9. Know when to ask for help.

If your own skills make you look wretched, chubby, or lame with a hot iron, lean on people who can make you seem pretty, slim, and not smell like burnt hair. Always give them credit for this, or you'll seem like a tool. And then no one will be there to fix the streaks from your self-tanning experiments except you.

10. "Having it all" means holding your baby in one hand and drinking a Bloody Mary through a straw in the other, while your sweet and hunky husband massages your neck.

Bonus points if you can do this while running a conference call on your cell phone, taking the Xbox controller from your other, misbehaving kids, and keeping your slicked-back ponytail in place. (Note: I only achieved this once. But, man, that day I really had it all!)

11. If you get caught carrying sex toys through airport security, hold your head high and own it.

This goes for vibrators, furry handcuffs, and any sort of edible undergarments. Maybe you wanted a snack for the plane ride; they don't know. Lots of women have worked hard to earn us these sexual freedoms, and no TSA person can ever take that away from you.

12. The only regrets you should have are for the things you didn't have the guts to do.

Don't let fear get in the way of speaking your mind, kissing your coworkers, or jumping off cliffs with thirty-foot drops. Keep reading, and you'll know what I mean.

Love,
Melissa

Chapter 1

CHAMPAGNE WISHES AND CLAM-FREE DREAMS

Actors often joke that show business should be called "the broke business." *Us Weekly* only writes about celebrities who've made it big enough to have massive homes, designer clothes, and swank personal lives. But most entertainment people actually struggle their whole careers to succeed in music, movies, or TV—only to end up as background artists, stand-ins, and piano men at their local pubs. Lucky for me and my family, my career started rolling at four years old and hasn't stopped since. In fact, it helped rescue us from being broke, rather than caused it.

I come from a long line of blue-collar folks who pride themselves on their hardscrabble work ethic. Dad was a twenty-year-old cabdriver in Northport, New York, when he met my mom and got her a job as a cab dispatcher at the age of sixteen. Four years later, when they got pregnant with me and decided to have a shotgun wedding in the backyard of my grandparents' house (I guess all that "free love" of the '70s came with some consequences), Dad had just started working with his brother Charlie, breeding clams and oysters at Charlie's shop on Long Island. Every night, Dad came home from work in his dirty T-shirts and cut-off jean shorts, with grime under his fingernails and smelling like low tide. But Mom didn't mind at all. She knew what it was like to pound the pavement, too, since she occasionally sold trippy tie-dyed baby tees at street fairs, and after I was born, spent the next ten years either pregnant or breast-feeding my siblings, Trisha, Elizabeth, Brian, and Emily, all while managing our acting gigs. Mom and Dad were also following in their parents' footsteps. Dad's mom, Ethel, worked as a phone operator to support her four children when her husband died just weeks after my dad was born, and my mom's father was a plumber, willing to build or fix anything for anyone to help support his wife and kids. So from a young age, I was aware that you had to work hard to pay for the things you needed or wanted—and for what your family needed or wanted, too.

My parents never let on about any financial stress or struggle when I was young, though times were hard with a baseball-team-size family and seasonal careers, at best. In fact, my mom almost didn't take me to my callback for Splashy, my first acting gig, because the thirty-dollar train ticket was too expensive. She changed her mind when my manager convinced her I'd make good money if I got the part. But I always felt secure, since we had a house, a car, and food on the table. I never had a reason to feel that other people's lives were better than mine.

My parents did a good job helping us feel happy and safe, so I'd have had to look really close to see how frighteningly broke we were, though the signs were there. For instance, every night Dad dropped his pocket change into a five-gallon water jug in his closet, hoping to save up for his dream boat, a Bertram yacht; Mom routinely dumped it out to give us milk money and pay a neighbor to cut the lawn (the jug never got more than a quarter full). We ate simple homemade meals mostly made with clams, since Dad brought them home from work for free. (To this day, Anthony Bourdain himself couldn't convince Mom to touch a slimy mollusk, in any recipe.) Even at Christmas, when my siblings and I made really long wish lists, thinking Santa was our ticket to rake it in, we were fed the super-confusing line, "Pick five things. Mommy has to pay Santa for the presents." But it really wasn't until the owner of my dance school called me out for wearing torn ballet tights for the third day in a row, in front of all the other girls in their new Danskin wardrobes, that I realized how bad things were and how upset it could make me. Her words stung, especially since I took dancing very seriously and didn't want to be judged for anything but my skill. At least we were able to pay for my classes, and when they exceeded our family's spending limit, this same owner let me student teach the four-year-olds on Saturdays to pay for an extra day of pointe lessons. The little ballerinas called me "Miss Melissa" back then, as I taught them to jeté across the studio. I was only ten years old.

Acting and modeling were mainly how I contributed to the family pot, though it never felt like "work." To this day, I have no clue about how much money I made on a commercial, guest star role, or any other gig until well into my *Clarissa* years. All I remember is that at an early age, I booked a lot of jobs, partly because Mom rewarded me with toys when I did. By the end of my eight-year commercial acting career when I was twelve years old, which nicely corresponded with the age I outgrew plastic figurines, I'd acquired over a hundred Barbies, plus dozens of Strawberry Shortcakes and a bunch of My

Little Ponies. Holidays may not have been lucrative, but working sure was.

While I loved the idea of winning a job, I never worried too much about losing it, for money reasons or otherwise. I liked acting like a goof during auditions, letting nice women do my hair and makeup, and then shooting the commercial, TV show, or movie with encouraging and creative people. Some of my favorite shoots were also very kid-centric and involved junk food, which helped—like a Twinkies commercial at seven years old and a Life Savers Fruit Flavor spot at eleven. In this last one, I played paddleball and checkers with giant Life Savers and kids I knew from the audition scene. (Nobody you'd know, unless you followed kids' commercials.) We did this wearing neon outfits and eating rolls of sticky Life Savers, so I basically rode a major sugar high for eight hours, while dressed like a young Debbie Gibson. What kid wouldn't love to spend her day like this—plus take home the clothes every once in a while?

As soon as they could gurgle and coo, my other four siblings began landing jobs, too. In their own ways, they helped our family pay the bills, and if Mom was shlepping one of us into the city for auditions, she figured she might as well give my siblings the option to join in the fun. My sister Emily's ultrasound was even used in *All My Children* for a pregnant character on the soap (our agent knew about Mom's baby bump and passed along Emily's first "head shot" to the producers). Once she was born, she was supposed to play the baby, but production moved up the shoot date, and since Mom wasn't due for another twelve weeks, she couldn't save the job, short of a scheduled C-section. My siblings and I collaborated sometimes, as when Trisha and I did a Tylenol commercial playing sisters. One of our most fun family performances was a silly little Showtime movie my mom produced many years later, in 1996, called *The Right Connections*.

It starred me, Elizabeth, Brian, Emily, our two-year-old sister Ali from Mom's second marriage—and believe it or not, MC Hammer. We knew it wouldn't win us an Emmy, but it was a blast to be on set with family, cracking jokes and doing our best white-kid rap with Hammer. By then, the guy had blown most of the fortune he'd earned from his music career, and if that wasn't embarrassing enough, here he was being upstaged by my two-year-old sister in a cable movie.

Like anyone, my parents were always trying to move up in the world, so they moved a lot when I was young—first from a friend's converted garage when I was born, then to a condo, and finally to the ranch my dad still lives in. This last house was on a dead end, with only five other homes on the block, and the street was close enough to the railroad that the house shook like an old roller coaster whenever a train passed by. The surrounding woods made it feel like we owned more property than we did, especially in the winter, when the whole neighborhood came over to ice-skate on a nearby pond they thought was ours. (We never corrected them.)

I was in my twenties when my friend Joe, who also grew up in Sayville, teased me about literally living on the "other side of the tracks." This was when I realized that my family raised us in the less affluent area of a rich town. We swam in other people's pools and admired their beautiful homes and pesticide-rich yards. I also coveted their wheels. My sisters, friends, and I played a lot of MASH, a game that's meant to predict the home, spouse, number of kids, and car you'll have as an adult (MASH stood for *man*sion, *a*partment, *s*hack, *h*ouse). This is how I learned about luxury cars like BMWs, Mercedes, Jaguars, and Porsches—all of which made my MASH list, and as an adult, turned out to be the order in which I owned each one. But back then, my parents were often on the outside, looking in. It's hard to keep up with the Joneses when your Oldsmobile doesn't burn rubber.

By contrast, my childhood BFF Nicole, who I met in second grade, also lived in my town but seemed to have it all. She was sweet, gorgeous, and an only child—an enviable trifecta, even for a confident actress with awesome siblings. Because her Dutch-born mom worked for an airline, and her dad was a football coach during the school year and a lifeguard on Fire Island in the summer, Nicole traveled a ton—Paris, Hawaii, Holland— and had a boat. In the summer, she'd invite me to the beach, where we'd sunbathe on her skiff and eat butter-and-Dutch-chocolate-sprinkle sandwiches from a real picnic basket. What a difference from the PB&J my own mom threw in an old Macy's shopping bag when we hit the shore.

Nicole always got a kick out of spending time with my huge, loud, and crazy family, as I envied that Nicole got all her parents' attention and could travel on a whim, since they were a small unit. Meanwhile, my family's vacation splurge was to a corny Poconos time-share at a family ski resort, once a year. My siblings and I thought we were rolling with the homies because we had a "vacation home." After a day on the slopes, we put on our swimsuits and dove into a deep, cherry red bathtub, which we called our "hot tub." We spent hours splashing around and talking about how many times we skied Renegade, the only "serious" black diamond run on the mountain. Years later, my sister Trisha and I went back to the resort during her college winter break and couldn't believe what an anthill Renegade really was. Another surprise: that our tiny "hot tub" only fit two kids, much less five.

As a grown-up, I live on the right side of the tracks, in a well-off coastal suburb outside Manhattan, not so unlike the one I grew up in. I'm not oblivious to the similarities, or the fact that I upgraded from my childhood. But the life my parents gave me offered a perspective I'm grateful for and that some of my neighbors lack. I can see the value of making my boys share a room (in a six-bedroom house), wear hand-me-down clothes, and learn to fix a bike chain and a clogged toilet. So I don't regret my beginnings, because they helped me become a grounded mom, wife, and friend. They also helped me appreciate pool-hopping. Why deal with all that time, money, and maintenance when you can slide on your Havaianas and head to the neighbor's?

By the time my brother was born in 1984 (my mom's fourth child), my siblings and I had found our showbiz grooves—commercials, modeling, voice-overs, soap operas, miniseries, feature films—and thus, began upping our collective finances. And as it worked out, around the same time, Dad started a construction business that began making good money, so our lifestyle got much better. He built an addition to our house, which went from squishing six people into three bedrooms to seven people into four. We only added a second floor and whirlpool tub in my parents' room, but it felt like a mansion. With more gigs coming in, my parents could also put away some of our earnings for college and weddings for the four girls.

The income my siblings and I made now helped with fun "extras" like trips, better holiday presents, and other comforts. Suddenly, Santa was a little more generous, and the shrubs outside our house were full of twinkle lights, since we could afford a higher electric bill for a month. We started trading our Poconos time-share for upgraded locations in Breckenridge, Colorado, and Waterville Valley, New Hampshire. If we wanted a new bike, we bought it ourselves. I could also afford to start collecting Franklin Mint Shirley Temple dolls, though I paid in installments. The irony is that now that I have money, I get them free from fans for my birthday.

One of my proudest moments as a kid happened when I was about eight years old, and I asked my dad to build me a clubhouse in our backyard. I was big on naming and forming clubs at the time, which I blame on my love for *Romper Room, The Mickey Mouse Club,* and *Grease*'s Pink Ladies, and I was constantly trying to get neighborhood girls to join. I clearly remember my dad saying, "Sure. If you get three national commercials, I will build you a clubhouse." Perhaps this was our equivalent of "Get straight As, and I'll take you to Baskin-Robbins." I also think Dad was placating me so I'd leave him alone and let him watch his beloved *60 Minutes,* but he shouldn't have doubted the Hart work ethic.

Two months later, I had shot those three commercials, and though Dad was floored—he thought the challenge would take me a year to complete—the man sure did deliver. In just a few weeks, he built me a towering room on stilts, six feet off the ground, made from cleverly reclaimed goods from our yard. He used our old greenhouse roof, complete with skylights, and turned an upside-down picket fence into the clubhouse's exterior walls. Though the place could use a remodel and a fireman's pole, it's still around and has withstood tough hurricanes and rowdy sleepovers with screaming, giddy girls. It will always be my oasis in the sky.

I know it's easy to assume that the Harts had a *Toddlers & Tiaras* situation going on, with parents who got work for their kids to give their own lives purpose and cash flow. But that wasn't the case. Mom and Dad weren't like Joe Simpson or Kris Kardashian-

Jenner, who've been accused of using their kids as a bullet train to success and to making their own situations better. For us, acting was something my siblings and I wanted to do, and Mom made it happen. We were a pretty lively bunch, and acting let us ham it up in front of an audience that gave us more attention than our parents did when we performed dance routines in the living room. What began as entertaining a little girl's dream became a family business, with the perk that the residuals from one national commercial covered an entire year's worth of mortgage payments. Okay, so we walked a fine line—but I did score an awesome clubhouse and a kickass, lifelong career from the deal.

While a lot of "child stars" can become pretty confused or resentful as adults, maybe one of the reasons I turned out so sane is that I wouldn't consider myself a "child star." I was a child with a serious hobby that segued into an amazing career—in the same way the kid who loves to swim becomes an Olympic gold medalist, or the child who practices piano every day becomes a Carnegie Hall performer. As Malcolm Gladwell would say, I put in my ten thousand hours. I simply loved to act, and I didn't care about the rejection, which for me has been key to having such a long career; from a young age, Mom taught me that if I didn't manage my expectations, and take the good with the bad, life would feel like a real pisser. Between work and auditions, I enjoyed a "normal childhood," like other kids on Long Island. I played in the sprinklers in our backyard, climbed trees, hunted frogs, and rode my bike to get Italian ices or to a friend's house to play Battleship.

While our whole family clearly benefited from the money I earned, showbiz was never all about the cash, or else my childhood would have played out very differently. My family would have moved closer to Manhattan or to L.A. for more frequent auditions, and we'd have spent anything we had left on a high-profile publicist instead of refurnishing the cramped home we'd grown to love. All that pressure would've also caused me to obsess over whether casting people liked me, or how upset I'd be if I didn't get a part or a new toy. This would've killed the childlike glee that made me so good at peddling cereal and snacks—and nobody likes to buy Twinkies from a desperate, beaten-down child. The only upside to this fantasy is that I might have dated another child star like Fred Savage, who I always wanted to be my first on-screen kiss. Hey, Fred, if you're reading this, let's grab the families and do dinner. It's on me.

Chapter 2

ROOM TO ROMP

Ask most actors what inspired their love affair with The Business, and they'll tell you about an amazing film or play that made their hearts skip a beat. Octavia Spencer, for example, has said she was first moved by the inspiring and heartbreaking work of *E.T.* Gary Oldman remembers belting out the score to *A Hard Day's Night* when he was just five years old. And both George Clooney and Viola Davis say that 1976's *Network* made a huge impact on their future dreams. When Peter Finch's character roars, "I'm mad as hell and I'm not going to take this anymore!" Viola, for one, says it just blew her mind.

I also remember the stirring words that moved me to be an actor. They went like this: *Romper, bomper, stomper, boo. Tell me, tell me, tell me, do. Magic Mirror, tell me today, did all my friends have fun at play?*

Okay, so it's not Shakespeare. But to a four-year-old, the final monologue of *Romper Room* sounded pretty deep. I especially loved how the cheerful host said these words just before looking into the camera, and then listed all the names of the kids that she said she could see through her special magic mirror—"I can see Jane, and Molly, and Billy, and Gina . . ." Sadly, "Melissa" wasn't too common a name back then, so she never said mine. But while most of my friends just stared back at their TVs, willing this woman and her mildly creepy bumblebee sidekick to notice them, *I* knew there were better ways to be recognized. I had my aha moment.

I need to be on that floor with those kids, I thought. *I need to be on TV.*

I told this to my mom, who was always looking for new ways to entertain me—I was her first child of what would eventually be seven, so she had a lot of energy to spare back then. She called her friend, whose daughter had recently been booked for a small part on a soap opera, and asked her for the name of her manager. Just two weeks later, we met the man on New Year's Eve, and after taking one look at my blond hair and blue eyes, he took the last three hundred dollars my mom had in her savings account to snap some head shots and book my first audition for Splashy, a bathtub toy. Our empty pockets also meant I didn't get a new dress for my big afternoon, so I wore one from my first day of preschool that made me look like I'd jumped right off the pages of an English picture book: a navy blue smocked dress with small, embroidered red roses. It was perfect.

The audition was at 1515 Broadway, in the heart of Times Square. This landmark now houses the Viacom headquarters, including Nickelodeon, which would later produce *Clarissa Explains It All*—but in the early '80s, it was just a random office building dwarfed by Forty-second Street's booming porn and prostitute business. Once I got inside, I quickly scanned the waiting room and noticed that all the girls looked like me—blond hair, blue eyes, big smiles.

Even so, I was booked for the Splashy job. I partly credit my lucky dress, which I'd continue to wear to most of my auditions until I outgrew it. (It still hangs in my closet, in case I ever have a daughter.) But at this, my very first shoot ever, I had lights, cameras, and what felt like a hundred people staring at . . . my four-year-old boobies in a bubble bath. I was mortified. In the end, though, it didn't matter how I looked naked because the client only used shots of my hands in the commercial, and then featured another blond-haired, blue-eyed child's face and body in the ad. I didn't even know I had been replaced until Mom recently told me the story. I've been telling talk show hosts for years that the little nudie girl in that bubble bath is me, even though I secretly wondered why she didn't look familiar.

Splashy was a win for my early career, even if our manager did turn out to be a real swindler. (Rule number one of showbiz: Never give an agent or a manager a dime before booking a gig.) Mom fired him after my fifth audition. She began managing me herself and quickly learned how to promote my all-American looks among the industry's top agents. I became a pro at acting like a little adult to make my mom and the casting people happy. I was officially a working girl (not in a *Pretty Woman* kind of way).

When I was just starting out, I worked mostly in commercials, and my parents rarely fussed over my ability to land the jobs over and over again. They never told me I had a special skill or called all the relatives when I booked a gig. So to me, acting was just something I did in my free time, the way other kids play sports or take ice-skating lessons. In fact, I acted, danced, and joined Brownies, though acting always took priority. Sometimes I'd even miss a dance recital, talent show, or graduation to Girl Scouts so I could make it to an audition or shoot a commercial. But I never thought this happened because my parents were positioning me for a bigger career. More like Mom was learning that our business thrived on relationships, and if we skipped meetings or opportunities, our agents, managers, and casting directors would stop sending me out for jobs.

Commercial auditions were a blast for me, and it helped that they were quick and dirty. My parents didn't have a fax machine and e-mail hadn't been invented yet, so agents sent Mom scripts in the mail or read them to her over the phone, and she'd write down my lines. Then she'd recite them to me (I couldn't read yet) and I'd memorize the part at home, in the car, or in the waiting room of the actual audition. I had the memory of a Bronx Zoo sea lion—I learned my tricks fast and performed them with ease and grace. In the audition room, I'd be in front of two to ten gruff grown-ups, including a casting director, director, producer, and the discerning client. I'd stand on a masking tape X that marked my spot, look right into the camera like the host on *Romper Room,* and say my lines with enthusiasm and boatloads of charm. Ta-da!

"Great, thank you, *next!"* the casting director would shout. On to the next blond kid . . .

After my audition, Mom always treated me and whichever sibling came along to a snack, like a blueberry turnover from Au Bon Pain, broccoli pizza in Midtown, or an ice-cream Chipwich to split. (Seriously—we were too thrifty to buy one for each of us.) Once after an audition in Harlem, I wanted KFC, which meant taking a detour home through a sketchy part of town. Mom told us to roll up our windows and lock the doors, and then she freaked out when a group of men began chasing our car down an alley. She swore up and down that they were after us, but as it turns out, we were just on a one-way street and they were trying to tell us to turn around. We couldn't hear what they were saying because our car was so tightly sealed, but even still, we never trolled for goodies in that neighborhood again.

After a long day in the city, I'd zone out on the ride home. We spent up to twelve hours a week in transit for my jobs, and once a year I'd hear Mom scream about clocking so much time in the car—usually when she reached her breaking point, often during tax season. Don't even get her started on how she went into labor in the Midtown Tunnel when she was pregnant with Lizzie. Usually, though, I'd just close my eyes and fantasize that all the '80s lyrics on the radio were about me. I'm never gonna dance again either, George Michael. I just called to say I love you.

Back on Long Island, elementary school life was significantly less glamorous than I let my peers think. After a few ads ran on TV and in the local papers when I was in fourth grade, and I began to noticeably miss school for auditions and shoots, kids began to ask a lot of questions. Do you ride in a limo? Do you live in a mansion? Do you know ALF?

I dodged answering most of them, usually by changing the subject or rolling my eyes, since it all sounded so stupid and suck-up-y to me. The truth also wasn't half as interesting as their perception. My mom drove a white Oldsmobile station wagon with a wood panel down the side. We lived in our cramped ranch at the end of an isolated block and used my dad's lobster traps as end tables and his old ship's wheel as the top of our coffee table. It would be a few more years before my girlfriends would care that I knew Joey Lawrence but not a puppet alien.

I think all this bobbing and weaving is why I liked running into my audition friends in the city—Joey, Sarah Michelle Gellar, Jennifer Love Hewitt, Soleil Moon Frye, and Lacey Chabert, to name a few. Since we shared the same acting "hobby" and saw each other a lot, I felt like we had this time-consuming interest in common that I didn't share with the kids at home. They just got what I did, and I didn't have to explain it to them. It also helped that I was too young to view my city friends as professional competition, though we were often going for the same roles. (The parents, on the other hand, were in it to win it. Most saw dollar signs from the start.) A lot of times, the means to a job was acting like a kid—like trying to roller-skate for a part on *Another World,* or riding bikes with Joey Lawrence and Soleil Moon Frye during a Ron Howard audition for *Little Shots*—so it hardly felt like we were working. We were encouraged to just be ourselves, so if we got booked for doing our best, we thought we deserved it. Years later Soleil told the press a story, while I was sitting next to her, about how she ran into a little girl in the elevator after auditions for the *Punky Brewster* pilot and was so worried that she didn't get the part because the child told her mom that *she* did. After the interview, I confessed to Soleil that the elevator girl might have been me. I never would have said this to be mean, but I did land a lot of jobs because I was such a confident child. That said, we all know who scored *Punky,* so clearly bravado only goes so far.

Between the ages of four and twelve years old, I booked more than a hundred commercials, including national spots for Life Savers, Twinkies, Arnold Bread, Tylenol, Barbie (sadly, no freebies here), and the first Chrysler minivan. I also kept busy with regional work. I crammed so many lines into my child-size brain that some of them decided to stick around forever, like the commercial I did for Connecticut Natural Gas: *"You can probably*

tell just by looking at me that I've been a homeowner for years! Nice,
isn't it [while gesturing to my giant dollhouse]—Dutch colonial, three
bedrooms, very up to date. But believe me, a big responsibility. Especially
when it comes to saving energy . . ."

I'll spare you the rest, but suffice it to say that reciting ads
took up a lot of my time and gray matter in those early years. In
between, I did some TV work, took on modeling jobs for cata-
logs and ads, acted in feature films, and started to do theater
too. I was an aspiring Shirley Temple—that quintessential child
actress whose success story I worshiped, and whose signed pictures, movie posters, and porcelain dolls I collected and still
have today.

I accomplished a lot of different stuff at a young age, but
commercials could be the most grueling, though not because I
learned pages of dialogue or worked eighteen-hour days. One of
the most challenging jobs I did was a Barbie pony commercial,
because it tested my young discipline and self-control in a big
way. Here, two other girls and I were asked to peek over a table at a row of beautiful, shiny plastic horses. Each one had a
silky mane and a foot raised, as if it were frozen in mid-canter,
but we girls could only *look* at these toys—no touching allowed.

Every time the director yelled "Cut!" a prop stylist rushed to
the table to brush, style, spray, and essentially play with the
horses' hair, which was torture for me, because I wanted in on
the action too. Instead, I had to sit still and do my job on cue.
I'd learned about self-discipline early on, when I worked with
Bill Cosby in a pudding commercial. Every time a giggly, Jell-O-
eating child "misbehaved"—say, mentioned that he had a stom-
achache or asked to trade his chocolate dessert for vanilla—Bill
promptly gave 'em the boot. So from then on, I always respect-
fully did what I was told while flashing a camera-ready smile,
even if it drove me insane.

Sometimes I could go too far in my eagerness to please. I once shot a Fritos ad that sold the salty corn chips as an incentive for children to clean their plates during meals. For this spot, I had to eat chunky forkfuls of meatloaf, peas, and mashed potatoes—and after every bite, drink from a tall, cold glass of whole milk. For three hours, I did nothing but bite, drink, bite, drink, bite, drink. We did these takes no less than what felt like fifty times, and although the director offered me a spit bucket after I chewed my food, I swallowed it all down instead. I was too embarrassed to spit in front of strangers, and as a result, Mom said this was the only time she's seen a person literally turn green. As if things weren't nasty enough, the director then asked me to cram my face with nothing *but* Fritos—one at a time, in handfuls, throwing them in the air and trying to catch them in my mouth . . . By the time we wrapped, I'd eaten enough meat and potatoes to sustain an army of lumberjacks, and to this day, I still have an aversion to corn chips. I can't even smell them without gagging. Good thing Fritos had yet to invent some of the flavors they have now, like Chili Cheese and Chutney. Chutney! I'd have barfed peas for days.

It was during these adventurous and influential years that my parents insisted I was just like all the other kids, that my friends thought I would be the next Elisabeth Shue, and that I saw compelling signs that both impressions were legit and meaningful. I'll never forget the time that all my worlds seemed to come together in a way that made sense, felt really good, and validated the person I wanted to be when I grew up. And yes, it had to do with a commercial job.

For some reason, I don't remember the audition for my favorite Rice Krispies ad, but I do recall loving the actual shoot, because I was asked to play an upright piano that made no sound as a make-believe Snap, Crackle, and Pop danced along the ledge. I really had to use my imagination to pull this off, instead of simply memorizing lines, since I talked to three invisible cartoon men who danced on soundless keys while singing, "It's fun to put Snap, Crackle, Pop . . . into your morning!" The animated characters and the piano music were added in post-production.

The commercial aired a few months later, around the time that my second-grade teacher, Mrs. Tresham, had a baby. Although she was in her thirties, I fantasized about being her best friend—she was pretty, kind, and really young compared to the frumpy old schoolmarms who stalked the halls at Cherry Avenue Elementary. When she was out on maternity leave, all of the students, especially the girls, couldn't wait for her to get back and tell us about the new addition to her family. It was a huge event in the life of a seven-year-old.

The day Mrs. Tresham returned, she called me to her desk after class.

"Melissa, I'll never forget seeing you on TV while I was in the hospital having my son," she said. "Your smile really helped me get through labor!"

As an adult who's given birth three times now, I can't fathom having a warm association with anything that happens when you're in that much pain. But as a child who looked up to Mrs. Tresham, I remember feeling so important to be part of such a big, happy moment for her. My hobby was actually special enough to help someone I really liked, and she first recognized me on the television and then acknowledged me in real life. The kids also gave me the adoring nickname "Rice Krispie Girl"—which I guess you could say was my first "character name," long before I'd become known as Clarissa or Sabrina. It was my *Romper Room* dream come true.

Chapter 3

THE DAY MY TIPSY DAD WENT
PUNK AND HIT MY MOM
(OR, MY YEAR IN TV MOVIES)

Though cereal commercials and magazine ads made me a local celebrity among teachers and friends when I was young, my reel truly started to fill up when I did a succession of TV guest appearances, movies, and miniseries from 1985 to 1986. I think the TV movie and miniseries genres were particularly significant to boosting my early career because they played such a big role in mid-'80s television. Back then, Sunday was the most popular night for TV watching for families, and the miniseries and made-for-TV movie formats were all the rage.

I'm no cultural historian, but I suspect the reason for this was twofold (at least). First, both genres were self-contained stories, even if told over multiple episodes. Studies say sixty million households had cable in 1985, 88 percent of whom subscribed to an extra cable service like HBO or Showtime and already tuned in to prime-time soaps like *Dallas* and *Knots Landing.* So the notion of a movielike experience on TV was more popular than a Rubik's cube in study hall, especially since they covered dramatic topics like eating disorders, kidnapped children, and murderous teens. Second, one 1986 poll said the average American household had their boob tube on for seven hours a day, so sinking into a network movie or series was a welcome part of their routine. As a busy mom of three who loves to DVR *Grey's Anatomy* and *Friday Night Lights,* two of the closest shows we now have to a popular miniseries, I can relate.

Personally, these genres meant a lot to me for less thinky reasons. Unlike when I shot commercials in New York, a lot of guest roles and TV movies and miniseries let me travel, and this was when I began to appreciate hotel rooms for their free soaps, chlorinated pools, and pillows that felt like a piece of heaven. Traveling also allowed me to eat a lot of ice cream. No matter where we went, Mom and I explored the sweet shops in every new city we hit.

Remember racing home from the bus stop to watch the *ABC Afterschool Special*? They had serious and often controversial story lines that dealt with big-deal, coming-of-age topics like drug and alcohol abuse, divorce, bullying, interracial friendship, and teen pregnancy. They also had ridiculously dramatic names like *Just Tipsy, Honey*; *The Day My Kid Went Punk*; *My Dad Lives in a Downtown Hotel*; and *Please Don't Hit Me, Mom.* Well, on Saturday mornings, ABC also aired the much lighter *ABC Weekend Special,* a half-hour series for kids. Unlike their more emotionally charged big-sister shows, these episodes were all based on innocent storybook and literary elements or characters—and, hold the phone, I was in one with Drew Barrymore.

In 1985, Drew and I starred in *The Adventures of Con Sawyer and Hucklemary Finn.* (Who wrote these titles?) This was basically a female take on the classic Tom Sawyer and Huckleberry Finn tale, only here, two teen girls try to prevent a robbery and get into lots of rambunctious trouble in the process. Drew won the main role as Con Sawyer, while I was a character named Cindy, who was Con's spoiled, bratty younger stepsister. About 75 percent of the cast were kids, so it didn't take long for us to have our own adventures on location in Natchez, Mississippi—with Drew, of course, as our real-life Huck.

Though I was only nine at the time, Drew was ten and still in her contentious, wild child, dope-smoking stage. She was an intrepid little girl with an audacious personality who'd yet to grow into the sweetheart we all love now. One day, she took the group behind our motel to watch her give a French-kissing lesson with costar Kimber Shoop, who went on to play the title role in *The Ted Kennedy Jr. Story* (yup, a TV movie). I'm bummed to report that she didn't let me come watch her wiggle her tongue in Kimber's mouth, because I was a year younger than her, but she did teach me how to backstroke in the motel pool and ask me to her room to watch her on TV in *Firestarter*. All I remember is her enormous earring collection laid out by the motel sink. She had these dangling skeleton ones that struck me as a little daring and creepy for a ten-year-old.

Drew also planned a trip to the mall to see *Desperately Seeking Susan* with the rest of the cast. It was during this field trip that I caught a small but telling glimpse of how Drew likely ruled her family's roost, when she wasn't controlling our set. As moms and their kids piled into vans to catch Madonna's 7 P.M. film debut, Drew announced that she wanted to do some shopping first, so we'd all need to see the 9 P.M. show instead. A lot of the moms were thrown by this little spark plug's audacity, but of course, it was my Long Island mom who spoke up.

"My daughter has to learn her lines and then get to bed at a reasonable hour, so she'll need to see the 7 P.M. show," insisted Mom in a firm but rational way.

"What a bitch!" yelled the star of our movie, once Mom was out of sight.

Though Drew's mom tried to calmly explain that my own mom was just looking out for me, Drew didn't apologize or look ashamed. I would've had a bump on my head the size of the Appalachian Mountains if I'd muttered such an ugly word at that age. She just got back to gossiping with the other, older girls. She also didn't realize I was in the back of the van, and that I was upset that she'd called my wonderful mommy the b-word. I'm sure she'd take it back now, if she could.

Much more glamorous than shooting on that backwoods Mississippi lot was a job I scored soon after *Con Sawyer,* a CBS miniseries called *Kane & Abel.* It was about two strangers who share the same birthday—and while one comes from a privileged background and the other a poor one, they both get filthy and serendipitously rich in New York City. I appeared in one scene of this movie, but it mattered for two reasons. First, we shot it in the middle of the night, from 11 P.M. till 6 A.M., and I wasn't even allowed to stay up this late during slumber parties. Even more exciting was shooting in the lobby of the Waldorf Astoria, one of the grandest hotels in New York City.

Though I was nine at the time, I played Abel's daughter, named Florentyna Rosnovski, during her seventh birthday party (I always played younger than I was). In the scene, my "dad" and I look out at the elaborate room—with its marble floors, glittery chandelier, and black-tie guests—as he reminds me that the night is "all for me." I wore a flowing pink party gown, and as a child who couldn't even afford multiple audition dresses, I could hardly contain myself. I was so excited to be in such a fancy room, wearing a fancy gown, *in the middle of the night,* that there was no need for me to act when the director cued me to show Florentyna's enthusiasm. For seven hours, I was a mini-Cinderella at an elaborate ball designed all for me—at least until sunrise.

As a break from all the dramatic roles, I also liked guest starring on popular TV shows. Two that I loved were *The Lucie Arnaz Show* and *Saturday Night Live,* which I appeared in three episodes of, with hosts Jim Belushi, Roy Scheider, and Billy Crystal. Working on *SNL* came with the best perks of any project I'd taken on so far. I was allowed to stay up late (again!); met musical guest Billy Ocean, who performed my favorite song, "Caribbean Queen"; and took home a Barbie Dreamhouse from the set (they no longer needed the prop, which meant I really scored).

My all-time favorite guest role, though, was for the cop drama *The Equalizer*; I couldn't get away from the heavy stuff for too long. This hit was the *Law & Order* of its time and starred stage and screen actor Edward Woodward. Between Mr. Woodward's sophisticated British accent and dashing silver hair, he was like a warm and fuzzy 007. No wonder he became a hero to little boys everywhere. For my part, I played Laura Moore, a young girl who'd hired the Equalizer to help me and my mom, played by Caitlin Clarke, escape an abusive father, played by Kenneth Ryan. This was my first real taste of an episodic show's demanding schedule, since we worked long days for about two weeks, on multiple locations around Manhattan.

I enjoyed every minute of it, particularly watching how fast the stunts and dramatic physical performances could turn into bloopers, some of which were never reshot. For example, in one scene, Kenneth hits Caitlin's character with a right-hand slap, but instead she falls to her left; this is so obvious, they redid it. But in another, Kenneth kidnaps me and then carries me up an on-ramp to the West Side Highway and dangles me over it. I felt so bad for the actor who had to lug my body up an incline and then hoist me into the air that I decided I'd help him try to kill me. If you ever catch the scene, you'll see that as soon as we reach the railing, I throw my feet up on the edge to relieve some of my body weight. My mom held her breath down below, as she watched her baby hang over an eight-lane highway, without a stunt double. After this harrowing experience, she became much stricter about what I was and wasn't allowed to do on a set.

At the end of my one-year TV blitz, I couldn't have asked for a better finale—a month in Vancouver shooting a terrific television movie called *Christmas Snow* with my mom and new baby sister, Emily, who traveled with us. This was the first time I'd ever traveled outside the country for work, and I couldn't wait to get my passport stamped. If you get the chance to see the movie, it's about a mean-spirited landlord who goes missing during a snowstorm but learns how to be happy when a woman and her kids, me included, rescue him from the bitter cold. The movie stars Katherine Helmond, aka Mona from *Who's the Boss,* and the unforgettable comic legend Sid Caesar, who I'd adored since he played Coach Calhoun in *Grease.* Sid was the only star I'd ever worked with who I recognized. The first time I saw him, I was intimidated for sure, but I found him to be serious and kind. We didn't have a lot of scenes together, though I did with Katherine, who was lovely.

I spent most of my time on the set of our TV family's candy store and dressed in 1920s costumes. If it wasn't thrilling enough to wear old-fashioned clothes and watch the crew make falling snow from bubble machines, Mom took me and Emily to the World's Fair on weekends, and I got to ride the log flume as much as I wanted.

Another thing that really stuck with me about filming *Christmas Snow* is how quickly and effectively it rescued me from feeling the impact of my first career-related rejection. I was lying on the floor, watching bad Canadian TV, when Mom got a call that I'd been cut from a scene in *Crocodile Dundee* in which Paul

Hogan magically fixes a cut on my knee. I'd shot in Central Park, just weeks earlier. When she told me, I didn't lose sleep or stop eating my bag of salt-and-vinegar potato chips. I shrugged my shoulders and put on a pout, and then got distracted when Mom asked if I wanted bubble-gum ice cream from the shop down the street. I can't believe how quickly I bounced back as a kid, and how little it took to get me there. But I was in the middle of a tremendous run, and even at their worst, my childhood blues couldn't keep me down for long. They were nothing compared to an *Afterschool Special*.

Chapter 4

COMING OF STAGE

Like most preteens, I spent my middle school years trying to figure out how I fit in and who I fit in with. But for me, this went beyond wondering if the football star wanted to "go out" (he didn't) or if the popular kids would ever ask me to sneak out of flute practice to smoke with them in the hall (they did, once, but I guiltily looked over my shoulder the whole time like a nun taking a pregnancy test). While these tween worries were real, they were compounded by the fact that I was living two parallel and very different lives—one in suburban Long Island, and one among Manhattan's theater community. In retrospect, it was probably good practice for straddling my two worlds today in suburban Connecticut and Los Angeles. Except now I'm trying to impress soccer dads with my orange slices and fight Hollywood's It girls for roles.

On Long Island, I loved school but had trouble finding my niche. Though I was outgoing, social, and admired by my peers in elementary school because my face constantly popped up in commercials during *The Care Bears* and *He-Man and the Masters of the Universe,* in middle school, my previous classmates were mixed in with kids from two other large schools. That meant four hundred students, few of whom knew me or cared about my reputation, were tossed together like a salad—and I somehow became the raw onions that get pushed to the side. My closest friends began hanging out with girls who snuck out of the house for make-out parties in the woods and had wittier attitudes than mine, so I was rarely invited to bonfires or to play spin the bottle. And while I excelled at impressing teachers, handing in homework on time, and getting good grades—my sharp memory and that Hart family tenacity helped me through trickier subjects—it wasn't effortless, so I couldn't claim "the smart kid" as my identity either. I did excel in math and science, and being on Student Council and playing flute in the band made me burst with pride. But in my quest to become a "nerd," I fell off around "dork."

Consequently, I did my own thing and kept a few friends from elementary school that I'd see at lunch or on weekends. While most of my peers experimented with beer, pot, and blow jobs after 3 P.M., I went into Manhattan every day. I'd moved on from commercials by age twelve, so the distinguished arena of Off-Broadway theater became more and more my thing. Few of my classmates knew about my other world. The stage was where I began finding my people, and it was soon more interesting to me than anything the kids on Long Island could come up with. Let 'em have their cliques and near-miss attempts at popularity and dating. I had a whole secret life, filled with eccentric and smart adult role models, and an audience's applause every night.

Theater was a different beast than commercial work. The

lines were obviously meatier, but the hours were long, budgets were meager, and the critics' expectations were elusive. It's similar to being in an independent, extremely low-budget film, where everyone pools their talents to make a piece of art that they hope will resonate with an audience. It's not like theater is a great moneymaker for actors either, especially Off-Broadway. I think it actually cost my family money for me to do so much stage work, since we put about a hundred miles a day on our car, paid for gas and tunnel tolls, and then hired a wonderful English au pair named Sarah to spend time with my siblings while Mom was with me at most rehearsals and performances.

When I was around twelve years old, I began working with big-name actors, directors, and writers. Three performances stuck out as having the most impact on the person and actor I was becoming. The first was a small lab reading of *The Valerie of Now*, written by Peter Hedges and directed by Joe Mantello, for the prestigious Circle Repertory Company. For those who don't know, a lab reading is like a one-week rehearsal and performance for theater members, to decide whether the funders want to produce the play—kind of like a TV pilot, but for the stage.

In *The Valerie of Now*, I played a little girl who "rides" a bike (it was attached to a contraption that let me pedal in place) while performing an emotionally gutsy monologue. It was about twenty minutes long and included a lot of '70s songs like "Stand by Your Man" and Minnie Riperton's "Lovin' You," which I had to listen to over and over to learn the lyrics. (As a twelve-year-old, I'd have much preferred to spend QT with Bon Jovi.) So as I biked down the street/stage, I talked and sang to myself and to the neighbors I passed. It can be hard enough to walk and talk on a stage, but try riding a bike that's going nowhere, while delivering lines and hitting all the right notes to music you've never heard before—including the falsetto in "Lovin' you/I see your soul come *shinin'* through . . ." I mean, thank God I don't do musicals.

This was also the first time I worked with serious artists so clearly destined for great things. After our lab, Peter went on to write the novel *What's Eating Gilbert Grape* and adapt it as a screenplay, receive an Academy Award nomination for adapting *About a Boy* for film, and cowrite and direct the poignant and hilarious film *Dan in Real Life*—among other admirable coups. As for actor and director Joe Mantello, he's perhaps best known for his work with *Wicked, Take Me Out,* and *Angels in America,* and is one of the great theater directors and actors of our day.

Shortly after the lab, I moved on to a full-length play called *Beside Herself* for the Circle Rep, which gave me more of an education in the arts than I could've received in a decade at Juilliard. *Beside Herself* had a small cast of six, including Lois Smith, Susan Bruce, Calista Flockhart, and William "Bill" Hurt. I threw myself into weeks of rehearsals, while watching celebrated talent and directors "find the character" and "explore the stage"—two things every actor needs to understand. It was also intense and intimidating to be around people so focused on their craft, especially since at thirteen years old, I didn't have any real sense of anxiety or pressure. I just went in, followed the experts' leads, and looked forward to my daily Snapple-and-Smartfood snack when I needed a break. I especially liked watching the cast center themselves with pre-show rituals—especially Calista. She'd do a series of yoga-like breathing and stretching exercises, and every night before the show, I'd do them with her behind the stage. It helped me find a few calm, pensive, and reflective moments to quiet and focus my mind before performing in front of such an enormous and daunting crowd.

I'll be honest, Bill Hurt could've benefited from our de-stressing techniques. During the show's run, he battled in a very public custody trial with the mother of his child, and there was a constant mumble about this. The paparazzi that hung outside the theater day and night, waiting to pounce with questions and cameras, were actually my first encounter with these shutter-bugs. I found it fascinating to watch people whose job was to watch people.

And though Bill was even-tempered to me and my family—he taught me how to blow enormous bubbles with a soapy wand and showed my brother Brian how to shoot rubber bands—he could also be unapproachable and serious. A lot of his conversations were way over my head, especially as a kid whose favorite activity was making mindless mix tapes. I remember telling my mom that I didn't understand what he was saying half the time, which prompted her to ask Bill to speak to me with a more simple vocabulary. He shot back that if I wanted to be around adults, I needed to learn to talk like one. And that was the end of that.

My mom did her best to be a team player during my *Beside Herself* run. Four times during the play, Lois Smith's character entices Bill Hurt's character into her house with a fresh pie. So to help the play save money, Mom offered to bake four home-made apple pies, for nine shows a week. (We needed fresh pies for each performance because Lois pulls pies out of the oven four times during the show for Bill to eat.) That's thirty-six pies a week! So between baking pies and coordinating schedules for me and my siblings, Mom was busier than Snooki on Cinco de Mayo—though sometimes we left the pies sitting on the kitchen counter due to our hurry to beat rush-hour traffic and make it to the theater by my call time. One time we were an hour into our drive into Manhattan when Mom had to make a U-turn to go home to get the pies she forgot on our kitchen counter. And though she spent all this time playing Betty Crocker, Bill never thanked Mom for her pies. He just complained when they were slightly burnt or said all that sugar was starting to give him a spare tire.

Bill's occasional gruffness did teach me a valuable lesson about how to interact with fans. One weekend, I invited six Long Island girls to come see the show. I'd just told them about my theater work a few weeks earlier, so it was new and fun for them, and for me, to see how my two worlds would mix. Most of the girls had strict requests from their parents to get Bill's autograph on their playbill, and while he did this for five of them, he accidentally skipped my shyest friend, Nicole. When I told Bill that he missed her, he said that if Nicole wanted her playbill signed, she had to ask herself. This made Nicole feel even more timid. I'm not sure whether my friend ever got that autograph, but Bill's reaction left such a big impression on me about how not to treat young fans. Since then, he's famously proclaimed, "I'm not a star, I'm an actor," and while I get where he's coming from, being an actor doesn't excuse you from being a good person. When kids are terrified to approach me and struck mute, even though they're fans, I call it "The Santa Effect"—and like the jolly character, I reach out to them more often than not. Rob Lowe has said that "the effect famous people can have on other people's lives is not to be underestimated"— and I'm sure his fans are more rabid than mine and Bill's put together. Our industry has given us a larger-than-life presence to a lot of people, and it's not okay to let them down or be dismissive when they've helped us attain the status and privilege we have. As an adult, I do admire Bill for his incredible body of work and efforts to keep his private and public lives separate and am grateful for his lessons on professionalism, but I really hope he's found a way to take life less seriously. After four Academy Award nominations, I think we're all aware that he's "an actor."

Perhaps Bill's unpredictably stern and aloof presence throughout the show is one reason I was so surprised when he handed me a note, written on the play's stationery, at the end of our run. He did this with all the cast members. Mine said:

Dear Melissa,

It's been swell, swell, swell . . . working beside you. You have an angel in you. Not just pretty but also strong and wise . . . I see she will be there for you when you need her . . . [May] happiness and serenity visit your days abundantly.

Bill

I had no clue what most of this maturely worded note meant, even though Mom told me it was meant to be sweet. I'm sure Bill thought he was doing me a major favor by talking to me like I was a member of Mensa, and I wonder now if Bill had a softer core than he'd originally let on. Of course, the note was also his idea of a wrap gift while the rest of us handed out thoughtful jewelry and candles, so any points he gained for benevolence were kind of lost for being cheap or forgetful.

While Bill was no doubt an uncertain figure, I felt most at home with the beautiful women in our cast. Backstage, in the privacy of our group dressing room, it was lady central, and I loved it. Every day, I put myself to work with little tasks, while the women applied their makeup and all kinds of hair products. My favorite job? At a long mirror, in a room no wider than a railroad track, I'd slip between Lois, Susan, and Calista and collect any flower arrangements that had begun to droop. I'd then hang the flowers upside down for a few days until they dried perfectly straight. Finally, I'd put them back into their original vases, their beauty forever preserved.

It was among these women that at the age of thirteen I developed my first girl crush. I was mad about Calista, who was twenty-four at the time, the way young girls are when they look up to their prettiest babysitter or their most awesome camp counselor. Beyond teaching me how to physically and mentally prep for public performances, Calista became the big sister I always wanted, since I was the oldest of five at the time and needed a break from being a constant role model myself. She was honest, trustworthy, and open-minded, and she made me want to be a better version of me. As a young teen, the best way I knew to do this was to emulate her. On the non-school days that we rehearsed or performed, I spent the night at Calista's Manhattan apartment with its view of the Empire State Building. Every time I drove into the city with my siblings, we competed to see who could see the skyline first, but out Calista's window, it was always within reach and I never had to share it.

Calista also influenced my style a lot. She gave me her funkiest hand-me-downs, including a pair of black leather lace-up Kenneth Cole flats that she called "fence climbers," since they had extremely pointy toes. Mom and I usually shopped at Daffy's on rehearsal breaks, where I tried to channel her style. Back then, the discount clothing store carried the best designer stuff for kids and adults, so we really cleaned up. Daffy's clothing was also a big difference from my usual preppy gear from Kids "R" Us. So much of a tween's identity is linked to her clothing, so Calista's suggestions and validation mattered more to me than she knew. Spending time with her felt like I was hanging out with Molly Ringwald in a John Hughes flick—complete with us as self-doubting, mildly neurotic characters and a Simple Minds soundtrack in my head.

When we had time to kill before a matinee, rehearsal, or evening show, Mom, who was only nine years older than Calista, came with us to Seventh Avenue and Bleecker Street for our favorite pre-show meal at John's Pizzeria. This place has been famous for its brick-oven pies since 1929. I thought their pizza had the most delicious thin crust, rumored to taste so good because of New York City's tap water. Mom, Calista, and I could each eat a whole pie by ourselves. Years later, when Calista was rumored to have an eating disorder, I was tempted to leak shots of us surrounded by some big ol' pizza pies to prove the gossipers wrong. I suspect she's always been thin because she has a lot of nervous energy, and every time I read about a study that links fidgeting to weight loss, I think of Calista. Sometimes when she focused on a scene during rehearsals or listened to a director give notes, she crossed her arms around her body and rocked back and forth. I've always had a lot of energy myself, and if people diagnosed kids in the '80s with clinical conditions as thoughtlessly as they do now, I'm positive I'd have been labeled ADHD and prescribed some serious meds. Though people just said I had "excess energy" back then, Calista's rocking still looked appealing to me, so yes, I started to mimic her. Once she noticed it, she told me to stop, and said I shouldn't rock like her. She never explained why.

Looking back, I realize that Calista probably felt nervous and insecure about her first role on Broadway. She was always hard on herself and concerned about other people's impressions of her. On the night our *New York Times* review came out, she was particularly anxious. Mom drove Calista home most nights, since she lived near the Midtown Tunnel, which we took to Long

Island. In the car, she was really concerned that the critic Frank Rich's feedback could negatively impact her career and the show's run, since his was the only review that seemed to matter. I remember how Calista's adrenaline was pumping, and how confused she was about his review. It said:

> Among the younger alter egos, Ms. Flockhart, in her New York debut, shows unusual promise. She brings consistent emotional clarity to messy post-pubescent effusions, not the least of which is the line, "No wonder this place is such a slushy dung heap of a horror!"

Impressive, right? Mom told her this, over and over, but I could tell from my mother's insistent and strict tone that Calista's nerves were on overdrive. Maybe Calista needed to hear how good she was from my mom, whom she admired, in order to believe it herself. I thought Calista was perfect, but nobody asked the thirteen-year-old in the backseat.

While my own reviews on stage were top-notch, my peers at home gave me questionable ones about who I was becoming, and what I began looking like, without their influence. As my wardrobe gradually took more cues from Calista's closet, mixed with influences from our show's young and punk backstage crew, Long Island didn't celebrate my inner riot-grrrl. I'll never forget when one chick came up to my locker to let me know that my black tulle skirt with red felt polka dots clashed with my black-and-red-striped shirt. She was so sure that dots and stripes were a bad mix, but I was so secure in my NYC-inspired outfit that I wore it again the very next day.

Of course, this faux pas was nothing compared to the ridicule I faced for wearing a pin on my jean jacket that said "Latent

Thespian" among all the Hard Rock Café and George Michael buttons that covered its pockets. A theater friend gave it to me as a joke, but my dumb schoolmates didn't know what a "thespian" was and assumed I was coming out of the closet. The truth is, I wanted to go completely goth or punk, but it always seemed like too much work to wear so many layers, all that makeup, dread my hair . . . so I settled for a leather coat, tight jeans, and a big, heavy, black men's watch that I scored during a reading of *For Esmé—with Love and Squalor* for Broadway's Circle in the Square. It was a prop, but the director let me keep it as a memento.

Yet despite my notice-me looks, most of my classmates were clueless about my second life, minus a small handful of friends. Once when I was miserably failing French class, I tried to translate, from English to French, "Jacques fell off the windsurfing board," and this kid named Karl, who'd been a friend until middle school, decided to pick on me. After I did my best *"Jacques est tombe de la planche a voile,"* he called me out in front of everyone as being terrible at French and then tacked on the line ". . . besides, you're a has-been. I haven't seen you in a commercial in years!" Karl was right that I no longer did commercials, but I was also the youngest honorary member of the Circle Rep Company, so I didn't feel like a has-been until he said this. It was a weird moment for me, because while I enjoyed spending time with adults who gave me respect and made me feel like a princess, I was still a tween, so I also wanted to impress the hormonal dipshits. Karl's comment stuck with me for many years after, as I continued to be a sweaty, blubbering mess around people my own age.

It was always adults, especially creative ones, who had my back. They didn't care if I wore men's shirts, combat boots, and a scarf at the same time—in fact, they encouraged it, because they valued self-expression and being a good person. I'm so grateful that I didn't feel the need to give in to every bit of peer pressure at school, because I had other role models to show me who I could become. It frightens me a little to think who I'd have turned into without them.

During middle school, theater gigs happened at break-neck speed: *The Valerie of Now* lab was in the spring of 1989 and *Beside Herself* began that fall. In the winter of 1990, my monologue from Peter and Joe's *The Valerie of Now* became a thirty-minute intro for the Off-Broadway play *Imagining Brad* at the Players Theatre on MacDougal Street. Our "pilot" was picked up!

Rehearsals for *The Valerie of Now* monologue were much more relaxed and enjoyable than those for *Beside Herself.* And what an incredible acting exercise for a thirteen-year-old. Since a monologue by definition is one actor on stage performing solo, I spent most days in a room with just Peter and Joe—and we had a really good time. For this performance, I'd moved from the bike during our lab to a sofa now, explaining what was about to happen in the play by pretending to talk to myself and to friends on the phone. They cut all the songs except "I Am Woman," probably because they weren't impressed with my vocal skills. Here, I burst into Helen Reddy while jumping up and down on the sofa as the lights faded. (I made couch-jumping a thing, before Tom Cruise did it on *Oprah*.) This ending was different from what the guys had originally written, which was me making out with a pillow as if it were a boy. But as a kid myself, I was too embarrassed to perform this in front of two older men, much less an audience. I shyly confronted Peter and Joe about my trepidation to kiss a pillow onstage, and they listened to my fears and changed the scene so I'd feel more comfortable.

I learned my entire monologue so fast during rehearsals that

Joe and Peter needed other interesting ways to fill our time. We did great acting exercises, similar to the ones I've heard that you learn at NYU's Tisch School of the Arts. I ran around the room saying my lines as lots of different characters with all kinds of voices. The intention was to loosen me up and help me feel free and comfortable with the words I was saying. I repeated my lines as a baby, as Oscar the Grouch, as Jessica Rabbit . . . so fun.

Another clever activity was supposed to get rid of my harsh New York accent. For this, Joe and Peter asked me to repeat the phrase "calling all dog daughters" over and over again for days, until it went from sounding like "cawling awl dawg daaaawters" to the stripped-down, nonregional diction that's become natural to me ever since. Well, once in a while, I do slip up. Years later, on the set of *Clarissa Explains It All,* the word "paranoid" always came out as "paranawd," and on *Sabrina, the Teenage Witch,* I once said "Santa Claws." If you catch me after four tequila shots or cut me off on the 405, my inner New Yawker also rears its ugly accent. Then again, my diction is easily malleable. Because I married an Alabama man, I often speak with a Southern lilt. I basically went from Fran Drescher to Delta Burke—with a theatrical respite in between. But no matter how much my husband tries to correct me, a Florida orange will always be a "Flarrada awrange."

In the eventual performance, my monologue in *The Valerie of Now* came across as the very grown-up and humbling text it was, but I couldn't have done it without the skilled and inspiring support of my industry role models. My monologue was about how I'd gotten my period for the first time and had no idea how to handle it except to "stuff a bunch of tissues up there!" This was a pivotal line in the piece, because after my best Helen Reddy, the play went on to portray my Valerie character all grown-up and married to a blind man with no arms as a way to deal with her father physically and sexually abusing her on her birthday, when she got that first period.

I was secretly mortified to talk about menstrual blood and abuse implications like this, but I pulled it off with maturity. In fact, Frank Rich wrote in *The New York Times*, "Melissa Joan Hart delivers a precocious comic monologue with the worldly showbiz verve of a stand-up comedian more than twice her age. If she's not careful, someone may write her an *Annie 3*." This review, plus word-of-mouth buzz, is one of the things that helped me score my *Clarissa Explains It All* audition that summer, just a few months later. In fact, Mitchell Kriegman, *Clarissa*'s creator, joked that one reason he hired me was because his vet saw *The Valerie of Now* and named his stray dog after Valerie. I'd like to think that in a few years, when I went on to understudy three roles in *The Crucible* at the Belasco Theatre on Broadway with Martin Sheen and Michael York, this part played a role in getting that job, too.

The most surprising thing to me about the people who impact us most, especially during an influential time, is how long their imprint lasts. In 2001, I bumped into Calista at Madison Square Garden, when we were both performing in Eve Ensler's *The Vagina Monologues* V-Day fund-raiser to end abuse against women. I'd only seen Calista once since we worked together, when I briefly ran into her as she was walking her dog. But here we were again, backstage for a show, and it felt surreal. We hugged and then bolted into a tiny bathroom to have a smoke. We were both jittery about being on the same stage with Meryl Streep and Glenn Close while reciting lines about orgasms and rape.

I took in the moment, as we puffed and caught up. Just two girls ashing their Marlboros into a locker room toilet, trying to beat their nerves and play it cool.

Chapter 5

BEING CLARISSA

In the summer of 1990, my agent, who always booked my jobs, called my momager about having me audition for a new sitcom called *Clarissa Explains It All* for Viacom's children's cable channel, Nickelodeon. Until then, Nick aired mostly kids' variety programs like *Dusty's Treehouse* and *Livewire,* and game shows like *Double Dare,* which was loved for its gooey slime pranks. Their Nick at Nite programming included mostly live-action sitcom reruns like *The Donna Reed Show, Dennis the Menace,* and *The Monkees* that appealed to adolescents, but there weren't any non-syndicated sitcoms specifically targeting teens except for *Hey Dude,* a Western series with a male lead, whose first episode ran in 1989. So when *Clarissa* was set to debut in March of 1991, it was nicely positioned to make an impact with a new audience. The creators hoped the teen sitcom would appeal to boys and girls by casting a clever, compassionate, and free-thinking female lead. Not only was that a first for Nick, but a groundbreaking concept for network television programs at the time too.

I remember the *Clarissa* audition process like it was yester-day. All Mom and I knew about the character was that she was a tough-minded teenager, so we decided I should wear my pink T-shirt and faded blue denim short-overalls—sweet and tom-boyish. The first audition didn't feel any different from others I'd been on, but I nailed it nonetheless. Maybe that's because I'd just finished playing a strong girl in *The Valerie of Now* and my head was still in a spitfire place. Acting like a willful sassypants was becoming second nature to me.

The producers and casting people called me back for a sec-ond go, and I repeated the pink-tee-and-overalls look. Once I chose an outfit for an audition, I always wore it for callbacks, hoping it was a look that the producers liked for the character; seeing me in it again also helped them remember me. The waiting room felt like an intense pressure cooker this time around, and my competitors' faces were more focused and less friendly than I'd remembered. I made it to a third callback, and while wearing my good-luck outfit yet again, the show's cre-ator and executive producer, Mitchell Kriegman, sat me down for a talk after I reread my lines to him. He asked me if I liked New Kids on the Block, the newest boy band to hit the radio waves.

"Euuuuch," I groaned. "I hate them."

Though I was being honest, I immediately clammed up with regret. This was a popular group, and for all I knew, Mitchell was a huge fan like the rest of America. What if he listened to "The Right Stuff" on his way to the studio? Or had a daughter with New Kids bedsheets and posters of their greasy faces, just like my cousins did? Mitchell paused before asking me what music I *did* like. I told him I liked They Might Be Giants. I couldn't get enough. This wasn't a band that most thirteen-year-olds listened to, but I spent a lot of free time lying next to my tape player singing, *"Istanbul was Constantinople/Now it's Is-tanbul, not Constantinople . . ."* Mitchell smirked and seemed to make a mental note, but all I could think was that I'd blown the audition.

The next day, when Mom and I were on our way to a different audition, my agent paged Mom's beeper. We ran to the nearest pay phone, on the corner of Fifth Avenue and Nineteenth Street, to ring her and quickly learned that I had been offered the part of Clarissa. We screamed like crazy, jumped up and down, and celebrated with a Chipwich. I did the pilot for *Clarissa* in the fall of 1990 and by January, we were in production on our first thirteen episodes of the show. We shot at the Nickelodeon studios, a TV studio/attraction at Universal Studios that had opened in Orlando a year earlier. I was going to Hollywoo—er, Florida!

Years later, Mitchell told me it was the one-two punch of my outfit and disdain for popular music that helped him choose me to play Clarissa. That, and the fact that he liked my performance, especially when my overall strap dropped at the exact same part of my monologue during all three auditions—a move he assumed was intentional, but was really the result of how I gestured while reciting my lines. Funny enough, Mitchell had been hard-set on Clarissa being a brunette, since blondes rarely fit his idea of the nonconforming, feisty, smart, and relatable type he wanted to depict on his show. But by being myself, I was able to charm him into admitting that blondes could be all these things too.

While I was auditioning for *Clarissa,* I simultaneously tried out three times for the NBC show *Blossom,* which was about another strong-willed teenager and her family, but I was going back for the role of her ditzy best friend, Six. I thought this character was quirky and silly, but also more naive than Clarissa. If given the choice, which character would I prefer to play? I prayed late into the night, asking for guidance to figure out exactly what I wanted for my future. I was raised Catholic, after all.

In my head, I weighed the pros and cons of being on both channels. As a fan of NBC's Thursday night lineup, which at the time included *The Cosby Show, A Different World,* and *Cheers,* I knew and liked the kind of programming NBC delivered. I also loved Nick, but I wasn't sure I wanted to be on a kids' network. Would teenagers actually tune in? Would I limit future jobs by endearing myself to such a niche audience? Then again, I knew *Clarissa* would be my show on Nick, and on NBC, I'd be the sidekick. Well, God answered my prayers like He always does. *Clarissa* it was. I was catapulted into the world of sitcom TV for the first time, and spent the next four years shooting sixty-five episodes of a very funny show that to this day makes me crazy proud.

Clarissa was about a spunky girl with typical preadolescent conflicts that mostly revolved around family, school, and social situations—driving, first crushes, sibling rivalry, drinking, babysitting, bullies, that kind of thing. She had a best friend named Sam, played by Sean O'Neal, who was an optimistic foil to Clarissa's get-real attitude. There was no sexual tension between them, which was and still is a rare dynamic when you put a boy and girl on a bedroom set together. Clarissa's parents trusted her to make a lot of her own decisions, but gave her advice when she needed it. This was a newer way to portray the American family, as well. Clarissa looked up to her mom and dad, but more often than not thought she was smarter than her daffy folks, like most teenagers do. I think teens liked watching that dynamic play out. Others watched to hear the "Na Na" theme song, to identify with Clarissa's friendships, and a lot of fans thought it was fun that she invented her own video games. I think this last point made her relatable to guy viewers, who tuned in to see a pretty, smart girl who was also into a hobby they were.

Today's tweens have been weaned on girl-centric shows like *That's So Raven* and *Gossip Girl,* but casting a young female as a sitcom lead was still a risky, innovative move in 1990. *Square Pegs* and *Punky Brewster* helped pave the way, but before *Clarissa,* most teen female sitcom characters played sidekicks, girlfriends, and sisters. Girls on *The Cosby Show, Family Ties,* and *The Facts of Life* were smart and sassy, but they didn't have the energy and attitude that Clarissa did. Mitchell has even said in interviews that he named the character Clarissa because it was so distinct she could also hate it—which is what she says in the series opener. Who couldn't identify with that? (Her last name, Darling, was inspired by Wendy Darling from *Peter Pan.*)

The way *Clarissa* was shot also helped the show find its place in the zeitgeist. The movie *Ferris Bueller's Day Off* had just broken the fourth wall—that's when you acknowledge the audience through the camera, which is said to allow the actor to bust through the imaginary boundary between the fictional work and its audience. This was a theatrical technique that, when used on TV, was mostly done on variety shows like *Saturday Night Live* or *In Living Color.* But when Ferris did it, it caused a commotion, and our show followed suit. More than anything, though, when Clarissa delivered her lines down the barrel of the camera, it was a way for her to bond with the audience. Mitchell has said that he wanted this to make viewers feel like they were in the room with her. Clarissa's connection was essential, since both sexes would only watch a female lead if the girl were cool enough that boys liked her and girls wanted to be her.

A lot of fans tuned in to see what Clarissa wore every week. Her clothes were original, playful, and not at all provocative—Keith Haring graphic tees, scarves, peasant tops, and more vests than you could find in Diane Keaton's closet. Most of her outfits included layers of color and pattern, paired with colorful Doc Martens or Converse sneakers. The stylish ragtag look was a skillful mix of Punky Brewster, Cyndi Lauper, and the sweeter side of urban punk. I think our show's designer, Lisa Lederer, did for trendy teens what Patricia Field later did for fashionable twenty-somethings who watched *Sex and the City*. (In fact, I think Lisa did some shopping for the show at Pat's store.) To this day, people still tell me that Clarissa inspired them to work in the fashion industry or revamp their wardrobe. I could never follow the character's unpredictable style, so while I loved her clothes, I never duplicated the looks in my own life. I could rock dangling earrings and army boots, but forget the psychedelic leggings and painted jeans. I did keep a lot of custom-made wardrobe pieces like a blue paisley vest, mix-matched pajamas, and any Betsey Johnson piece I could get my hands on. My friend Michele, who worked in wardrobe, made me a great keepsake picture, constructed from many pieces of fabric and material that were used to make some of my clothes. It still hangs in my office at home.

Like Clarissa's personality, her look was elaborate without being flashy, and liberating without seeming pretentious. I wasn't made to look like today's girls on *Hannah Montana, Lizzie McGuire,* or *Wizards of Waverly Place,* who wear a full face of makeup, hair extensions, and daring clothes. I'm floored to learn that some of them are younger than I was when I started on *Clarissa.* In fact, Mom insisted that my character never wear mascara or have tweezed or groomed eyebrows; she hoped to preserve what little-girl charm I had left in my big-girl world.

(This is how she earned her nickname, "Dragon Lady," around the set.)

Because the show was about a preteen's life, and I was a young teenager, *Clarissa*'s writers occasionally turned to me for input and help shaping Clarissa's character—albeit in small, but significant, ways. Right off the bat, Mitchell made They Might Be Giants Clarissa's favorite band, with their posters on her set wall, even though it wasn't the most popular group at the time. He's also said that he wrote in slang I used in real life—like "obee-kaybee," which some of my girlfriends and I used back home, and now there's an OBKB.com fan site dedicated to the show. Clarissa also always had a plan—and five backup plans, if those didn't work out—which is exactly like me, though I'm not sure if that was art imitating life, or vice versa.

When any television show gets the green light for its first season, the showrunner, who's responsible for day-to-day decisions, typically sits with the actors or sends them a questionnaire to learn about their passions, hobbies, and interests. This way, story lines can benefit from the actor's real outside pastimes and talents. Because I'd played the flute since fifth grade, our writers penned an episode about Clarissa's nerve-wracking flute recital. That said, they didn't always take advantage of my interests. In our third season, I told one writer that I wanted to write an episode about Clarissa babysitting the biggest brat in the Northern Hemisphere, inspired by my little sister Emily's antics. I helped flesh out the idea in the writer's room, and then one of the people on the writing staff took over and within a few weeks, my idea became an episode. This was bittersweet for me, though, since I wanted to help develop the episode further and my sister wasn't cast. I did get to meet the talented and sweet Michelle Trachtenberg, who played the little horror, so that was fun. My ego never got in the way of remembering that the show had writers and producers for a reason.

As such, Mitchell was hugely instrumental in making my time at *Clarissa* so great. He created a show about a girl who stood up for herself, went after what she wanted, and did things her own way. I've always been grateful that he saw enough of that in me to let me play her. He is a brilliant man with a bit of a kooky mind, which is exactly what you need to be a success in his business. He also treated me like a daughter, and I needed that. Mitchell was very protective and very concerned about my money being put away for college and my future. He made sure my guardians and the crew and network were treating me well. Whenever he came to Florida for a taping (after the first season, he mostly worked from New York), Mitchell took me to my favorite restaurant at Universal Studios and let me order anything on the menu—lobster, steak, chocolate ice cream, you name it. It was great to be in mature company, and at a nice establishment for a change, since I ate most meals at the commissary among characters from the Universal theme park. It's hard to enjoy your burger with Beetlejuice flinging boogers at you.

Nickelodeon was also very conscientious about making sure I didn't miss out on big moments during my adolescence, and I have to think that a lot of this was Mitchell and my mom's doing. During the last season, Nickelodeon rearranged our shooting schedule so I could be in New York for my sister Alexandra's birth, and then again for my boyfriend Mike's prom since I didn't have one of my own to attend. The network and crew also gave me a private graduation with a podium, "Nickelodeon High School" diploma, cap and gown, and six-foot cold-cut sub. They invited my family, including my six-week-old sister Alexandra and my boyfriend. Mitchell gave a commencement speech. After being named valedictorian in my class of one and voted "most likely to have her own series," I gave a talk, too, with funny anecdotes about the cast and crew. I can't tell you how much it warms my heart to remember the lengths they all went to in order to ensure I had as close to a typical adolescent experience as possible. Years later, on the *Melissa & Joey* set, I duplicated the graduation idea for my young costar, Taylor Spreitler, who was also homeschooled and didn't have a proper graduation. She was as moved by the gesture as I was. It's good to pay it forward.

On set, I also wasn't oblivious to the fact that adults put me on a pedestal because I was the show's lead. They laughed at all my jokes and answered every lame question that crossed my mind. They let me be a curious kid and turned my incessant queries into lessons. When the camera wasn't rolling, my favorite part of being on set was learning the ins and outs of TV production and realizing how many skills went into putting twenty-two minutes of script on air. The crew's talents were also personally handy. If my earrings broke, props fixed them. If my jeans were too long, wardrobe hemmed them. If I needed pictures hung in my dressing room, the grips helped, and for random needs, hard-working production assistants, or PAs, were on call.

I remember running amok between shots and on rehearsal breaks, too. One time I chased down a crush who worked in promos because he stole my popcorn, but when he made a sudden 180 at the end of the hall, I rammed my nose into his forehead. This gave me my first and only bloody nose, and he swears he still has the tissue; I'm waiting for it to show up on eBay. I also flirted with the lighting guys who taught me how to properly dim an Inky or Tweenie—giant industrial spotlights used on Hollywood sets—and let me lower the baton so they could adjust a lamp. I liked goofing around with the directors and asking them to explain how they knew what camera should be looking at which actor, and when to switch cameras for the edit. They occasionally let me work the cameras and sound booms during rehearsals. I would have loved to help create the replicas of the *Enterprise* from *Star Trek* sets, or mix the colors for *Double Dare*'s slime, but those were a big deal.

Outside the studio, I wasn't as crazy about the attention I received. Around the start of our second season, I began getting recognized for the first time, and I didn't like it. Nothing bad ever happened to me, but I felt generally uneasy about being approached by strangers in public. Cable television was still newish to some Americans, the paparazzi wasn't as ubiquitous as it is now, and nobody had cell phones for videotaping celebs or snapping their uncensored pics, so I didn't have much experience interacting with fans the way teen stars do now. I also hated when people mangled our show's title to *Clarissa Tells It All,* which happened all the time and still does.

As much as I truly loved the work on *Clarissa,* my shoot and travel schedule made it a real challenge sometimes. I worked seventy-hour weeks with a laser-like focus. I shot in Orlando for three weeks straight, traveled home for two weeks, and then came back for three—until we'd completed ten to fifteen episodes in a season. My workweek began on Saturday night, when I read the latest script, given to me on Friday. Then with the cast, director of the week, writers, and producers, I spent Sundays at the table reading for that week's episode in our enormous, dark, and damp soundstage. The good lights didn't go on, and the thermostat wasn't regulated until we started shooting on Wednesday. I often got strep throat and colds from the stage, and there was never time to heal completely. A few hours after

I'd be sent home by the doctor, I'd get called back to rehearse, shoot, or go to school. Sunday table reads were the first time the cast and crew heard the script read aloud, as we noshed on bagels and coffee around a plastic folding table. After our reading, we dove into rehearsals scene by scene, and worked out the blocking (how we moved around the set). If any of the three kid characters were not in a scene, we were sent to the schoolhouse trailer attached to the side of the stage to work on our academics. This was the only time of day we saw sunlight, unless we ventured offstage for our one-hour lunch break.

Besides my hectic work schedule, I was frequently wiped from the intense energy I had to exert when we rolled tape; subscribing to the Nickelodeon school of acting was no stroll in the park. We'd have long, twelve-page scenes that we arduously rehearsed, and when it was time to shoot, we'd easily work on them for another hour and a half. I'm sure you've noticed that child actors on kids' networks are abnormally peppy and overly expressive. My *Clarissa* peers and I were already energetic kids with a ton of personality, yet for some reason, this was never enough to satisfy directors. They wanted us to act like we were hyped up on nondrowsy cold meds. One of my favorite directors, named Chuck, was great at getting us pumped after ten draining takes by joking around, and if that didn't work, telling us to "Shoot this one out of a cannon!"—as in, the scene—which became known as "Cannon take!" for short. Every time I heard those words, I had to blast 'em with more pizzazz than what felt natural. No wonder I had a hard time transitioning to more subtle and serious roles later in my career.

The cast and crew worked six days a week, but only rolled cameras on Wednesday, Thursday, and Friday. When it came time to shoot, I was terrified that I'd mess up the five long monologues my character had to deliver, straight into the camera, every week. Because of this shooting style, there was no room for error, and if I made a mistake, we couldn't do pickups, since monologues can't be spliced together in editing. I had to get every single word correct or start over. That kind of pressure, in front of seventy-five-plus adults just watching and waiting to go home to their families, was intimidating. And though the monologues scared me, I also loved the adrenaline rush of nailing them in one or two takes. It was a welcome challenge, and I never back down from a challenge. I took great pride in knowing my lines, blocking, and even knowing other peoples' lines; and I rarely, if ever, went blank when the cameras were rolling (or when I was up on stage earlier in my career, come to think of it). I also really loved shooting the flashbacks and dream sequences, since they let me act a little ridiculous, take on another character, and learn only a half page of lines, as opposed to the usual ten-page scene.

My *Clarissa* cast and crew made it a memorable place to spend four years. I've always been so lucky to work on shows that have a close-knit group. It sounds clichéd, but like a lot of actors who spend years on a hit television show, I thought of my *Clarissa* coworkers as a second family. They were all warm, caring, and loving to me in a way I'll never forget. When you spend more time with over seventy-five new friends than your eight-person family, it can either be really special or really horrendous—and *Clarissa* was definitely special.

We worked hard, but we also knew how to have a good time. Our young, mostly single crew went to a bar called Florida Bay nearly every Friday night, which gave me the social life I craved. Though I was underage, the bar let me tag along with my co-

workers once they realized I wasn't there to get wasted, not that
I could convince anyone to sneak me some booze anyhow. It
wasn't until the show was about to end that my friend and
dresser Michele, and her fiancé, David, ordered me my first tequila shot at Florida Bay. It was my drink of choice for years.

Sean O'Neal, the actor who played my friend Sam, was a particularly good sport and sidekick. His role on the show was to be
my close friend, and because Mitchell didn't want him to go up
the stairs or through the front door and talk to her parents every
time, he made him come up a ladder through the bedroom window so we could start interacting faster. Sam was one of the first
sitcom buddies who refused to use the front door, besides Vinnie on *Doogie Howser, M.D.* Joey on *Dawson's Creek,* Bruh-Man on
Martin, and Shawn on *Boy Meets World* soon followed. That ladder was only three rungs high and attached to hinges on the cement floor, so poor Sean had to lie flat on the floor with only a
furniture blanket to cushion him, with the heavy and awkward
ladder lying across his belly, for as long as it took us to get to his
part of the scene. When his cue came, he'd throw the ladder
against the windowsill, wait about three seconds, and then
slowly crawl to his knees and eventually up the three rungs,
over the sill, and into the room. If Sean was not a young able-
bodied teen at the time, I doubt he would've been able to do this
for four years without a lot of wear and tear to his body. And no,
we never hooked up in real life, though I may have had a minor
crush on him when we first started. Of course, after two days of
working together, I knew we were more like brother and sister.

My other on-set cohort was Jason Zimbler, who played my
brother, Ferguson. He was always up for hanging out. We were
both Yankees from the North who traveled to work, and when
the show ended, we met up in Paris for the bat mitzvah of our
foreign language teacher's daughter. It was the last time we

really hung out. We always got along, but believe me, we also knew each other's secrets and how to push the other person's buttons, much like real siblings do. Sean and Jason were the only peers I had for four years, so if I wanted to spend time with people my own age in Orlando, they were all I had. Sometimes I tried hanging out with the kids from *The Mickey Mouse Club,* like Keri Russell, but with our crazy work schedules and no driver's license, it was logistically too hard to be friends.

For a while, I kept in touch with the warm and wonderful Elizabeth Hess, who played my mom, Janet Darling. She introduced me to yoga and the ancient art of "breathing from your knees." This was an inside joke between us. Elizabeth had taught me how to use my breath to relax parts of my body, and though it was a head-to-toe effort, I could never seem to loosen up below the knees. So during long, tedious scenes when we'd get the giggles, the only way we could calm down and refocus ourselves was for her to announce, "Breathe from your knees!" I still think of this when I'm tired, punchy, and need a minute for myself on set or at home. Years later, I also worked with my hilarious *Clarissa* dad, Joe O'Connor, when he guest-starred in a Christmas episode of *Sabrina, the Teenage Witch*. The rest of us just went back to our regularly scheduled lives. We have different interests and lives than when we worked on the show.

I'll also never forget that little beast Elvis! Clarissa's pet baby alligator was only on set a few times, though it seemed like more because we used the same close-up shot of him multiple times each season. I was fascinated by his reptilian ways, but I wasn't allowed to touch him. It was for his good and ours. For safety reasons, the animal wranglers made sure that nobody had a chance to upset the alligator. I was also told that if he ever got his chompers on my fingers, he'd hold on so tight that when I tried to pull my hand away, the force could potentially yank out his itty-bitty teeth. Of course, after shooting an episode about bullies, I might have been able to show Elvis who's boss.

The bully episode was one of my favorites. Here I fall for the jock Clifford Spleenhurfer, who picks on Ferguson at school, but I enjoyed shooting it so much because I really learned how to box! I still have a mean right hook. The absolute best episode, though, was the Brain Drain episode, where Ferguson and I compete in a *Double Dare*–like game show. We slid down a small slide, covered in slime, and into a pool of goo. Usually when you do stunts, you only have to do it once. But we went down the contraption twice, with a shower in between, and we were a complete mess both times. It was disgusting for sure, but still exciting to get paid for being so sloppy. I'd never been slimed before, even though it was Nickelodeon's signature move.

At the end of every season, there was always the chance that the show wouldn't be renewed, so every finale of *Clarissa* came with a tearful good-bye and an excuse to cut loose. Most networks that aren't too cheap throw the cast and crew decent wrap parties with music, alcohol, and food. I treated ours like the mixers I was missing out on in high school. I planned my outfits, danced the night away, and bugged people to sneak me a drink. They never did, since they wanted to keep me, and their jobs, safe. At the end of every wrap party, the crew gathered around as the DJ played The Allman Brothers' "Melissa." This was always a special but difficult moment for me, since good-byes came next. Halfway through *Clarissa*'s fourth season, we learned the show would end. I knew I'd miss everyone, but I was turning eighteen and anxious to start my next adventure. At this wrap party, "Melissa" was especially heartbreaking. It was now our swan song.

Being Clarissa was a great learning experience for me. I can't exactly say that she knew it *all,* but the character sure did teach me a lot as I internalized my lines. She repeated famous quotes by people like the Dalai Lama and Queen Latifah, way before people did this on Twitter. During one of the first episodes, I had to say something about Tibet, but I'd never heard of this place before, so I said it quickly and rhymed it with the sound a frog makes—"ribbit." This happened over and over, no matter how often the producers corrected me. (I also got tongue-tied saying "sibling relationships," which came out "sibwing rewationships." We must have done fifteen takes before I stopped sounding like Elmer Fudd.) I was even schooled in Wall Street 101. One of my favorite lines in the show was when Clarissa wanted to be an anchorwoman like Jane Pauley and was reporting the day's news to the viewers. She starts by giving the financial report and talking about the Dow Jones, and then says, "Now who is this Dow Jones guy, and why does he keep going up and down?" I couldn't have agreed more with this line and Clarissa's POV as a kid, so my delivery was flawless. At fifteen, I had no idea what the Dow Jones was, and to be honest, I'm still hazy on it.

It's hard to let go of something special, but you have to know when to move on. We shot the pilot for a CBS spinoff called *Clarissa Now* in 1995, about Clarissa's internship at a Manhattan paper. After production wrapped, Mitchell and I felt that we didn't have as much freedom on a network as we did on cable to keep it going the way we liked. I think fans would have been disappointed if it went to air. Same goes for a reunion show. I don't think it could ever be as fresh or relevant as the original *Clarissa* was. I don't even know how I'd play the character now that I'm so much older, and I think it's better to reminisce about the old days than try to recapture or reinvent them. People are always disappointed with a reunion anyway. Few people like high school reunions, let alone ones on TV. It would make me feel old and fat. And we'd all get that theme song stuck in our heads again.

Na na na na. Na na na na.
All right! All right!
Na na na na na. Na na na na na.
Way cool!

Guess we know what you'll be humming for the next two chapters.

Chapter 6

IS THAT TEEN SPIRIT I SMELL?

I worked on *Clarissa Explains It All* from January of 1991 to December of 1993, from fourteen to seventeen years old. This age window is when most teenagers spend 90 percent of their time worrying that if they're left out of anything—a conversation, a party, a double date—they won't collect enough memories or feel amply prepared for what comes next. According to *Glee,* Taylor Swift, and my much younger siblings, navigating high school is a really significant part of being a teen. But bouncing between New York and Florida in high school meant I didn't have the experiences that I hear all about. Even so, I didn't miss it, and in a lot of ways, I think I was better off. I was too busy enjoying my early independence.

I never cared about school-related traditions like homecoming, prom, or football games; I did like junior high dances, but more for the music and dancing than anything else. And while *Clarissa*'s stellar reviews meant instant cred to the show's execs, I liked that I could be part of a great collaboration in another part of the country. When I did miss my family and good Chinese food, I reminded myself that I could make my own decisions in Florida, and that was huge. In Long Island, I never decided when to wake up, what to wear, what to eat, or even how to get out the door with clean hair and teeth. Until I was thirteen years old, Mom got my day started with chipper and instruction-packed drills: "Get up, buttercup! Wear the clothes on your bed, brush your teeth, and eat the Shredded Wheat on the table!" But down in the Sunshine State, I had to set an alarm at night and make grown-up choices, like what shampoo to use (Aveda) and which skincare products would keep me from breaking out (Clinique). I had to look like the competent pro everyone wanted me to be.

Since I shot *Clarissa* in Florida for three weeks and then spent two weeks in New York on break, Mom hired a series of guardians to look out for me in Orlando. When I first got the part, she and Dad had four other kids to take care of, and Mom had to go with my sister Liz on a three-month job where she sang Broadway tunes on a Caribbean cruise ship. So I spent a lot of time with a rotating door of parental stand-ins. I had a new one every season. Mom and I can't remember the order of my guardians, but I had some influential memories with each one.

There was Marissa, who my mom found through a friend. For one season of the show, we lived together in a studio-owned condo, with two bedrooms and two bathrooms. This was the first time in my life that I had my own room, let alone my own toilet. I was also stoked to have a roommate who wasn't a relative. Marissa and I had a ton of fun together, and since the apartment wasn't ours, it felt like I was crashing at an older cousin's new pad, away from the chaos of home.

We mostly spent time together at night, after I finished shooting for the day. Neither Marissa nor I knew how to make a proper meal, so most dinners were like a science experiment in our attempts to make something edible. We ate English muffin pizzas and fried zucchini, which counted as a vegetable. We also watched a lot of TV like *The Cosby Show, A Different World,* and *Golden Girls,* and she helped me "run lines" for work the next day—i.e., memorize my dialogue. Some nights, I'd take a dunk in our hot tub with whoever else I could rope into going, usually one of the writers or cast members like Jason. He and I lived in the same apartment complex and spent a lot of platonic time in the tub. Marissa didn't worry. She knew we were never up to any shenanigans.

Then there was Vicky, who also worked at Nick in the PR department. I got to know her when she and her team shot the *Clarissa* ads on the iconic itchy orange couch, which was used for promo pieces. I spent a lot of time hanging out in her cube when we weren't shooting, so I begged Mom to let her be my guardian. She was probably ten years older than me, and about five years older than Marissa was, but we got along like peers—this time in a different fully furnished condo. (They moved me every season, though I'm not sure why.)

As an adult, Vicky talked to me like an adult. She told me terrible date stories, like the night she went out with a tampon salesman who opened his trunk to offer her boxes of free samples. She came home with handfuls of the cotton plugs. Treating me like a peer, though, didn't mean her decisions were always mature or responsible. We ate cookie dough for dinner while watching *Beverly Hills, 90210* and *Melrose Place.* And once I convinced her to let me see *Basic Instinct* on opening night at the Pleasure Island Disney World movie theater. When the ticket guy wouldn't sell her a ticket for me because I was underage, she dropped her voice a few octaves and whipped out the signed document that my mom had left her. It said she had full guardianship over me.

"So you're telling me that I can give permission for her to have open-heart surgery, but I can't say that she can see *this stupid movie?*" she asked.

Her argument got me into the film, though Vicky regretted the decision when we both crossed our legs tight during the scene in which Sharon Stone opens hers wide. Shortly thereafter, and unrelated to this incident as far as I know, Nickelodeon execs decided it was a conflict of interest for one of their employees to look after me while I was working there.

Next up: a friend my mom met on a cruise, named Christine. She was a magician's assistant, and my whole family called her "the Babe in the Box." The Babe was a sexy, wild twenty-three-year-old, with long blond hair and even longer legs. Picture Jenny McCarthy during her say-anything/go-anywhere MTV *Singled Out* days. Mom thought the Babe was loads of fun, and when her tour was over, she asked her to be one of my guardians. I think Mom's unlikely choice for a role model shows how much she trusted me to make sound decisions alone.

What Mom didn't count on was that the Babe's hot body and bottle-blond looks would be tough for me to handle when it came to guys. I had such a crush on an older guy named Brandon who worked at the studio, and though the Babe knew it, I woke up one morning to learn he'd slept over. In her bed. He'd taught me how to drive a stick in his Nissan, but all along, he was hoping to take my nanny for a ride. Sex was constantly on my mind as a teen, and her having it with Brandon stung. The babe had practically stolen my man, like when Kelly stole Dylan from Brenda on *90210*, except we weren't dating and I was more of an Andrea. It hurt too much to split hairs.

During *Clarissa*, I worked six days a week with scheduled days off, and on one of the few Saturdays I had free, one of the grips invited me and the Babe to go Jet Skiing on a nearby lake. I got such a rush pushing the machine to its limit that I repeatedly raced through the water until I was thrown off. Then I climbed back on before I let imaginary water moccasins or alligators get hold of me. When we got home from the lake, I noticed when I changed out of my bikini that I had my first "red dot special," as I liked to call it.

I was fourteen at the time, and all my other friends back in New York had already gotten their periods. Without my mom, sisters, or friends my own age to share this experience with, my only option was to tell the Babe. How did she handle my newfound womanhood? Well, after a few months of using pads, she decided I needed to graduate to the big leagues and use a tampon. She directed me to the bathroom to figure out how to use one, and it wasn't fun. Though she thought she was being helpful, I found the whole experience to be terrifying and stressful. Thank God my female castmates and "the glam squad"— the wonderful girls in hair, makeup, and wardrobe—took a much gentler approach with me. Elizabeth Hess was so happy Aunt Flo visited that she gave me an African bead necklace she said celebrated a female's womanhood. Between Elizabeth's gesture and the copy of *Our Bodies, Ourselves* given to me by Erin Cressida Wilson, a fellow actor in the play *Imagining Brad,* I was set to be a lady. Looking back, I probably told too many people about this milestone. But that's a recurring theme in my life—I rarely keep private moments to myself, because I like to celebrate them with others. I could never be a Hollywood bouncer: I let way too many people into my private parties.

By my final season on *Clarissa,* the only person I wanted to live with was my best friend from the set—a girl named Michele, who'd been my dresser for all four seasons of the show. Nickelodeon didn't object to the arrangement, since I was so close to my eighteenth birthday, and Mom said I was practically an adult. Michele's job was to bring my clothes to my dressing room, make sure they fit well, and then just before we'd shoot, pick and pull and tape me into fashion perfection. Most actors have a very close and intimate relationship with their dressers, since they're the ones who see you buck naked numerous times a day, and know how to camouflage every big and small flaw on your body.

Michele was tall, gorgeous, and wise—a clean-cut, carefree, all-American sorority-girl type. She knew how to have fun but stay out of trouble. When we weren't attempting to cook dinner or Rollerblade, we'd hang out with our friend Bruce, the stylist on our show and a movie buff well versed in black-and-white films like *His Girl Friday* and *All About Eve.* As a child, I had considered Shirley Temple and Judy Garland charming actresses, but I had no idea Audrey Hepburn and Bette Davis could be so enchanting, too. Since I spent a lot of time stressing about my SATs and filling out college applications while we lived together, Michele took me to her old sorority house for pledge week—just to show me that college could also be fun. The atmosphere was so congenial, supportive, and inclusive—unlike any girl group dynamic I'd encountered so far—that I made the mistake of pledging a sorority at NYU the following year, only to quickly learn that on city campuses, nobody does this. I guess Manhattan coeds don't need to wear Greek letters to get them drunk or laid, since the city's bars and clubs offer this without asking for dues.

Michele was, and still is, like a dear sister to me, one who knew how to look out for my safety but let me act like a free-spirited teenager. She showed me through her own example how to have an adventurous life, while also being a responsible, good-hearted person. She taught me that happiness comes from the people you choose to be around—a lesson she stood behind when she got engaged to her longtime boyfriend, David, who was the assistant to *Clarissa*'s creator, Mitchell Kriegman. Back then, David and Michele cheered me on for everything from my first sushi (California rolls), to my first taste of hard-earned luxury (a first-class trip from New York to Orlando), to my first Philharmonic performance (in Central Park). And let's not forget that first tequila shot! I admire their marriage so much that when my husband Mark and I were looking for a town in which to raise our family years later, we chose one thirty minutes from Michele and David. I thought this would be a sure-fire way to have a life as wonderful as hers. I also made her and David godparents of our first son, Mason.

When I wasn't on set, my teen years weren't all girl talk and movie nights. In the summer of 1991, the first year I shot *Clarissa*, my mom spent a few months on a cruise ship (yes, the same one where she met the Babe) with my sister Liz and baby Emily. She met so many people with crazy lifestyles—a juggler, a singer, a Broadway showgirl—that being a Long Island housewife suddenly paled in comparison. She was also already by herself so much that she decided she'd had enough, should divorce Dad, and then reinvent her life as we all knew it.

Here's how it went down.

After a few weeks of being at sea with just Liz and Emily, Mom wanted the rest of the family to join them on a weeklong jaunt around the Bahamas. But with all the kids gathered on the dock, my parents got into a humongous fight about the T-shirt my dad decided to wear for his first visit to see his wife since she left for Liz's gig. The shirt had a bull on it, with tiny poop drop-pings spilling out of its rear, inside a red circle with a line through it. The unsubtle message? "No bullshit."

Dad thought it was hilarious, but Mom was horrified that this was the man she was about to introduce to her fabulous new cruise friends. She flipped out. It didn't take long for us kids to realize their marriage was over, but we were also stuck on a big boat with them and forced to watch it play out until they announced they were splitting up. They argued and slept in separate rooms, which made me feel so helpless. To get our minds off the drama, my sister Trisha and I hit the disco to learn new dance moves from other teens on board. Lucky for me, when the trip was over I went back to Orlando to tape our last six episodes of the season. I didn't have to wit-ness the mess that ensued once the Harts hit shore. I've never been back on a cruise ship since. I have such vivid memories of feeling trapped.

During the wrap party for that first season of *Clarissa*, when everyone said their good-byes, I really absorbed the magnitude of what was about to go down at home when our designer, Lisa, gave me a tight hug and whispered in my ear, "I don't envy what you have to return to." I felt sick about leaving my *Clarissa* fam-ily to encounter a shit storm with my biological one, on top of the harassment I thought I'd get from the local Long Island kids for my dual life.

Each time I went back to New York, Nickelodeon paid for a town car to drive me from the airport to Long Island. It was al-ways an hour late and I'd constantly have to drag my bags to the curb, and then around the airport, and eventually to a pay phone to call the dispatch a few dozen times before my car would find me. At fourteen years old, this really pissed me off, but since I didn't know that I could make a formal complaint, it never failed to happen the same way, month after month. On that trip home after we wrapped, the car picked me up after an hour, as usual—but before I could notice we were headed west instead of east on the LIE, I was taken to Sixth Avenue and Eleventh Street in the city, across from the famous Ray's Pizza in Greenwich Village.

My mom was waiting for me outside a beautiful town house. She told me she'd truly left the 'burbs, and my dad, and that I'd be living with her. She never asked me if I wanted to. I knew they were getting a divorce, but I didn't know how the specifics would play out. Mom helped me inside with my bags, up a tall set of stairs, and into an empty high-ceilinged living room with a tiny white kitchenette. She told me the furniture, my sisters, and my brother would arrive the next day. Oh, and by the way, she met a gay Broadway singer on the cruise ship, and he'd be our roommate to help with the rent. For two weeks, the divorce and move made me really blue. I moped around the apartment, trying to make sense of it all. I also didn't want to live in the city. It was nice to visit, but that's all I thought I could take. It was dirty, smelly, loud, and now I had to call it home.

As if my life weren't already splintered from living in Florida and New York, I was now asked to spend hiatus weekends on Long Island with Dad and weekdays in New York City. But it actually sounded more annoying than it was. Children of divorce usually have a hard time with their parents' separation, but after those two initial weeks of ennui, I got over the sad part and did my best to work through the anger that came with having a severed family. I'm not sure if I could compartmentalize these feelings because I was old enough to talk about what had happened with my siblings, or because I could see how unhappy my parents really were on that cruise ship. I'd noticed that their fights were becoming more regular and heated—there's a fork mark still in my father's kitchen cabinets from when Mom threw one at him in a huff—but we never knew it would end in divorce.

City living wasn't as bad as I thought it would be. I loved discovering new bookstores and boutiques; and the A/C/E train was the ticket to getting out of my head. Our town house grew on me, too, especially the attic room I shared with my sister Trisha. It was hidden behind closet doors on the third floor and had skylights instead of windows, though it was also the only room without a window AC unit. I spent long, hot summer days covering my walls with my original paintings, mostly inspired by the Keith Haring and Andy Warhol art for sale that I walked past on the streets. On one wall of my room, I painted a giant Earth as the center of an even bigger sunflower. I asked guests who visited to add their favorite quotes to the nine-foot staircase wall, until it was covered in many colors, handwritings, and inspirational sayings. My favorite line was, "What's a weekend, if you ain't knockin' boots?"—a lyric by A Tribe Called Quest. It was scrawled by a Sayville buddy named Joe, who'd become a closer friend now that I lived in Manhattan. On the security bars that covered my skylight, I hung long necklaces that had made their way into my suitcase from the *Clarissa* set. I collected combat boots from Eighth Street and knickknacks from St. Mark's, and displayed both for all to see.

Trisha's side, on the other hand, was extremely girly, with a floral Laura Ashley bedspread and wallpaper on her half of the room only. This was funny to me, since she looked more Salt-n-Pepa than Rachel Ashwell (though *she'd* tell you she drew her inspiration from the Wu Tang Clan). Influenced by her classmates in the Bronx, Trisha wore men's Polo shirts, Hilfiger oversize jeans with boys' boxers sticking out the back, and Nike sneakers or Timberlands. The cherry on top was a slick ponytail and giant gold "door-knocker" earrings. Maybe the best comparison of all would be Jennifer Lopez, when she was still "Jenny from the Block." I can't blame Trisha, though, for embracing the anonymity and "anything goes" style that comes with living in Manhattan. I could be anyone I wanted to be here, too. And even though my sister and I had very different looks and interests, we helped each other out when the divorce got to us. Trisha and I have always been close, even when we couldn't stand each other, because beyond our carefree childhood, we had the experience of sharing those tough years and that wild room together. I always say that the best part of having such a big family is all those built-in friends, and Trisha was no exception.

Moving to the city also meant changing my New York–based school. The bummer was that I took my studies so seriously and was doing really well until I was forced to move around so much. So far, I'd worked with Florida tutors while attending public school in ninth grade and then private school in tenth, and then for the last two years of school, Mom and I decided that I'd simply work with tutors to get me through the curriculum as fast and easily as I could. It was the most difficult to balance school and work on set, though, because I worked on one or two subjects a day, for four to six hours—on top of rehearsals, wardrobe fittings, learning lines, and whatever else I needed to do for that week's episode. It's not easy to learn calculus for 320 uninterrupted minutes, once a week, and retain it. When I wasn't in a scene, I worked in the school trailer with Jason and Sean. "Recess" was running around the Universal Studios lot and jumping on the Back to the Future ride whenever possible.

One of the few major benefits to my DIY schooling happened

in ninth grade. I was on a huge soundstage, surrounded by capable, creative people, and they were always willing to help with projects for my Long Island classes. I owed my English teacher a model of England's famous Globe Theatre, though I had no clue how to turn wood and nails into a diorama. But my friend David, our set designer who built *Clarissa's* weekly sets in short periods of time, had years of experience making models. In just twenty-four hours, he made me a to-scale cardboard Globe, which I then surrounded with pieces of green strawberry baskets to represent the theater's balcony rails.

Because of my wonky schedule, enrolling in Professional Children's School, or PCS, in tenth grade was a no-brainer. PCS is a private school for students simultaneously pursuing artistic careers, which was helpful and necessary when I was shooting *Clarissa.* (Trisha went to the esteemed Bronx High School of Science, while Liz, Brian, and Emily attended public schools in the area.) Located on the Upper West Side, PCS was like a skinny converted apartment building, only the apartments were classrooms, and the halls with our lockers doubled as a break area. There was also a tiny outdoor yard where we'd occasionally shoot hoops, but it was nothing like the giant grassy fields, tennis courts, or Olympic-size pool I'd known in Sayville. Not that physical education was important to PCS kids. We were just there to get our diplomas, so we could pursue our creative dreams or get into a decent college; we were also too young to know our life experiences and résumé would get us into any school before straight As did. Unlike my Sayville classmates, who seemed uninterested in my acting, what made PCS students special were their jobs. My classmates included ballerinas, stand-up comics, and actors like me, including some famous names like Sarah Michelle Gellar, Jerry O'Connell, the Culkin brothers (Macaulay, Kieran, and Shane), Dash Mihok, Donald "Shun" Faison, and my best friend while I was there—Tara Reid.

Even though some of us were in different grades or classes, PCS was so small that I mingled a lot with these kids in the halls or on the really steep stairwells between floors. (Who needs PE when you have to walk a dozen flights up to get to trig?) And even though the acting kids all did the same thing, we never talked about our work, which was refreshing to me.

Compared to the teens I knew from Long Island, my PCS classmates were also more self-confident, and significantly less judgmental. This also could've just been city kids maturing faster than the rest of the country, especially since we were around adults so much at work.

Though it was a specialized school, a lot of typical high school stereotypes and superlatives played out at PCS. Macaulay Culkin was most popular, since it was well known that he was a mega-million-dollar movie star and probably the most recognizable student for being Kevin in *Home Alone*. His brother Shane was in my grade and became a good friend for a minute, but Mac and his brother Kieran were wild, arrogant boys who seemed spoiled by too much attention from fans. They got away with wearing two different color shoes at the same time, Kris Kross style—who does that? As for Shun, Dash, and Jerry, they were the "hot" seniors. I still run into Dash, who went on to do supporting roles in *The Perfect Storm* and *Kiss Kiss Bang Bang*, and Shun, maybe best known as Dr. Christopher Turk on *Scrubs*, on studio lots or at occasional Hollywood parties. Or we keep up with each other on Twitter.

Sarah Michelle Gellar might as well have been known as "most likely to be my professional doppleganger." She was a year younger than me and though we always got along at auditions and commercial shoots, I wouldn't say we were super close. We began our careers at around the same time, and hung out during commercial auditions, but rarely crossed paths at PCS. Our lives went on to mimic each other's and still do. When I shot *Clarissa,* she dazzled on *All My Children* as Susan Lucci's daughter. I used to randomly turn it on and feel proud that I knew her. Then about six months after *Sabrina* first aired, Sarah began slaying vampires as *Buffy,* and a decade later when I began shooting my third sitcom, *Melissa & Joey,* her third show launched, too. The tabloids have kept me posted on similarities in our personal lives as well. We got our first tattoos around the same time, got married a year apart, and seem to have timed a few of our pregnancies simultaneously. Isn't that strange? Whenever I hear something new about my cosmic twin, I stop to wonder if I've had, or will have, similar experiences in my own life.

Then there's Tara Reid. She was a lively and naughty friend. Unlike the skin, bones, and boobs she is now, Tara was a plump young thing in high school. And the wild side that's made her infamous? You could say she honed her rebellious skills at PCS. Any trouble I got into in tenth grade can pretty much be traced back to Tara, though I rarely did anything wrong. One time, we both got scolded for her copying off my test (my teacher thought we were in cahoots), and when she smoked cigarettes on the church steps near our school and I went with her, we both got in trouble for it, even though I hadn't lit a cancer stick. One of my favorite memories of Tara was when we both quit an acting class after just one improv skit. We could both be outgoing, yet neither of us had the nerve to invent a workable scene on a whim. It was too much pressure to be funny without a script and not embarrass ourselves, especially in an artsy school.

Like most teenagers, I began to really collect and covet my friendships during my teen years, though I didn't form many long-term relationships from PCS, since I felt so invested in the time and energy I spent working on *Clarissa* for most of the year. That said, fans always want to know if I stay close with past costars after wrapping a show or movie. I rarely do. Most actors' lives are a traveling circus that isn't conducive to regular coffee dates. I've worked everywhere from Surfers Paradise in Australia, to Baton Rouge, Louisiana, to Provo, Utah, and up into Calgary, Canada, for weeks to months at a time. Actors also live in really close quarters, sometimes six days a week, so it doesn't take long for us to get a little tired of each other. We see each other in the makeup and hair room, at the craft services table, and on set. But our top priority is to work. I know this may be disappointing to hear, but when you see actors getting along in a scene, don't assume that they're best friends in real life—more often than not, they're just acting. They've probably had some nice chats between takes, or maybe gone to lunch, but they're not talking late into the night about their hopes and dreams (or at least, I'm not). I've simply grown to trust that some people just come into your life for a lifetime, a reason, or a TV season, and I'm grateful for every experience.

I did become very tight with a lot of people from the *Clarissa* crew during my high school years, and I think this is because of my background. I've always had more in common (at least I think I do) with the grips, camera department, makeup, hair, and wardrobe people, boom operator, sound guys—the technical folks who get their hands dirty. In the business, people like to say there's an imaginary line that separates those who influence the creative direction of a film's story from those who perform duties related to its physical production (this line is used for matters related to the show's budget). "Above the line" people are those who guide creative direction, including your screenwriters, producer, director, casting director, and actors. The crew is said to be "below the line," since they perform the physical production of a film. The first group was always more interested in who I knew, what I could do for them, and what car I was driving, but the second group reminded me of my family. They wanted to work hard and then head home to what was really important. They never had time to chitchat or feed my ego when they had recitals, graduations, and basketball games to get to. In fact, I always thought befriending the crew was much harder, but more gratifying, than trying to win over a network exec, producer, or actor who was always too quick to compliment a day's work. To me, there's no better feeling than having a dolly grip run into me at the craft service table and say, "That scene was hilarious!" I appreciate that the crew is the first to arrive and the last to leave; they're the ones who do the grunt work for no credit and little pay. And they don't care who you are or what you have done, because they've worked with The Best, and this is just another paycheck to feed their families. They also know your every tantrum, mentally record every minute you're late to set or delayed from lunch, and are well aware of sex- or drug-related antics, since they empty your garbage at night. So if they love you in spite of all that, that's saying a whole lot.

When *Clarissa* wrapped in December of 1993, so did my atypical high school experience. It's a wild thing to work through adolescent growing pains while playing a character doing the same. I think living out Clarissa's dramas—in which every problem comes with a solution—kept me from feeling like I had to experience a lot of them on my own. And some situations, like when Clarissa obsessed over what to wear for her school picture, were so outside my reality that I didn't relate. I did, however, *really* understand Clarissa's unrelenting desire to drive a car. I shot so many episodes about Clarissa itching to get behind a wheel when I was fifteen that because of her need to experience horsepower, I wanted this, too. I'd like to say it lifted when I got my license, but my need for speed continued well into my twenties, when I graduated to race car driving (more on this later).

Rather than revel in the fact that I played the lead in a sitcom, which means my world literally revolved around me for four years—a teenager's dream come true, right?—I somehow came out of these years feeling more responsible and introspective than smug and insufferable. I was also totally exhausted. Seventy-hour workweeks, spending tons of time in airports, changing schools, my parents' divorce, shifting friendships, studying for the SATs, and then finally applying to New York University made me eager for a fresh start. Of course, I'm leaving out perhaps one of the biggest energy-sucks of all—boys. But they're up next.

Chapter 7

STRAIGHT FROM THE HART

Teen girls are like Hormone CNN: all guy thoughts, all the time. I was boy-crazy back then like everyone else, but I was also an underdeveloped pixie. Most dudes barely noticed this people-pleaser with a late-bloomer's body—particularly when there were other gals around, flaunting their self-confidence and burgeoning curves. To young hornballs, hanging out with me didn't feel like headline news, though I did hit a few make-out milestones like everyone else.

At fourteen years old, it felt like I'd waited forever for my first kiss. Most of my friends had already played tonsil hockey, and I wanted to do the same. But for my big moment, I wasn't going to settle for any zit-faced kid with a tongue, so I held out until I had a real crush to make a memory. Enter Chris, a grade younger than me and skater-boy cute. He had dark, straight hair that was combed over to the right side of his head and revealed a shaved scalp beneath. For '90s teens, this was as popular a cut as the Bieber style was for a bit. And like most boys his age, he gave me just enough attention to keep my hopes up, but then pushed me away, which held my interest.

The pilot for *Clarissa* had just been picked up, so I was about to shoot thirteen episodes in Orlando and embark on a grueling and unfamiliar schedule. I knew this first kiss would take planning, but I could handle it. My closest friend that summer was a girl named Jessica, so I asked her to have a one-on-one talk with Chris. She told him I really wanted him to be my first, and that I'd be in Florida for the rest of the year, so I wouldn't want to "go out" or anything.

Chris agreed to these conditions and met us in Gillette Park, a popular spot for locals to carve their names into picnic tables, attend our town's annual Oyster Festival, and make out like nobody's watching (though they usually are). On this big day, however, it was all about my Bonne Bell strawberry-flavored mouth. While Jess disappeared with the other boys, Chris and I awkwardly sat on his skateboard, trying not to slip off, and shared an amateur and sloppy kiss that was over in a flash. I don't think I ever ran into Chris much after that, but with my first significant smooch out of the way, I was free to make out to my Hart's delight.

Though my first real kiss went smoothly enough, I can't say the same for my first *on-screen* kiss. The professional rite of passage happened during an episode of *Clarissa* in 1993, when I was sixteen, with a character named Paulie. This was also the first time I had to lock lips as Clarissa, so the show's producers were careful to let me know, before I read the script, that I'd be puckering up that week. I was really afraid it would be embarrassing and awkward to do this in front of hundreds of people, including the crew I'd grown close to. I also knew I'd have to do the scene over and over, until we got it "right." It's not like I'd kissed a ton of boys in my own life so far. Frankly, we could be at this all night.

Though the producers said I could help choose Clarissa's "love interest" from three head shots, when they laid them out I suggested we go with anyone but an actor called James Van Der Beek. (Oh, come on. I know people think he's dreamy, but I never got the appeal.) This was five years before he began getting naked with most of the cast on *Dawson's Creek*. But despite my objections, guess who they cast? Yup, my opinion didn't weigh as heavily as I'd hoped. On top of not being hot for my costar, I was dating my first serious boyfriend, Mike, at the time (more on him later), so I had to overcome a nagging feeling that I was about to cheat on my man—in public, with a stranger, for all to judge and watch.

During rehearsal, James and I both got really uncomfortable as I went in for the kill on the Darlings' sofa. And then, before I could reach his thin lips . . .

"My girlfriend is not going to like this!" he blurted out.

"Neither is *my* boyfriend!" I shouted. I said this in a snotty-teen-girl-rolling-her-eyes way I'd learned from my sister Trisha; she always pulled off more attitude than I could. It's not like *I* wanted the kiss to happen! I needed to make it clear I wasn't happy with this. He was no Mike.

I'm sorry to say that I don't remember a lot about the kiss itself. I think I buried that memory in a deep, horrified place reserved for times I passed gas in school and flirted to get out of speeding tickets. But to this day, I still have a small panic attack—call it PTSKD, Post-Traumatic Screen-Kiss Disorder—when I read a kissing scene in a script. Even if I swish with Listerine and use a lip stain coated with Chapstick to avoid a mess—a trick I learned from the makeup gals on *Clarissa*—it's rarely a sexy thing. In fact, in my newest show, *Melissa & Joey*, Joey Lawrence uses enough lip balm for both of us, creating such a thick barrier that there's hardly any skin-on-skin contact. It's hard to get turned on when it feels like you're kissing one of

Madame Tussauds's wax statues. Not smoking or eating onions at lunch is also a kindness. On a recent episode of *M&J*, one actor had to bite into a chicken leg and then mack on me. He really housed that bird and, with a mouthful of greasy flesh, immediately swooped in for the kiss. I was disgusted by the scene and couldn't understand why he didn't take a tiny, fake nibble for my benefit. Meanwhile, Joey chuckled off to the side, the thought of it making him reapply his Carmex, I'm sure.

At least Van Der Blah and I got it right in six takes. In a film, a director and DP might ask you to do it twenty-five times, to get the most beautiful shot. It requires choreography. *Put more light on your lips. I need your face toward the camera. I need more space between your faces while you kiss.*

Then there's the question of whether to use tongue, and how much. When I was single, I went for it—but seeing that I'm now married with little boys who've watched Mommy's work, it's super embarrassing to act like I'm into the kiss when I know my spouse and kids are going to watch it while sitting right next to me on the couch. I don't even want to consider what my mother-in-law thinks of all this. So I just try to throw myself into the character and push everyone else out of these racing thoughts.

It's also hard to do a passionate, open-mouthed kiss without tongue, yet scripts call for it all the time. It feels like you're eating an ice-cream cone with fish lips. Mario Lopez still swears I got frisky trying to do this in the final scene of our movie, *Holiday in Handcuffs*. When the director yelled "Cut!" Mario jumped around yelling, "You slipped me the tongue! She slipped me tongue!" The more I protested, the louder he got—not unlike the way my six-year-old throws a tantrum over a candy bar at the grocery store checkout. The way I see it, either A. C. Slater deviously slid his slinky Latin tongue into my mouth, or we accidentally "bumped" into each other. As for my best on-screen kiss? Balthazar Getty and I had some wild and spoof-worthy make-outs in a pilot we did called *Dirtbags,* but the suave Adrian Grenier (my costar in *Drive Me Crazy*) tops the list.

Though some girls might have taken more advantage of going to a high school with famous actors, I usually kept my mouth and legs closed to them. I was so busy making new friends, keeping my grades up, traveling south all the time, and working on *Clarissa* that I didn't really make time for PCS boys. Plus, the ones I crushed on—like Donald "Shun" Faison and Dash Mihok—treated me like a sweet little sister, so I never let myself get too caught up in daydreaming about them. Now the big, strong electric guys on set who saw me the same way? They took over my dreams day *and* night. I was hot for men in their twenties who lifted heavy stuff. Maybe it's a Freudian thing, since Dad owned a construction company, or a Long Island thing, since everyone drinks beer from the can—God forbid they get caught with a frosty glass.

I did date one budding actor when I was fifteen years old, but he wasn't from school. I first saw him when I went to watch the rehearsals of a small stage production of *The Sound of Music* with my sister Liz, near our apartment in Greenwich Village. My mom and her best friend/our agent Ayn wanted me to check out two brothers she knew. The younger was Lizzie's age and in the play, and the older always took him to rehearsals. When we all left the theater that day, with the boys a few steps ahead of me and my sister, I dragged Lizzie as fast as I could, so that when they held the door for us, we'd be able to make some eye contact. Big Brother let the door slam in my face.

I bumped into him there the next week, however, and we casually started dating. I don't remember how it happened, but I never told him about the theater incident. He had a stupid way of flirting where he'd try to surprise me with a quick shove into a pile of trash or a street lamp, and then say, "Watch out for that garbage!" I somehow found it charming, even if it was gross. Being with him was also one of the first times I'd hooked up with an aggressive, hands-y kind of guy, so I dressed in layers to make it more difficult for him to get what he was after. I'd wear a trendy leotard top with a snap crotch, tight jeans, a big belt, combat boots that took forever to unlace, and finish the look with a flannel shirt tied around my waist. This was during Nirvana's reign, and I liked mixing their grunge influence with punk styles, though all the extra clothes were really meant to slow the boy down. I think of our tricky make-out sessions when I flip past Fox on the TV, since the boy in the story was Danny Masterson, who played Steven Hyde on *That '70s Show*. His younger sibling was Chris Masterson, who played Francis on *Malcolm in the Middle*.

Not every meaningful man in my life at that time was a booty call or love connection. In 1992, I got to know Joey Lawrence while I was working at Nick in Orlando. This was decades before he could hold me at arm's length with his shiny lips. We saw each other at auditions throughout our childhood careers, and he'd been starring as Joey "Whoa" Russo on *Blossom* for the past two years and was in Florida to visit his girlfriend Kellie Martin, who was about to wrap her part as Becca on *Life Goes On* and was working with John Goodman on *Matinee*, which was shooting at Universal Studios. Joey asked me if I wanted to join them for dinner, and Kellie and I became fast friends. I had no idea then that these two people would make such a huge impact on my life in very different ways—one as my costar on my favorite project to date, *Melissa & Joey*, and one as a lifelong friend. Joey then came back to Orlando, not long after that trip, to bury a time capsule with me for a televised Nickelodeon event. (The capsule, which won't be opened until the year 2042, includes VHS tapes of both *Clarissa* and *Blossom,* as well as a disposable camera with pictures of me and some random *Clarissa* friends on the Universal lot.) At this affair, Joey brought his new girlfriend, Jennifer Love Hewitt, with him, and we had yet another chummy dinner together.

I have to admit—one of the best things about Joey was his taste in women. I was so deprived of girlfriends my age on *Clarissa* that when I met Kellie and Jennifer, I grabbed on to them and didn't let go until I was pried away. I did the same with JoAnna Garcia and Sheeri Rappaport when they were on *Clarissa.* In fact, I gave all the female guest stars, upon arriving at our Sunday table read, an invite to a sleepover at my condo on Monday and Friday nights, plus lunch every day with me at the commissary, a ride on Back to the Future during break, and a trip to the Slime kitchen to taste the goo they had backstage on the studio tour. Was I desperate for camaraderie or what?

For all the fun of teen flirting, lust, and friendship, these feelings had nothing on that of my first love. I fell hard in the summer of 1992, when I was sixteen years old and back in Sayville visiting my dad. A bunch of my on-again/off-again Long Island go-out friends were hanging out in town by the local pizza place, where most kids met up at some point during a night out. I was there with a boy named Tim, who was a super cute, popular guy who wouldn't have given me the time of day when we were in public school and before I was on a TV show. I'd been casually dating him for a few weeks, but that night while Tim was off skateboarding somewhere, a group of guys pulled up in a white Chevy Celebrity. They were from Patchogue, the town just east of Sayville.

Among them was a boy named Mike, who was very tall, skinny, and had an extremely outgoing personality. Like my first kiss, he had long, floppy, dark, skater hair. I clearly have a type—if they didn't look like Danny Zuko, they looked like Pauly Shore. He also had a quirky sense of humor and self-confidence like I'd only seen in the older men I crushed on around the set. Even though he was only a year older than me, Mike knew how to flirt like a man—he was big on flattery and eye contact—and I liked that he could drive and had his own car. He asked me, my sister Trisha, and two of my girlfriends if we wanted to go for a ride, without a real destination, which meant ditching Tim, but oh, well. I thought this was dope because it reminded me of when people cruised in the 1950s. (See: every other scene in *Grease*.)

We ended up at my dad's house, and the whole gang came inside to hang. Dad was now a bachelor and didn't have a lot of rules. He is also the ultimate smartass, so he didn't hold back on joking around with my crush. As soon as Mike and his buddies walked into the house, Dad began his interrogation.

"How tall are you?" he asked, in a deep, fatherly tone.

"About six two," said Mike.

"I didn't know they piled shit that high," Dad said with a snorty chuckle, to let us know that he thought he was hilarious.

Good thing Mike's humor was on par with Dad's, or he might have run for the hills. I also wouldn't have known how to read him. That night, Mike told me his name was Jimmy and gave me a fake number, but I saw right through his prank because it was so Dad-like. I showed him my number in the phone book and told him that I could get us on MTV's *Hanging with MTV* to see his favorite singer, Morrissey, perform if he wanted to come visit me in the city. (MTV and Nickelodeon are owned by the same parent company, so I took advantage of my connections.) He called the next day.

I broke up with Tim, and for the rest of the year, Mike and I acted like a clichéd, first-love, "nothing else matters" teen couple. We were naive to heartbreak and adored each other with abandon. It only took a few weeks for me to fall head over heels in love with Mike, and we spent as much time together as we could. He was a high school senior, so he visited me in Florida when he was on break, and I spent more time in Sayville than Manhattan when I was home. At Dad's house, the fridge was always stocked with Bud, there were no curfews, and I knew where he hid the spare key, so I could easily come and go as I pleased. Though the scenario might have led to discipline issues with other kids, I was already living as a responsible adult for most of the year in Florida. I could handle the autonomy without getting pregnant or arrested.

I was in love for the first time in my life, so I decided it was time to lose my virginity to Mike. Six months had passed, which was the amount of time I'd promised myself I'd wait before having sex with someone I dated. Not so unlike how I orchestrated my first kiss (or most pivotal moments in my life, really), I carefully planned this night to be perfect. Mike's birthday happened to fall on the same day as the Young Artist Awards ceremony in Los Angeles, so a lot of special moments would be happening at once. My mom and her new boyfriend, Leslie, got us our own suite at the hotel; they probably thought that we were already "doing it." For the ceremony, my *Clarissa* stylists helped me pick out a Betsey Johnson strapless lace baby doll dress and thigh-high boots. For extra oomph, I wore a Victoria's Secret corset underneath. It not only looked sexy when I won the award (the first of three for me as *Clarissa*), but it turned Mike on, too. I packed a Victoria's Secret teddy for what would come later.

It was a happy birthday for Mike, and our night unfolded just as I'd hoped. That's all I will say, though. I rarely knock go-go boots and tell, unless I'm five gin-and-tonics deep.

After consummating our relationship, Mike and I were even *more* enamored with each other and found every possible moment to be together. When I went back to work, we spent countless hours on the phone, talking about boring and useless topics, like young people with few real problems and responsibilities do. We also paged each other a lot. Before we had cell phones, rappers and clingy teen couples hung little black boxes off their belts that beeped with phone numbers, urging people to call them. We sent each other messages on these things, using a series of numbers that, when read upside down, looked like words. For instance, 07734 became "hello." Or we typed "69" as a dirty way of saying, "Hey, I'm thinking of you, if you know what I mean." It was a crude form of sexting, but effective nonetheless.

Mike and I were together for fourteen months before he went to Fordham University in the Bronx. As a college man-child living in coed dorms, he partied a lot, ate too much White Castle, and hung out with his brilliant but bizarre roommate Kit (Mike and Kit—insert *Knight Rider* joke here). Shortly after he moved in, I visited his room and was sitting on his bed, taking in the sights and smells of a guy's dorm (basically filth, beer, and sex), when a girl busted in wearing nothing but a towel and asking for Advil.

Right away I knew something was up with this chick if an entire dorm of PMS-ing female students didn't have a single pill to spare, and she came to *my* boyfriend's room, half-naked, like a whorish damsel in distress. As soon as Mike awkwardly introduced her to me, she said "never mind" and left the room. Sur-vival instincts kicked in, and I sensed a threatening female on my playground. (I've had a sixth sense for bitches since I was young.) However, I also get jealous easily, so it can be hard for me to tell who's really menacing and who's not. Was my first love really cheating on me?

On the night of my eighteenth birthday, and the end of Mike's freshman year, I began piecing together the clues that suggested Mike might not be the faithful prince I thought he was. He constantly broke plans, offered fewer invites to stay over on campus or hang out at college parties, and then finally on my eighteenth birthday, when I suggested we go back to his dorm, he wouldn't let me and didn't want to stay over at my place. On my birthday! Mike also refused to admit he was act-ing weird, so a few weeks later, when his friends went to the Jersey shore for the weekend without him (he said he was going home to his folks'), I invited myself to join them. I was a woman on a mission. I drove for four hours, in my busted-up Jeep with no top or doors, down the Jersey Turnpike on my way to the beach. It wasn't the safest decision I've ever made. But I was trying to make Mike jealous by hanging out with his boys, and maybe do some recon on the side. When Mike didn't seem to care, I blatantly asked Mike's two buddies if he was cheating, and sure enough, they'd seen him canoodling with the tart up-stairs.

I was so livid, I couldn't breathe. And since this was my first real relationship, I also didn't understand what I was feeling. I didn't know a heart could literally ache, while simultaneously making me want to throw up. I was also angry as hell. As the sun came up, I sped back to my dad's house in record time and told Mike that I was coming to his house for a talk. Though I was only five minutes away, he left before I got there and his mom answered the door. She and I were as close as any girl and her boyfriend's mother could be—a warm, loving Italian who'd whip us up homemade penne alla vodka at 11 P.M. after a concert or party. God, I loved her pasta. Anyway, I told her I thought Mike was cheating on me, and she promised to make him call me at my dad's that night, since she could see how hurt I was. When Mike rang, I went back to his house and confronted him about what I'd heard. Of course, like most red-blooded American teens who like having their tarts and eating them, too, he lied and said he wasn't dating the trashy coed.

"Calm down," he said. "I just kissed her."

As I drove my doorless death trap home that night, listening to The Smashing Pumpkins sing "Disarm" for the gazillionth time and with the summer air whipping my hair in front of my face, I knew I had to end the relationship. For a long time after, I cried in the shower, tore up our cutesy photos, and returned gifts to him by way of my father, whom he'd started working for. Dad refused to fire Mike, and I couldn't get closure since my siblings stayed close to him and kept calling me with sightings and updates.

As a birthday present from my parents, Dad bought me a bike and Mom got me a plane ticket to Paris, so right after *Clarissa* wrapped, I took off on a bike tour to lick my wounds and burn calories. It was a long, lonely, and physically demanding ride through the French countryside with a bunch of spoiled, immature teens from rich towns in Long Island for four weeks. Not the salve I needed. It was like *Under the Tuscan Sun* meets *Amélie,* but starring an angry, confused, and broken-down young woman. A cigarette, red lipstick, and possibly a mime could have turned this into a moody black-and-white film. *Quel dommage.*

Chapter 8

MOMS DO THE DARNDEST THINGS

Mother/daughter relationships are notoriously complicated. There's Joan and Melissa Rivers, Debbie Reynolds and Carrie Fisher, and how about those Judds? My own mother, Paula, is no Mommie Dearest, but she's certainly thrown me for enough loops to keep my girlfriends entertained by her stories. Even so, our relationship has gone through a lot, both good and bad, that's helped turn me into the person I am today. For that, she gets her own chapter.

When Mom had me, she was all about peace, love, and lactation. She was a '70s hippie, which was proudly marked by her bell bottoms, feathered hair, and the fact that she advocated for the natural benefits of breast-feeding over factory-made formulas. She loved having and feeding babies so much that she went on to have and feed six more over the next twenty-one years—six of them, without drugs during delivery. She basically spent her entire twenties in and out of the hospital maternity ward, and yet when she wasn't pregnant, her stomach was flat and she never weighed more than 110 pounds. I wonder if all that breast-feeding was her calorie-burning trick, because she's never been on a diet or owned a gym membership. One of my favorite things is watching Mom's face change when strangers ask her how many kids she has. *No way,* they say. *You look amazing.* And that's all it takes for Mom's expression to go from looking calm and controlled to unveiling a slow, knowing grin that spreads across her cheeks and reminds me of when the Grinch steals the Whos' roast beast in that Dr. Seuss cartoon. Mom's been fielding this comment for more than thirty years, yet every time she hears it, she gobbles it up like it's her first time.

We were a very affectionate family when I was young, though more into snuggling than doling out messy kisses. And Mom was the one who kept us in line, ruling with a tender heart and an iron hand. She had a great amount of patience, but once she hit her limit—look out. She'd spank us with a wooden spoon and put us in "the naughty chair," which felt like an eternity in exile. My sisters Trish, Liz, and I got a taste of this when we stayed up late making sure our Cabbage Patch dolls and Care Bears were safely tucked into bed; we were always preparing them for a disaster, like if the house caught fire or one of those famous Long Island tornadoes touched down. If Mom heard us giggling after she turned off the light, she'd burst into the room and let 'er rip. But we were only honing our protective Mama Bear instincts, which we learned from watching her.

Whenever I booked a job, she'd sneak on set and hang out in the back to keep a watchful eye on how I was treated. I was in a commercial with Doug Henning, a famous magician at the time, for the very first Chrysler minivan when I was seven years old. Mom overheard the director call me "the little girl in the red shoes" for three days in a row, so on the fourth, her claws came out.

"My daughter has a name," she said in her best make-my-day voice. "It's Melissa."

Though Mom lost her patience on those who deserved it (she also went crazy on families who cut the line at Disney), she kept it together impressively well for someone who juggled as much as she did. Beyond managing our careers, she handled everything around the house, since my father worked never-ending hours in the shellfish business, then with his construction company, and then back to shellfish. Though Mom wasn't a gourmet cook, we always had a decent breakfast on the table, lunch in a brown bag to bring to school, and a hot, balanced dinner with an occasional treat for dessert. She even experimented with making her own bread, which was always so warm and delicious next to the leg of lamb she'd cook for Dad but we kids detested. And while she was no Doris Day, Mom kept our house clean and comfortable, and expected everyone to do their part. We helped her dust, vacuum, take out the trash, wash the car, and weed the garden. Mom grew her own beautiful vegetables, and behind the corn, Dad planted rows of marijuana. They never smoked pot around me, but Mom and I did have open and honest discussions about her cannabis crop that made me uninterested in taking a toke of my own. Once I asked Mom what drugs she'd done and she told me, "Eh, I've tried them all, so you don't have to. None were worth it." She wasn't bossy or "because I said so" about this; she was sharing her experience and hoping I'd learn from it. I took her at her word.

Mom was also very honest when it came to taboo topics like sex. When I was in fourth grade, I was riding bikes around town with my friend Joanne when we came across a *Playgirl* magazine lying on the side of the street. We went back to Joanne's house, looked at the pictures, and split our favorites between us. I remember cutting out the tiny pictures of men with their big ol' shlongs bursting through their assless chaps—super hot. When I got home, I speed-walked through the kitchen and past my mom, who was all the while yelling, "Hey, how was your day?" I thought for sure she must have known the secret burning a hole in my pocket, because I looked and felt so guilty and ashamed scurrying past her to my room. But I've always had a strong gut reaction to right and wrong, and this time was no different. I couldn't imagine living with myself if I didn't tell Mom what I was hiding. I quickly crept back downstairs and spilled the beans.

"I have to tell you something," I said. "I have nudie pictures of men in my back pocket."

I expected Mom to scream or yell at me, but it took her an eternity to react. And then: "How about you just give them to me, and we can forget this ever happened," she said.

Seriously, that was it.

Mom's reaction made me realize how much she trusted me to make the right decisions and come to her if I made a wrong one; she probably wanted to giggle, the way I did when my son recently pooped in a toy bucket and guiltily handed it over. But she's always been candid with me and expected me to be the same with her, which I 100 percent have. I so vividly remember the hot-faced shame I felt that day, even if my indiscretion didn't faze Mom, that I never wanted to have a guilty secret on my conscience again. Because I didn't ever want to upset or disappoint her, I also took a huge parenting burden off her hands. She didn't have to be a strict disciplinarian or overbearing nudge. I'd play that role for myself.

With Mom's trust came freedom without much of a discussion, and I never abused that. Mom let me ride my bike to a friend's house, stay at the park until the streetlights came on, or watch television at night once I finished my homework and chores. This kind of independence gave me and my siblings the confidence to know we'd make good choices on our own, and I rarely let her down. Mom counted on us to be reliable and independent, which worked out well, given everything that needed to get done.

But even with so much on her plate, Mom showed up to every childhood event I can think of. Though she'd never hoot or holler at games or school plays, she was always in the audience or background with a very proud smile. She was also just as straight with me about my weaknesses, though she rarely gave direct negative feedback. I sometimes wonder if that kind of withholding is what kept me guessing enough to always want to please her. If so, I'm often glad she did it because it pushed me a little harder to make an impression on her, and I think that explains some of my professional drive and eagerness to excel in general. The thing with my mom, though, is that once you've done something great, and she tells you, it feels so amazing because you've really earned it. Beyond my parents and siblings, the only other person whose opinion matters to me is my husband, Mark. And you know what? Flattery doesn't come easy from him either. But when I've earned it, I know I've really done something terrific. (Mark swears he compliments me all the time and I ignore him, and maybe that's true too; I tend to blow off most kind words as inauthentic and insincere.) They say you marry your dad, but I think I married my mom.

The only time I remember Mom being actively tough on me, as a kid or otherwise, is when she'd ask me how it went on an audition during our drive back to Long Island. If I said, "I don't think I got it"—and if we were stuck in traffic or she'd had a rough day—she'd get pissed and tell me that's it, we're done with the business, because she was tired of me and my siblings wasting her time. She really believed in me, so it frustrated her when she thought I wasn't trying hard enough to live up to the potential she saw. But usually after the outburst, I'd actually book the job and then we'd do it all over again. One of Mom's biggest eruptions happened after I told her I thought I blew it with Mitchell on that third *Clarissa* audition. That's when she said we were finished with acting for good. Thank God fate didn't pay as much attention to Mom's flare-ups as we did.

Lots of books have been written about the fuzzy boundaries and strange oversteps of moms and their little girls, and for me and my mom, ours mostly happened during the divorce. I think this may have been a natural progression from Mom having me in her twenties, which always led her to say we "practically grew up together!" She also didn't have a lot of girlfriends her own age, the way I do now, and she always leaned most on family when she needed support. I suspect that both of these factors led to her treating me, more often than not, as a close friend. I couldn't get enough of it when I was eight or ten, as she was pumping out babies and I was playing with dolls. But I was thirteen years old when she and Dad got a divorce. I already had hormones, work, a commute, and boys to deal with—I didn't want to add moving, new schools, and all of Mom's issues to that list of stressors. Besides, I didn't know any real, live divorced people. My aunt Zippy was split and remarried before I was old enough to understand what happened, and my uncle Mark had four ex-wives, but he was a horny free spirit, so neither of them seemed to count. Other than them, I'd never watched a marriage fall apart or known any friends whose parents went through it, either.

Though Mom wanted me to be her confidante, or at least acted like she did, I was too young, angry, and selfish to be one.

The only people I wanted to help were me and my siblings, be-cause we were all on the receiving end of the chaos. We had that in common. I dealt by exploring the city, making new friends, decorating my room, and going shopping. And though Mom had always given me room to be independent, now I wished for her to be more hands-on. As Mom managed her new life as a single mother, she left me to make my own meals and pack my own lunches. It was to be expected at my age, but I still wanted her to take care of me in small ways.

She'd always kept close tabs on me and visited often when I was in Florida, but her monthly trips took an uncomfortable turn during the divorce. I spent hours listening to her gripe about Dad's faults and why the marriage got stale—and not even for some massive reason like drug use, abuse, or infidelity, but because he wasn't around enough, which, among other trav-esties, meant the dining room molding never got painted. It made me mad at Dad for being MIA and resentful toward Mom for splitting up our family. On top of it all, I didn't want to en-dure these incessant couch therapy sessions, when I had fifty pages of dialogue to learn for work the next day.

Though I could occasionally step outside the situation to an-alyze my parents' flaws, realize they were only human, and try to find some bright side to the whole mess, my overwhelming reaction was that of a typical adolescent. I used Mom's words against her, felt comfortable talking back and acting out, and yelled at her when I felt she was skirting her responsibilities as a mom to my siblings. It was suddenly clear that Mom didn't have all the answers I thought she did, because as she worked through the divorce, her flaws were on the table for everyone to see. And while I thought she deserved to have some fun with her new life and knew in my head that it took a lot of strength to divorce my dad and go after the life she wanted, my heart was still critical of her decisions because I wasn't her friend or therapist or drinking buddy. I was her child.

It's weird to think about this time in Mom's life without talking about Nanny. She was my mom's mother, and her best friend. Mom wanted a sister so bad but got three tough brothers instead, so she made Nanny her confidante. Even as an adult, Mom didn't make a move without consulting her, since she always considered Nanny to be wise and unconditionally loving. She was our family's matriarch for the first twelve years of my life, and when she wasn't ruling her roost, she spoiled us grandkids at every turn. Nanny traveled a lot and brought us handkerchiefs, dolls, and currency from exotic locations like Yugoslavia and Russia, where we still had family (I think I inherited her travel bug). She and Papa, my grandfather, built us hope chests for our valuable possessions and made us a giant Victorian-style dollhouse, which I still have and cherish. Nanny also sparked my fascination with Shirley Temple, since she bought me my first collectible pin at a Long Island flea market.

Nanny died in October 1988. She suffered three strokes and went into a coma. Our family held nightly prayer groups, but after a few difficult days, Mom took her off life support. It took Mom years to recover from the loss, since Nanny was always her brightest guiding light.

I mention this now because most of the Harts agree that Mom never would've had the courage to leave Dad if Nanny were still alive when it happened. Mom seconds this. She would have eagerly turned to Nanny for advice, and Nanny would have sent Mom back to her unhappy marriage because, as she used to say, "Divorce is not part of my vocabulary." But it seems that at this significant juncture for Mom, she needed to find her own way. To this day, we all hold Nanny in a very saint-like place in our hearts, and her name, Joan, will continue to be passed down through generations of our family (my mom, my cousin, and I all share the middle name Joan).

Mom definitely made the most of her journey toward discovering her new, grown-up self, especially since she never got to sow her wild oats when she was young. So despite having five kids between the ages of three and thirteen, she explored her new city, home, and men like the foxy broad she was. As I mentioned earlier, Mom made friends with a Broadway singer named Allan when she was on that cruise for my sister's gig, so she invited him to be our seventh roommate, and his social life gave hers a head start. As an adult, I'm still not sure why Allan agreed to this arrangement—he couldn't have found it too easy to bring men home to an apartment full of small kids and irritable teens!—though we all loved him and considered him part of our forever-changing family. And as Mom's social Sherpa, Allan introduced her to lots of Broadway backup dancers and singers. Her best girlfriend, Ayn, was also part of this scene, so she was Mom's partner in crime.

The major upside of all this, for me anyway, was that these Broadway guys became my guncles, or gay uncles, and had a strong hand in teaching me lots of adult lessons—particularly one guncle named Chris. I'd already read *Our Bodies, Ourselves,* so I knew how babies were made, but I also lived in Manhattan during the '90s when AIDS was rampant in the artistic community. When I started dating my first real boyfriend, Mike, in 1992, Mom didn't sit me down to clarify or expand on "the talk." She sent me to a Nine Inch Nails concert with Chris. On the car ride to the Meadowlands Stadium in Jersey, Chris explained how the birds and the bees worked, with a special emphasis on HIV. This was a topic he knew well, since he was infected with the virus.

Allan and my guncles introduced Mom to the gay club scene, at which point she turned into a regular Kathy Griffin. She partied with them on weekends, leaving behind her Dad-related frustrations and all those creepy straight men who'd otherwise hit on her. (Us kids went to Dad's house on weekends, which worked out perfectly.) Mom's clubbing wardrobe consisted mainly of short-shorts, bra tops, go-go boots, and the occasional neon wig. She bought them at Patricia Fields' eponymous store, which is now known for its women's clothing, but back then was populated mostly by drag queens. At the end of the weekend, I could smell my pillowcase and tell which guncle had slept in my bed after a night of club-hopping, based on its scent alone.

Sometimes Mom took me with her to the clubs because I loved to dance. Eventually, we became close to the doorman at Limelight's gay entrance. (At the time, some clubs had separate doors to keep belligerent heteros at bay. This also made it easy for me to take friends there on my own.) One night when my mom and I were out dancing, a fake-tattoo artist was hanging out near the main entrance, and I asked him to give me a Celtic cross on my left breast. I loved the design so much that I used a permanent marker to keep it going for days, and five years later, I got the real deal inked on the back of my neck. I didn't want to scare future breast-fed babies with it on my boob and besides, Mom's big rule was that tattoos were perfectly okay as long as they didn't show in a wedding gown.

After almost a year of adventures in self-reinvention, Mom finally met a guy named Leslie at one of her gay bars. After a spat with her friend Eric about who Leslie was checking out— him or her—Mom decided to ask him and learned that he was a straight man on the hunt for unsuspecting women at gay bars. (It really scaled back on his competition.) Mom didn't expose us to a lot of her dates when she left Dad, though I don't think she dated much. But with Leslie, she made it a point to keep us away from the phone if he called, which made me realize she really liked this guy. Originally from the Bronx, Leslie was raised in a boys' home with some of his brothers after his mom died; her eleven children were torn in different directions.

Nowadays, you'd consider Leslie a metrosexual—but back then, he was just a handsome, generous man who took great pride in his movie-star looks. He was also a hairdresser and a plumber, so he could highlight my and Mom's hair one day, and fix our leaky sink the next. That first Christmas, he helped Mom play Santa for her five kids by giving me his old skis and lending a hand with shopping for my siblings. He began joining us for family vacations and soon moved into our apartment when Allan's lease was up. Before we knew it, Mom was pregnant with her sixth child at the age of thirty-seven. Leslie wanted a kid, and who was Mom to refuse? She adored being pregnant and was really good at pushing out the babies. My sister Alexandra, or Ali as we call her, was born in 1993.

We needed more space, so we said good-bye to our town house, and Mom, Leslie, and I went in on a gorgeous old home in Englewood, New Jersey. I was a proud homeowner at the age of nineteen. Our three-story house had plenty of room for the six siblings living there—me, Trisha, Elizabeth, Brian, Emily, and Alexandra—plus a massive backyard, pool, and tennis court. The house was also surrounded on three sides by a very old cemetery where the Lindbergh baby was supposedly buried. Our expansive digs were a big difference from our Sixth Avenue spot, to say the least. Mom and Leslie got married at a nearby church and threw the reception in our backyard, and all the kids were part of this beautiful event. Three years later, they had my mom's seventh child, Samantha, after moving the whole family to California to shoot the ABC series *Sabrina, the Teenage Witch*. Dad got remarried around the same time to a woman named Lisa, and they had my sister Mackenzie, the youngest of our brood.

After I finished *Clarissa*, I got a bunch of calls to audition for characters that were too racy for Mom's seventeen-year-old girl. So she brilliantly decided that we needed control over any project I'd be a part of and started our production company, Hartbreak Films. To get it going, Mom bought the rights to the Archie comic book series *Sabrina the Teenage Witch* and turned it into a Showtime movie as our first project. But Hartbreak wasn't just another job for her—it was a new layer to her evolving identity. Mom now had her first "real" career that strangers took seriously, since housewife and stage mom/manager didn't earn her a lot of positive attention. She also began to dress the part of an exec, though to her that meant wearing short Bebe skirt suits and snug tops to meetings, instead of navy blue suits. She was in her late thirties and felt young and feisty. Why not show it?

Co-owning a company with my mom had the makings of a messy and confusing nightmare, but we handled its launch seamlessly and it's thriving today. I can't think of anyone I trust more than my mother, so why wouldn't I trust her with our careers? In a lot of ways, my successes and failures have always been hers too, so our company just feels like a natural extension of that. At Hartbreak, I love to brainstorm kooky ideas for movies or shows, and she'll do the research to find out if there's a market for it and help me make it happen. For example, I'd always wanted to produce a movie based on Shirley Temple's biography, so in 2001, we turned the book into ABC's Wonderful World of Disney's *Child Star*. One of the highlights of my life was getting invited to Shirley's house to have lunch and discuss the film. (A lot of people think she's passed on, but she still sends me Christmas cards to this day.) Sure, Mom and I get in fights or occasionally disagree about a project, actor, or writer, but Hartbreak also gives us a reason to have lunch or get on the phone to discuss future projects. We're not the type of family that calls to talk about the weather, hear someone's voice, or gossip, so it's the perfect excuse. We're more likely to text, or, when we do call, forget the niceties and get right to the reason we rang in the first place. It's not unusual to hear anyone in my family answer the phone with, "What do you want? I'm busy."

In 2009, Mom had trouble keeping her left flip-flop on her foot. She and Leslie had moved to Malibu two years prior, bought a sailboat, and Mom traded her Jimmy Choo heels for flats. The flip-flop debacle went on for about a year, but she wasn't quick to see a doctor since she was nervous about how serious it might be; she was losing motor control on one side of her body, and she knew that could indicate a neurological problem. When Mom finally made an appointment, she was diagnosed with a large brain tumor called a meningioma.

I was in a meeting when my phone rang a few times and I didn't answer it. Then I saw a text come through from Mom that said, "I have a brain tumor. Call me." When I called her back, Mom didn't ask if I was sitting down. She immediately told me what was going on in her no-nonsense voice, though this time it was tinged with so much panic that I hardly recognized it.

My head began to spin, and it was hard to believe that such a scary health concern was really happening to our family. My first and sudden reaction seemed perfectly sound at the time. I told her we had to find Dr. Shepherd—you know, the dreamy TV brain surgeon on *Grey's Anatomy*—because he'd know how to handle this. Clearly, that wasn't a realistic option.

The next morning, I went with Mom to her neurologist in the city to further evaluate her MRI. All the prime-time medical dramas in the world couldn't have prepared me for what I saw on that film. The tumor was the size of a tennis ball and starting to cross what's called the superior sagittal sinus, which is a channel that drains the blood from the brain into the internal jugular vein. She needed immediate surgery to remove it and relieve the pressure it was putting on her nervous system. After surgery, the doctor would confirm whether or not the tumor was cancerous.

When news like this hits a family, usually life seems to stop until the situation resolves. But I'm a terrible nurse, as are most of my family members. Mom will be the first to tell you exactly what to do to feel better, but rarely do the Harts make chicken soup. And with an illness as severe as possible cancer, it's hard to know how to help even if you want to. So I did my best, at warp speed, while multitasking—which is just what Mom would have done.

During the week of Mom's surgery, a lot of stuff fell on my responsible shoulders. First, I had to fly all of my siblings into Los Angeles for her surgery, which was scheduled for that Wednesday. Since they were all going to stay with me, I also had to coordinate rides to and from the airport. Then in the middle of Mom's ten-hour brain surgery, my publicist called to tell me *People* magazine had put me on their cover for a weight-loss story I did, and to get ready for an onslaught of interviews start-ing that afternoon, though I was in no mental state for it. The following day was my sister Trisha's thirtieth birthday, so we treated her to a very somber dinner in between visits to Mom's recovery room. And on Friday, operating on no sleep, I had to do a live TV interview to promote SweetHarts, the candy store I was opening the next day. Mom was a co-owner and supposed to be there, but of course, she was still in the hospital and on bed rest for weeks after.

While I was at the TV studio, waiting to go live and forgetting I had on a body microphone, my partner at SweetHarts asked with some thick sarcasm how I'd managed to get the cover of *People* that week. I'd just read how the magazine had told *The New York Times* that they had Bristol Palin, some divorcing reality stars, a former teen star (me), and Farrah Fawcett, who was gravely ill at the time, all on hold for the cover, depending on what happened when. With this piece of information in mind, I made a tasteless joke to my partner that I thought was private—and let's not forget my delirium over everything that was going on with my mom. I told him Farrah didn't die, so *People* picked me. I know, I know. On Saturday, with a heavy conscience and Mom in my thoughts, I hosted the mayor and a few hundred people at the SweetHarts store opening, in a striped Betsey Johnson dress that made me look like I'd just ridden in on the Good Ship Lollipop.

Mom's surgery was a success, and the tumor was benign. But just when I thought I was out of the woods, I found out that some jackass on the other end of the mic sold the Farrah comment to the press. When it hit the blogosphere, hate mail began rolling in. Angry bloggers called me "Melissa Joan No-Hart No-Soul." But Mom was on the mend and that mattered more than anything a bunch of anonymous jerks could take out of context. After her surgery, Mom had some sickness from her seizure meds, trouble controlling her emotions, and lots of residual pain as her brain stretched back into the space that had been impeded by the tumor. After a year, she got her memory and sense of humor back, though she told me the Farrah incident was definitely not funny.

Now that I'm an adult with a family of my own, Mom and I can finally laugh at the complexities of our relationship. I know Mom's not perfect, but neither am I—though I don't think you'll find me in a neon wig and hot pants anytime soon. I can't rock it like she can. But we do share a close bond that can't be easily explained or broken. Without a doubt, we love, respect, and look out for each other. When we fight, we might hurl insults or the first thing we see (chairs included), but we often let it go the next day. We don't keep score or hold grudges. She's the mom my girlfriends said they wished they'd had, the MILF my guy friends still ogle—and to me, she'll always be a friend first, parent second, and business partner third. Rather than fault her for being Paula, I prefer to cut her some slack and make the best of her colorful ways. We have a lot more memories to make.

Mom's always been able to wear a lot of hats at once, and maybe because we're a little older now, I can finally laugh about how easily she flits from being a role model one minute to a good time the next. She's a wonderful grandmother to her five grandkids, no matter how much she wished that day would never come because it makes her feel old. After all, she was only forty-seven when she found out my sister Liz, the first among us to have a child, was pregnant. Mom spent all nine months of Lizzie's gestation trying out different names that made her sound delightful, and not like a little old lady who sits on the porch knitting afghans. She finally settled on GG, short for Grandma Gilliams (her married name), right as my nephew Christopher entered the world. Simple and direct, but with a casual wink. That's so her. As is the fact that I once gave her the keys to our house in Lake Tahoe so she could spend a quiet week there with Leslie, but thanks to our security cameras, I found out she had twelve people and two dogs over for the holiday without even telling me. It looked like a party and a half.

On a grumpy day, it's easy to echo what most daughters say, which is that we wouldn't want to turn out like our moms. But honestly, I'd feel so honored to send my children into the world as successfully as my mom did. My siblings and I have good values, have traveled the world, have supportive relationships, and we know how to have a good time. I'm grateful for Mom's sacrifices, admire her strength, and appreciate her unconditional love, support, and trust. She's also good with words. On birthday and congratulations cards, she always writes at the bottom, "If I could have gone to heaven and chosen a child, I still would have picked you." I save them all in my hope chest that Nanny and Papa built.

Chapter 9

AN A FOR EFFORT

At eighteen years old, I'd left my proverbial nests—a stable and happy television family on *Clarissa* and a regal new home in the Jersey suburbs with a new stepdad and baby sister. I was now responsible for myself and legally deemed an adult, but I also felt the extra pressure to decide whether I should continue on my current show-business path, take a break, or quit the industry altogether. I could totally see myself as one of those child stars who, as an adult, becomes a lawyer or an art dealer—why not? So I did what most high school grads do when they need to buy some time while discovering what comes next. I went to college.

When I was biking through France after *Clarissa* ended, with those rich brats from Long Island, I was trying to get over my first painful breakup. But I also had an aha moment that helped nudge me toward the coed route. From time to time, the other kids and I took breaks to rest our sore crotches by doing other outdoorsy things like ride horses, ski in the Alps, and sunbathe in Cannes. In this spirit, our group went rafting one afternoon and encountered a whirlpool. Since the swirling water made the raft circle for a while instead of rush down the rapids, our leader said that if anyone wanted to challenge themselves by jumping out of the boat, scaling a rock wall, and then leaping off a cliff with a thirty-foot drop, now would be the time to do it. The rafts would wait until we climbed the wall and found our way through the trees to the rocky ledge, and then once we saw the boats begin to move downriver, we'd need to jump in the vicinity of the rafts. Here, our leaders would then safely pull us back into the boats. Of course, there was a catch to all this— once you left the raft, it couldn't head back upstream to grab you if you chickened out; the river only flowed in one direction. I was terrified of this dare, but I went for it (I was the only girl who did, too). I had a hard time scrambling to the top, and I hesitated when I got to the ledge. But then I just cleared my head, held my nose, and jumped into the unknown. Scary, rushing waters be damned.

It was like that Alanis Morissette song, "Thank You": *The moment I jumped off of it/ Was the moment I touched down.*

I mention this because I always wanted to go to college, although I had other options in the acting world, and going outside my showbiz comfort zone was daunting. But like when I jumped off that cliff, my instincts told me that life wouldn't be complete without satisfying this urge. I liked the rush that came with learning new things and having fresh ideas—a feeling I remembered, and missed, from my public school days. So in the fall of 1994, I took a leap of faith and became a freshman at New York University. A lot of TV stars move on to feature films to feel the thrill of exploring new characters and psyches, and my decision to go to college wasn't so different. I needed a new adventure after *Clarissa,* and becoming a student could be my most exhilarating role yet.

I didn't choose my future alma mater based on much research, or college visits, or prestigious alumni. Rather, I put all of my eggs in one basket and applied only to NYU's Tisch School of the Arts (I later transferred to their Gallatin School of Individualized Study). When I moved to New York City during my parents' divorce, I spent a lot of time gazing out our town house window and watching the school's purple trolley go by. I think it's remarkable when we let the past juxtapose with the modern world—as with cable cars on a busy San Francisco street or cobblestone walks next to Manhattan's West Side Highway—so I became obsessed with watching this old-fashioned bus shuttle students around town. It also reminded me of Mr. Rogers. "It's a beautiful day in Greenwich Village . . ." always played in my head as it drove away.

But you know what my Bible study friends say: if you want to make God laugh, tell Him your plans. I sent in my tuition check to NYU, and just a few weeks before I was to start classes, I was offered an ABC TV movie called *Family Reunion: A Relative Nightmare.* This starred the late Norman Fell (Mr. Roper from *Three's Company*), Alley Mills (Norma in *The Wonder Years*), and Jo Anne Worley (from *Rowan & Martin's Laugh-In*). It was also the first time my agent had contacted me, instead of Mom, about a role and announced how much I'd be paid for the part. (When I did *Clarissa,* I never asked what I made and nobody ever told me; even now, I'm not clear on the numbers, but I don't care. I did it for fun.) So the movie seemed like a dream scenario: it was a short gig, I was being treated like an adult, and I was offered a nice chunk of money I could put toward college. I also thought the role was sexy. It called for a mysterious runaway who captures the attention of a young boy who's about to attend his annual family reunion, and I'd been gunning to play an enigmatic outsider for a while. On the other hand, I also feared that if I took this job and postponed my first semester, I might get distracted by acting and drop the academic ball altogether.

But . . . I ended up taking the job. I really struggled with the decision, but ultimately it was good money and NYU wasn't going anywhere. The movie began shooting the day after Mom's wedding to Leslie, so I left for the airport still wearing my bubble-gum-pink bridesmaid dress. Four weeks later, I was back in New York. *Okay*, I thought. *Let's try this college thing again.*

Because I've always bunked with guardians or siblings, I didn't want to live alone on campus. So I moved into the coed dorms, which happened to be literally one block away from our old town house and made me miss my colorful bedroom. At NYU, I slept in a lofted bunk bed, with my desk and dresser squished underneath. I plastered what little wall space I had with snowboarding posters. I also had two roommates, Lara and Marianna, who'd already been roommates for a semester without me. The best part of the deal was that we shared a private bathroom, since many of the NYU dorms are converted apartment complexes or hotels.

At least dorm living lent itself to a stress-free social life. I hung out with Lara, watched the sun set over the Hudson River, dyed my hair different shades of red, and went to Knicks games with my girl Jessie, who I'd befriended during my sister Emily's run with *Tommy*. At the time, Viacom owned Madison Square Garden and Nickelodeon, which produced *Clarissa,* so I could always score floor seats to watch John Starks shoot three-pointers and Patrick Ewing sweat all over the court. I also did bong hits with the guys in the dorm room next door, which is about as stereotypically collegiate as it gets, huh? (By this point,

I was enough of a big girl to reconsider Mom's drug advice.) When I was going to NYU was probably the only time between the ages of ten and twenty-five that I liked being around people my age. I think it helped that college kids are so busy trying to find their way that they didn't pay much attention to how, or if, I was finding mine.

What I loved most about being a student, though, was how relaxing and orderly it felt to eat a bagel every day on my walk to class or to know there'd always be an organized activity if I got bored. I was amused by college fashion too—or the lack thereof. I've heard about kids at other schools wearing pajamas to class, but NYU trendsetters took their lax attitude to new levels. I could literally wear boots, slippers, or shoes made from pizza boxes on my way to a Golden Age of Eastern European Directors class and nobody would look twice. People also didn't care that I was "Clarissa," unless they were spreading rumors that she gave some guy a blow job in a closet. (This was never true but still comes up occasionally when I bump into NYU students on the street.) To my peers, I was just Melissa, the short blonde who acted sometimes, but mostly danced on tables and went to women's rights rallies in D.C. I also took my sister Trisha to my first and last frat party, but it was no *Animal House*. The only thing I learned is that I like my beer to be lukewarm and flat. No, really, I do.

Though college let me curiously glimpse a whole new world, I kept getting drawn back into my old one. In January of 1995, two weeks into my first semester, I took a job in Salt Lake City, Utah, for two weeks to guest star on *Touched by an Angel*—and it was a learning experience in its own right. I'd never seen the show, so my interpretation of the character fell short of the producer's expectations. In fact, he called me into his office to talk about it, since I wasn't "reaching deep enough" into my character to keep up with the other dramatic actresses on set. Until now, my TV roles had been mostly comedic, and I wasn't prepared for scenes about impending rape (from Jack Black, of all actors) or an emotionally tormenting fight with the character's mom. I hadn't done that kind of acting since the play *Beside Herself,* when I was twelve years old. I was so humiliated, I burst into tears when I left his office and called Mom for a little TLC. I eventually nailed the kind of earnest acting my producer needed, but I always think of this experience when I start a new project. It urges me to really do my homework.

Between frustrating takes, I became friends with a sympathetic ski bum PA named Hoot, who later introduced me to his buddy James when I came back to visit him in Park City during winter recess. James and I began dating—I was a sucker for his tall, thin frame and giant, kind eyes. Funny how on the set of a show about angels and God, I experienced a little divine intervention myself. I can't help but wonder if the real reason life gave me the opportunity to do a guest role on that drama series was that it would lead me to my next boyfriend.

In September of 1994, Mom was on the playground with Brian and Emily when a fellow mother gave her the Halloween issue of *Sabrina the Teenage Witch,* published once a year by Archie Comics. She and her friend talked about how I'd be perfect to play the character in a movie or television show—the character's age, spunk, and hair color were clearly a match—and a week later, Mom licensed the rights to the characters Sabrina, her boyfriend Harvey, Salem the talking cat, and aunts Hilda and Zelda for just one dollar. Mom then sold *Sabrina the Teenage Witch* as a TV movie to Showtime for a whole lot more. Just as

Picture perfect, 1979

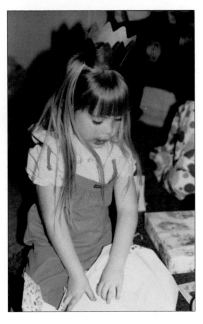

Always the princess, 1981

(Left to right) Me,
Liz (in stroller), and
Trisha with our beloved
grandmother Nanny

Rehearsing my first monologue, for the Connecticut Natural Gas commercial, 1982

"Live from New York...it's *Saturday Night!*" with guest host Billy Crystal, 1985

With actor Edward Woodward on the set of *The Equalizer,* 1986

One of my favorite commercial shoots, for Life Savers, 1987

Me, Mom, and Calista Flockhart at John's Pizzeria on Bleecker Street, sharing a pie, 1989

One of the last photos taken of Mom and Dad together, on the cruise before they called it quits

Just a few New York child actors hanging out: Macaulay Culkin, me, Wendy and Lacey Chabert, my sister Liz, Eden Riegel, and J. D. Daniels (on the floor), 1991

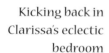

Kicking back in Clarissa's eclectic bedroom

The Darlings, my first TV family

TV Sweethearts Club:
(clockwise from top
left) Tia Mowry, Andrea
Barber, me, Tatyana Ali,
Tamera Mowry,
Jenna von Oy, and
Jodie Sweetin

A night of many firsts: me
with my first boyfriend, 1992

Climbing through "Sam's" window in my
Marlo Thomas look for the last episode of
Clarissa

My "graduation" ceremony on
the Orlando set of *Clarissa*

You say attic, I say penthouse: the NYC bedroom I shared with Trish

My Hollywood Hills bachelorette pad, where some serious partying took place

Hanging with dreamy Ryan Reynolds on the Vancouver set of Showtime's *Sabrina, the Teenage Witch* original movie

With my dear friend and *Clarissa* wardrobe dresser, Michele, on her wedding day

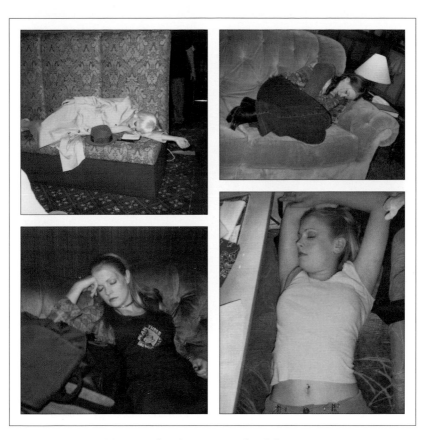

My narcoleptic years on the *Sabrina* set

Always curious: me, playing around with the camera on *Sabrina*

My twenty-first birthday, with Liz (left) and Trisha (right), pre-barf

Me, Mom, and Trisha, 1998

I was about to begin my second semester in the fall of '95, we hopped a plane to Vancouver instead.

Sabrina the movie was a great experience. I had a special place in my heart for Vancouver ever since shooting *A Christmas Snow* there, and I was excited to be back for a new role. The Sabrina character was bashful, cautious, and just wanted to fit in, which I could relate to, though she developed magical powers on her sixteenth birthday, which I could've used in real life. The cast was friendly and easy to work with, and I quickly became close to most of them. Since Sabrina's powers made her a track star, and I had to wear a bikini in one scene, I spent a lot of time at the gym with my first trainer ever, plus my costar Lalainia Lindbjerg, who played Sabrina's archnemesis, Katy. I also became close to Michelle Beaudoin, who played Sabrina's best friend, Marnie. Michelle went on to have a recurring role for a year as Jenny in the ABC *Sabrina* series, too.

Best of all was hanging out with Ryan Reynolds, who played Sabrina's heartthrob-y crush. Nobody looked as good with wavy blond locks and a thumb ring as Ryan did. Though I was madly in love with James, my boyfriend of six months by then, Ryan and I spent plenty of time together—him showing me Vancouver or driving down to Seattle with me and Michelle for the Bumbershoot Festival. Though Ryan was totally cute and charming, I couldn't get past the fact that he always seemed to be channeling Jim Carrey's oddball mannerisms and voices. Even so, he sure knew how to make a girl feel special. On our last day of shooting, Ryan dropped by the set to give me a wrap gift, since he'd completed his part on the movie. He didn't make a big show of the gesture; he just walked into my trailer, gave me a hug, handed me a box, and then walked out. But when I opened the box to find a gorgeous Bulova watch, I went weak in the knees. On the one hand, I knew that some people gave jewelry as wrap gifts, but on the other, no teenage boy had ever bought me such an expensive present before. Until then, I had suspected Ryan liked me and was flirting, but I never let my head go there. Men were always more into me when I wasn't single, so I didn't take him seriously.

His taste in bling, however, did turn me on.

There's a ridiculous moment in the *Sabrina* movie where Ryan looks at me and says in a throaty, whispered hush, "I think what we need is a little less talk and a little more action." When I opened Ryan's gift, I couldn't agree more with this statement. I ran out of my trailer as Ryan pulled out of the lot, jumped in front of his car's headlights, and demanded that he get out and talk to me. How dare he hand me a gift as thoughtful as that beautiful watch and then just disappear. Not sure whether to chastise or make out with him next, I decided to plant a big, fat kiss on his mouth without saying a word more. It was very dramatic.

That night, Ryan and I fooled around in my hotel room. I remember that his lips were pretty wonderful, plus he had these big hands and shoulders that completely swallowed my petite frame. It was a terrific distraction from how strongly he smelled of hair product. We made a plan for Ryan to visit me in New York a few weeks later, even though I felt bad about cheating on James the moment I left Ryan's arms.

The next evening on the phone, I confessed my make-out to James, who was in Utah. I made it sound like Ryan and I had just kissed a little instead of mauling each other all night. I told him I wasn't sure what I wanted, so Ryan could still visit—I'd hoped to keep options open, in case my instincts were off. After a few sleepless nights without both men, I decided that James was the guy for me.

I didn't clue Ryan in to any of this until he came to New York. He stayed with me at my stepdad's tiny studio apartment on the Upper East Side, where I'd been living during my second semester at school. I told Ryan that I wanted to be faithful to James, though we could still make the most of his visit without the touchy-feely stuff. He reacted as if I'd kicked his puppy—surprised, confused, forlorn. The rest of our week was awkward, since Ryan and I wanted different things from the trip and slept on our own sides of the same bed. We didn't even spoon. All my friends now think I'm nuts for ditching *People*'s 2010 Sexiest Man Alive, but I was in love with James and went on to spend four committed years with him. We had a warm, secure relationship that felt really mature. Around the time of Ryan's *People* nod, my sister-in-law Sally, a stylist, met Ryan on the set of *The Change-Up*. She told him how she knew me.

"Melissa let me make out with her once," he said. Let him? The guy could hardly stop me.

After we completed production on the Showtime movie, Mom sold *Sabrina, the Teenage Witch* to the ABC network as a sitcom. This put the final kibosh on going to college, at least with any regularity. I told myself that if the show was short-lived, I could go back or take summer courses. I even asked the dean for a leave of absence, twice, but he denied it both times. God clearly had other plans for me, and I was on board. I didn't want to walk away from a new challenge, plus there were the social perks and career opportunities that come with a network series. I knew *Sabrina* would open doors for me, yet in college, I hadn't even decided on a major. I also liked the idea of living in Los Angeles over New York, since it was closer to James in Utah.

When I first got into school, Dad used to joke, "It only took me two days of college to realize I didn't need it. How long's it gonna take you?" And though this comment sounded ignorant to me at the time, I finally saw his point. I had a profitable career in acting and producing, without a degree. Why kill myself for a diploma? Just like when I jumped off that cliff in France, I needed to prove to myself that I could do this and had nothing to fear. The difference is that my life raft was also an opportunity. For years to come, the entertainment industry would always be there to move me forward and give me the kick I needed to keep things interesting.

I stayed in the Gallatin program at NYU for seven years, on and off. I even studied abroad in Florence. But I never earned enough credits to declare a major, and I've yet to graduate. I hope to go back someday, don a purple commencement robe, and throw a black cap into the air with all the other graduates. Maybe I'll take the trolley to the ceremony. Until then, be patient. At the rate I'm going, I'll be one of those eighty-year-old graduates you see celebrated on the nightly news.

Chapter 10

ABRACADABRA! ANOTHER HIT!

Have I mentioned that my mom knows how to get shit done? After we wrapped on Showtime's *Sabrina the Teenage Witch* in Vancouver, she immediately flew to Los Angeles, pitched *Sabrina* as a sitcom to five networks, managed a bidding war with three of them, and finally sold it to ABC. She saw it as the next *Bewitched* or *I Dream of Jeannie,* but for teenagers. She wasn't alone. The show was picked up for thirteen episodes on a Friday night and initially slotted between *Family Matters* and *Boy Meets World* on its TGIF—"Thank Goodness It's Funny"—fall lineup in 1996. This was a big deal since TGIF cornered the family-friendly prime-time market.

Our ABC series was inspired by a comic book character, but the show also helped boost its printed legacy. *Sabrina* made her debut in a 1962 edition of *Archie's Madhouse,* went on to regularly appear in other Archie titles, and in 1971, *Sabrina the Teenage Witch* was published as a comic book series that ran until 1983. When our live-action sitcom debuted in 1997, Archie then relaunched the comic book series, which lasted until 2004 in various iterations and design styles (I even graced the cover of a few issues), with some stops and starts in between. Since then, Sabrina's made cameos in other Archie comic books yet still manages to retain a loyal, passionate crossover following from the show and comic book series.

Because Mom licensed the show's main characters from the Archie people—Sabrina; her two aunts, Zelda and Hilda; the talking cat named Salem; and a mortal human boy named Harvey—we respected their general identities. Yet our specific interpretations of these players mostly came from our writers' imaginations. I bobbed my hair to look like the print Sabrina's, but the nuances that gave Sabrina life on TV—how she acted shy around boys, tried desperately to fly under the radar at school, or zoomed through the air on a vacuum—were all original to the show. Archie did make some demands, though nothing major, like ensuring Sabrina wore a seatbelt in a moving vehicle or crossed the street at a crosswalk. It was a very fair trade-off.

The result? A madcap hit about Sabrina Spellman, a teenage witch who discovers on her sixteenth birthday that she's brimming with magical powers. She tries hard to blend in with her friends and enjoy a "normal" adolescent life, while still making the most of her extraordinary abilities. The problem is, she's a novice with her skills, so her well-intentioned spells often go awry. Sabrina lives with her five-hundred-year-old aunts, Hilda and Zelda, who are also witches, in fictional Westbridge, Massachusetts. Her on-again/off-again high school boyfriend, Harvey, is clueless to her powers, and her chatty cat, Salem, is really a warlock-turned-feline undergoing punishment for trying to take over the world. So while the show embraced teen-related plots like finding a date to the dance, Sabrina mostly explored her supernatural side. In her world, dolls talk, everyone has a secret twin, dates can be made from "man dough," witches become addicted to pancakes, and people split into four personalities to please everyone around them.

Mom had faith in *Sabrina* from the start, though success was never a given. We were always the little show that could. Though TGIF was a win for us, Friday nights are also typically referred to as death slots in the TV industry, since so many people go out on weekends. Yet *Sabrina's* ratings skyrocketed, squashing those of "competitive" shows like the highly antici-pated *Clueless,* which ABC expected to outpace us in the TGIF block. In fact, our numbers were higher and our run longer. (I actually met with producers about playing the lead of Cher on *Clueless* before *Sabrina* was picked up, but at the time, I couldn't nail the whole "airhead with a heart" shtick.) Even when CBS launched *Everybody Loves Raymond* the same year as *Sabrina,* in our same slot on Friday nights, its numbers never climbed above ours. In fact, star Ray Romano once told *Entertainment Weekly* in an interview, "My daughter watched *Sabrina.* I had a zero share in my own house." When his show moved to Tuesdays, how-ever, it had real longevity and success.

For us, it helped that *Sabrina's* audience was vast and de-voted. Whereas Clarissa was an independent teen with an edge, Sabrina related to those who didn't want to stand out in a crowd. She was self-conscious about her magical powers, which made her relevant to viewers who blushed over an awkward trait or growing pain in their own life. Yet one of my favorite things about the show was that we never pandered to viewers with a "very special Sabrina" episode. We didn't get into tough topics unless it was through a silly lens, since the show's purpose was to entertain, not preach or teach. Families and kids could watch it together, since the jokes were sophisticated enough for adults, kids were into the magic, and teens identified with Sabrina's persona. The witchy stuff also tapped older adults who missed the original spell-casting divas, Samantha and Jeannie. And finally, Sabrina appealed to her comic fans. As anyone familiar with Comic-Con conventions will attest, comic book enthusiasts are a devoted bunch. Franchises like *Star Trek*, *Star Wars*, and *Buffy the Vampire Slayer* will infinitely live on because of their hardcore followers. I recently went to one of these international conferences to sign autographs for fans, and you wouldn't believe how many adults like to dress up as Thor or Boba Fett from *Star Wars*—merging fiction with reality, in a very tangible way. Given that we turned an Archie character into a real, live, pretty teenager with a sci-fi twist, the show was a geek's wet dream.

My demanding *Sabrina* schedule was the same as it had been for *Clarissa*—three weeks on, with either one or two weeks off—which Mom had suggested to the network. We rehearsed Monday and Tuesday, with a table read on Monday morning and a run-through of the entire show on Tuesday evening. We began filming Wednesday at 8 A.M., which meant I was in the hair and makeup chair by 6 A.M., and worked Thursday and Friday until the episode was complete. We put in ten- to twelve-hour days, and on Fridays, sixteen to twenty. In the beginning, we killed ourselves ironing out special-effects wrinkles, like how to make Sabrina's spells look real or get that damn cat to talk. I've never felt more grateful to the Screen Actors Guild than I did during this period, since they have a strict rule that if actors work within twelve hours of a wrap time, the studio is fined a steep monetary penalty. No wonder I took frequent naps on any furniture I could find around set (okay, so my up-all-night social life didn't help). The crew thought it was funny to take Polaroid shots of me in umpteen odd locations and costumes and, at the end of each year, hand me a photo album full of my most embarrassing, mouth-wide-open snooze pics. As my husband says, I look like a Venus flytrap when I sleep. I'm sure a spider or two has made its way into my yap over the years.

Though *Clarissa* helped prep me for a taxing sitcom schedule, *Sabrina* was much more demanding in some ways, though at least I didn't have to find time for school between scenes. On *Sabrina,* we shot thirty scenes a week, compared to *Clarissa*'s ten, which was tough to fit into three days, especially with various talking animals, elaborate setups, and special effects. The upside of this was that the scenes were also shorter, which meant significantly less memorization—no more four-page *Clarissa*-style monologues for me. *Sabrina*'s tone also took some getting used to. While *Clarissa*'s episodes were clever, zingy, and sagacious with a happy ending, *Sabrina* was more about escapist fantasies—skiing on Mars or visiting my eccentric Aunt Vesta, played by the fabulous Raquel Welch, at her home in the Pleasure Dome. I didn't need to put as much effort into being a compelling, realistic, and relatable character with Sabrina, either. It was all about delivering the joke, which is a different type of skill and comes more naturally to me.

Though I was always a professional, knew my lines, and showed up for every rehearsal and stage blocking, I worked hard but rarely went that extra mile. Part of the reason for this is because *Sabrina*'s directors didn't push me as intensely as *Clarissa*'s did; maybe it's because I was an adult, or because I was the show's executive producer, or because I wasn't afraid to push back. Also, for the first time ever, my life was much bigger than just my job. I had a serious boyfriend, partied at night, and made the most of living in Los Angeles as a newly minted transplant. I often thought about that Bush song "Come Down"—*I don't want to come back down from this cloud/It's taken me all this time to find out what I need*—and hoped the other shoe wouldn't drop. I had Mom on set, James coming by, close friendships with the cast and crew, professional freedom—and it all felt really good. There was little work/life separation, but whatever. Why fix what wasn't broken?

The only unusual consequence of this overlap was that I sometimes internalized Sabrina's personality. If the character was in a crummy mood in my script, I'd be in a terrible mood all week while shooting. If Sabrina was addicted to pancakes, I found myself eating more of them that week, too. If Sabrina was having boy trouble, I'd get pissed off at whoever I was dating until we moved on to a new episode. In fact, Sabrina spent most of the final season in 2003 preparing for her wedding to Aaron, played by Dylan Neal, and sure enough, I'd also become engaged to my real-life husband, Mark, and was planning a wedding. I wish I could say I was going all method, but when work and life overlap the way mine did, it's bound to leave an impression on both. By the time my wedding day rolled around, I was a pro at lifting all that lace and taffeta to use the toilet.

During my first few seasons, I spent a lot of free time with Eryn and Christine in makeup, Ralph in hair, and Kimi in wardrobe. When your face sits inches from someone else's for as many hours as mine did, you can't help but develop feelings for them. I'd brought my friend Colleen with me from *Clarissa* as my key hairstylist, since we had a special bond; she was the first to inspire me to take care of myself with Denise Austin workouts, aromatherapy, massage, wheatgrass, and praying to Saint Theresa. During *Sabrina*'s hiatuses, I took lots of trips with friends from the glam squad. It wasn't hard to turn buckets of tequila, impromptu tattoos, and a black eye into "remember when?" stories with these women. They're all a little older than me, and were constants in my life, so our friendships grew at a healthy, steady pace. I made Kimi my son Brady's godmother, partly due to how close we became during a *Live with Regis and Kathie Lee* press appearance in the Bahamas, where we broke into a waterslide park after hours while wearing our jeans. And even now, Eryn, Kimi, Christine, and I keep a "ya-ya book," inspired by the one in the novel *Divine Secrets of the Ya-Ya Sisterhood*. We pass the scrapbook to each other when there's been a significant moment in our lives—childbirth, Emmy nominations, new homes, divorces, weddings—and record them for posterity.

I became fast and furious friends with the cast closer to my age too, though most of these relationships fizzled after the show ended. Even so, we were good for each other at the time. A lot of us were new to L.A., ready to take the city by storm, and in my twenties, that was plenty. I spent a lot of time with a red-headed stoner named Parker, who was a production assistant (PA) on set; a laid-back surfer named Todd, one of our camera assistants; my music-loving costar Nate, who played Harvey and was always up for anything; and Michelle, who I'd met on the set of Showtime's *Sabrina*, where she played Marnie but now was Jennie, Sabrina's best friend. (It was basically the same role, but with a new name.) My boyfriend, James, was also part of the gang, since like him, all the guys came from small or suburban towns and had that in common. Mainly, we threw hot tub parties and rowdy BBQs, and took trips to see bands and comics around the city. We also hung out at the beach, the lake, or the mountains. By the show's second season, Michelle was replaced by Lindsay Sloane, who, during our first season, worked on the soundstage across from us on a show called *Mr. Rhodes*, which was later canceled. She and Nate had already fallen hard for each other during his first season on *Sabrina* (no other on-set, or on-lot, romances—sorry!), so when she was part of the cast and our clique, she played my newest friend and became one in real life.

Sabrina's first four seasons ran on ABC from September 1996 to May 2000, and the final three on The WB Television Network from September 2000 to April 2003. While I had a great run on Nickelodeon, I was thrilled to learn how a big-time network gives your show every opportunity to succeed. We had loads of advertising and promotion, press, and a budget that made sure we were all well paid, our special effects wowed, and our guest stars were big names. ABC also personally treated us like royalty. Because its parent is The Walt Disney Company, they sent us on special trips to Disneyland for charity work or to shoot an episode that promoted their newest theme park, Animal Kingdom at Disney World in Orlando. Mickey Mouse is the ultimate boss.

ABC also gave me a chance to do more than act: this was the first time I'd executive produced a sitcom. In this role beside Mom, one of the things I enjoyed most was helping to round out the cast with the other leads and supporting actors. I loved being part of auditions, because as a fellow actor who's suffered through these intimidating and humiliating feats, I know it helps to have a real actor read the script's other parts, instead of the usual casting director. Too many times I've had to profess my love for a boy, while staring into the eyes of a middle-aged woman—who, by the way, was criticizing and judging my every facial twitch. Having me stand in also helped us all make casting decisions based on who I felt a great connection with.

Whether I was on a show or in a play, I'd always wanted to be at its helm and help impact its final look. And because of Sabrina, I got my Directors Guild of America (DGA) card. Though

Clarissa directors were always generous with their time and insights, most directors got annoyed with my constant refrain: "Wouldn't it be better if . . ." and "What about if I just . . ." So when Mom and the network asked me to direct an episode, I was ecstatic. Every time I read a script, I imagined the scene in a specific way, so I was excited to be able to make that visual come to life now—if only I could do it justice. I was also scared that I couldn't handle a cast and crew while acting myself. How would I prepare to say my lines *and* yell "Action!" at the same time? Could I perform and guide those around me? Was it possible to do this without pissing everyone off?

To watch me juggle two jobs at once, you'd think I was acting in some kind of farce—but believe it or not, this is how it's done. So first, I got my makeup done while positioning the cameras. I ran on set, had my first AD (assistant director) call "Action!" and then I delivered my performance. While I was acting, I watched the other performances with a director's eye and yelled "Cut!" when the scene was over, even if I was in it. Then I ran back behind the camera to either watch what we'd just done replayed on a monitor, or, to save time, trust the camera operators to tell me if we got the shot "in the can." This was physically and mentally draining, not to mention embarrassing when I got naked in front of the crew for a quick wardrobe change because I didn't have time to run back to my trailer.

The best advice I got about how to direct a good scene, which I still use to this day, is to remember that it's all about storytelling. As a director, my job was simply to build a narrative, one element at a time. Harder, I found, was learning to trust my instincts when I did this. I remember setting up a shot for a coffeehouse scene, and I wasn't sure how to open it. I asked Bill, our director of photography (DP), or cinematographer, for his input. Bill was my close friend when I wasn't directing and a bit of a bulldog when I was. His tough-love response: "I don't know. You're the director." I was shocked that he'd hang me out to dry on my first directing gig, but it was really his way of reminding me that I had to crystallize my vision, so I could manage naysayers and any challenges that came up. It's a lesson I still appreciate—that the director has to be prepared to make quick, solid decisions at a moment's notice. For the scene, I went with a dolly move right across some fake jack-o'-lanterns in the foreground and pushed into the cast at the coffee counter. It was a smooth move, I have to say.

Bill's words rang truest, though, during one of my proudest directing moments ever, ever, ever. During a Christmas episode, the script required a shot at the end of the show in which Soleil Moon Frye, who played my college roommate Roxie, and Kate Jackson, as her mom, ice-skated on a pool that Sabrina had magically frozen from her hotel room above. With me in the window, I wanted to shoot from Sabrina's point of view: looking down on the two women ice-skating below. But without a real pool, ice, or even ice-skates on set (it was a cement stage), Mom and the other producers discouraged me from doing it. They suggested I shoot from below the actors, chopping off their feet above the Rollerblades and tilting up.

Their idea didn't match my vision of the story, so I decided to trust my instincts. I got down on the floor with a broom, called in four chorus singers we'd used throughout the episode, and asked Cindy from set-dressing to bring me a very long swag of green Christmas garland from the living room set. I arched the garland, as if it was on the outside edge of a pool, swept all the clumped, fake snow against it as if they were frozen ice chunks on the surface of a pool, surrounded the area with the chorus kids, and finally put Soleil and Kate in Rollerblades, just below frame so that the shot started at their ankles and you didn't see their actual skates. A little ingenuity made the shot shine from above, just the way I wanted it. My mom and the producers were so impressed, and I felt beyond validated. The move gave me real cred with the cast and crew, not to mention the confidence to take chances during future directing challenges.

One of the reasons I think I get so much pleasure from directing is that I've always been enamored with "the magic of television," and the ability to make fiction look like familiar reality. A good example might be how *Sabrina* took place in Boston but was really shot in L.A. on Paramount's Stage 14, or on the New York backlot street. Every great Hollywood lot has a New York City street set—one of the many tricks of the trade. They're only a few blocks long and include fake storefronts and brownstone steps that resemble Manhattan's. Since Boston's streetscapes can look like New York's—if you tilt your head and squint really hard—we got away with fudging this when we needed a street scene on *Sabrina*. The rest of the time, we got visually creative. For Aunt Hilda's wedding, an episode I directed, we used a small, hedged area at the front of the studio by the main gate, and for the Spellman family secret episode, when my evil twin and I are about to be sacrificed on top of a volcano, we stood on a ledge made from two-by-fours and papier-mâché, in a parking lot where my car was parked two feet away. Possibly the best sleight of hand from that episode, though, was how you'd never know I spent most of the volcano shoot puking my guts up from a nasty flu. The glam squad kept my hair and makeup neat and smudge-free, and our wonderful key grip Phil stood behind the ledge the whole time to catch me if I passed out.

Some of *Sabrina*'s most fantastical stunts were about the magic, from a vacuum that flew to clothing that changed itself. Even during the opening sequence for the first three seasons, I posed in front of a magic mirror in the same three costumes and then—poof!—the fourth look was different every week and worked back to a quip about the outfit. We took this cue from *The Simpsons,* whose credits always began with Bart scribbling a new sentence on the blackboard and ended with the whole family on the sofa in an unexpected arrangement every time. Though the final result of our opening titles looked professional when it aired each week, the process did cause some unscripted giggles around set. We shot a handful of title shots at the end of one Friday a month, so I'd wear a baseball player costume one minute and change into a fruity Carmen Miranda costume the next. And since Fridays were our late nights during those first few years, we were already really punchy. As I tried stuff on, Eryn, Kimi, and I came up with dirty versions of what I could say about my outfit. One of my favorites went with a reindeer costume for the Christmas episode: "I'm a horny little piece of tail. Nice rack, huh?" Viewers never saw these, but the crew looked forward to when we'd air the gag reel at our wrap party each season.

Then, of course, there's the best trick of all: Salem, the talking cat—a clever, devilish sweetheart. Everywhere I go, people ask me about that animal. Was he real? Who made him talk? And of course, they always want to know as I'm bolting through the airport or down the sidewalk chasing my kids. For a while, I considered walking around with a black sock in my back pocket to use as a puppet when it came up to throw people off (and when I was busy, get them to leave me alone). But honestly, I was always amazed at how many moving parts brought Salem to life.

First, there were live felines. When we shot a real cat, there were actually about seven Salems per scene, plus our animal trainer, Cathy, and her crew of wranglers to help them "act" out their parts. Each cat had a different talent: one liked to be held, one liked to lie down, one liked to run, one liked to chase things, and so on. I was fond of Witch, the cuddly older Salem who liked lying in my arms, and one of its kittens, named Warlock, who never met a ball of yarn he didn't attack. Of course, the real cats didn't always behave according to the script. Sometimes they wandered, sometimes they scratched. By the end of each season, our sets reeked like tuna-flavored Fancy Feast from all the food placed under tables or next to props to entice the kitties to do their stunts.

In addition to the real cats, we had two animatronic ones and two stuffed kitties that shared the name "Stuffy." Stuffy looked just like the animatronic version but without the mechanics inside. He was mainly used during rehearsals to show the cat's placement and blocking, but once in a while, we'd tie a string around Stuffy to drag him behind a moving prop, or throw him across doorways or out from behind the couch. I always laugh at those scenes, because with all the money we spent on special effects, we still pitched toys across the room like in an *SNL* skit (Stuffy versus Laser Cats! I'd pay to see that battle). To make Salem look like he was talking, we had three highly trained puppeteers, two of whom stood off to the side with remote controls that looked like the kind that manipulated toy boats and trains. One puppeteer controlled Salem's mouth and cheeks, and a second, its ears and eyes. Then there was Mauri, our third hand, who had the least comfortable job of all: she moved Salem's body and tail from hiding spots, like under a cramped table or tucked inside a cabinet. Lucky for her, she was tiny. (Her big, red, curly hair was the hardest part to hide.) Every time we finished a Salem scene, the whole crew yelled, "Power down, Mauri!" to tell her she could shut off the cat and come out from her hiding spot. It became one of our inside jokes. Beyond the tight squeeze, Mauri's job was scary dangerous when other wild animals shared the spotlight with Salem. Cathy, our wrangler, also brought these each week—elephants, donkeys, and lions, oh my. Once an alligator snatched a sofa cushion and did the death roll with it, while Mauri was under the couch. The reptile's force shoved the furniture backward, and Mauri with it. When a panther got loose on set, Mauri had to stay in her hiding spot for an ungodly amount of time. I wasn't there for either fiasco, thank goodness, since I was never allowed on set with the wild animals. The network thought I was too expensive to be eaten.

As for Salem's voice, Nick Bakay, one of *Sabrina's* talented writers and still a good friend, did the honors. During the first few seasons, he recorded the voice live on set and later, he left us to work on *The King of Queens* (as a writer, not a talking animal) and did his voice-overs in a studio. When he was on set, his cat scenes were the highlight of my day—especially when he ad-libbed lines, like when a live cat went off-script. One time, a cat was supposed to sit patiently on a counter next to deviled eggs, but it got up to take a sniff instead. Blooper aside, Nick stayed in character and offered an unexpected, "Yum, eggs!" that reduced us to tears and made it to our gag reel.

By our fifth season, Sabrina and I were getting older, and we couldn't arrest our development any longer. The writers sent Sabrina to college and aged up the show by adding roommates— Soleil Moon Frye as an edgy and rebellious feminist, Elisa Donovan as a shallow ditz, and Trevor Lissauer as a sci-fi-obsessed nerd. Great timing, too—when we moved to the WB in our sixth season, we fit right in with its young-adult-centered shows like *Dawson's Creek* and *Buffy the Vampire Slayer*. It's not unusual for a series to change networks—for instance, *Buffy* later went from the WB to UPN, and *Scrubs* from NBC to ABC—though it usually happens when one network feels the show's losing steam and another thinks it still has legs. But ABC had offered us only one more season and the WB gave us two. More episodes meant longer job security for the cast and crew, plus more syndication, which was a financial perk for those who owned a piece of the show. We were lucky that a lot of our faithful audience followed us to the WB and liked the new angle and fresh blood.

One night at a bar in L.A. before we began working together, I ran into Soleil Moon Frye for the first time in about seven years. She and I had bumped into each other at auditions at various points along our career paths, and once at the Young Hollywood Awards in 1992, but this time, our relationship stuck. After that, we went to the gym, parties, and premieres together. When the new characters were being introduced to the show, I made sure the casting director and producers saw Soleil for the part of Roxie. When she got it, I was thrilled to have yet another good friend on set with me every day. Soleil fit right in with our loud, goofy, and laid-back crew. She caught the giggles when someone flubbed their lines and got carried away with physical comedy moments, which left bruises of love all over my shoulders. It was also nice to lean on her emotionally if I was having a hard day, and to joke around between takes.

Nearly all the girls on set, including Soleil, hung out at my trailer during lunch and breaks. It was on the Paramount lot, right next to an area called "the tank": a deep blue basin with a tall wall painted to look like a fluffy blue and white sky. The tank was mostly used as a parking lot, but when it wasn't packed with cars, producers filled it with water for scenes that took place on an ocean. Not only did I have "beachfront property," but the set designers gave me a wooden picnic table with an umbrella and laid Astroturf on the cement to create a small oasis.

The girls spent so much time here between scenes that we started a book club and read everything from *The Red Tent* to the Harry Potter books. We carved pumpkins at Halloween and snuck cigs on late-night shoots in our dreamy sanctuary. For privacy, the set people erected a lattice covered with fake roses at each end of my trailer. Too bad it didn't prevent a pervert from stealing my worn G-strings from the trash outside my trailer and selling them on eBay. I never wore butt floss before *Sabrina,* but Kimi would go bananas if she caught me with panty lines. Sometimes after a long day, I'd be so anxious to get them off that I'd just throw them in the garbage, never imagining they could end up on the black market. It didn't last long. Once Paramount caught wind of this, they and the FBI launched a sting operation to find the criminal and busted him when he came in for a fake interview to work at the studio. If we'd caught the shakedown on film, it would've been a good story line for that *Dateline* show: *To Crotch a Predator.*

When I wasn't with the ladies at my souped-up trailer park, I spent a lot of time with my TV aunties. I felt very close to Beth Broderick (Aunt Zelda), who liked to flash me her ta-tas as a joke, and Caroline Rhea (Aunt Hilda), who kept us laughing with tales about her ex-boyfriends and Irish gym teacher. Caroline was also a stand-up comic, so the cast and crew doubled as a sounding board for her material—no two-drink minimum required. I still use some of her best lines, like when she'd say she had "diarrhea of the mouth." Sometimes she told people her name was Caroline Joan Hart, and she'd go berserk when they pronounced "Caroline" with a short "i," as if the "e" didn't draw it out. Beth and Caroline also gave me invaluable advice, mainly having to do with men, and the importance of wearing a bra, which I ignored at the time but after having three kids, am now putting to use. One lesson that still resonates with me was about when to bite your tongue. When I was twenty years old, I rushed to the polls to "rock the vote," since MTV had beaten this into my head since I was twelve. I wore my "I Voted" sticker proudly to set on that Super Tuesday, feeling pleased with my civic duty. But when the aunties asked who I voted for, and I proudly told them Bob Dole, good grief if they didn't spend the next few hours heatedly explaining why he wasn't the best guy for the job. Once they stopped their yammering and we got on with rehearsal, some of the Republican crew pulled me aside and whispered, "Way to go." After that incident, I chose my political audience carefully, especially as a young red elephant in Hollywood.

Sabrina was full of talented recurring actors and guest stars. Among my favorites were Mary Gross, Alimi Ballard, and Paul Feig, who played Mr. Pool, Sabrina's overly enthusiastic science teacher, and went on to create *Freaks and Geeks* and direct *The Office* and movies like *Bridesmaids*. Phil Fondacaro was also priceless as Roland, a little person who lived in the Other Realm, was obsessed with Sabrina, and often stole her away from her aunts. He and I had some laughs while shooting the Rapunzel episode, where I was dressed in traditional princess gear with the long locks. We had to hold hands running through a meadow. Off the clock, Phil partied hard, and I often bumped into him in L.A., usually at the Playboy Mansion with "this annoying guy" he'd say was renting his guest house—Verne Troyer, aka Mini Me from *Austin Powers*. I was always impressed with how regularly Verne scored with the Playmates in those dimly lit mansion bathrooms. Martin Mull, who played the principal, Mr. Kraft, was my all-time favorite regular. He was already well known for his huge body of work and later became the luncheonette boss on *Roseanne*. He has an inspiring life and a love of art, and he once told me he always said yes to a job because he was afraid it could be his last, which I understood. Whether we were at his art studio or chatting on set about his balanced outlook on life, I always felt inspired by his passion for cultivating new interests, which encouraged me to feed mine. He was funny as hell, too.

Sabrina had its share of big-name guest stars, like Loni Anderson, Barbara Eden, Raquel Welch, and the cast of *Laugh-In*; I even got to tap dance with Dick Van Dyke (I wasn't half bad). Friends like Garry Marshall, Donald Faison, and Brian Austin Green also came by for an episode here and there, and once I met my future husband, Mark, the lead singer of the group Course of Nature, I made sure we invited his band to perform in an episode, and we took photos of them for the walls of the music magazine office where Sabrina worked during the seventh season.

As a music head myself, I was stoked when we brought on guest stars from this world—among them Paula Abdul, Davy Jones from The Monkees, Randy Travis, Hanson, Avril Lavigne, 10,000 Maniacs, Violent Femmes, Coolio, Goo Goo Dolls, and Debbie Harry. One fan favorite was Britney Spears. She and I had a big year in 1999, doing a lot of press together to promote my movie/her song *Drive Me Crazy*. On *Sabrina*, she also appeared as a "gift" from Sabrina's dad while Sabrina was visiting his apartment in the Eiffel Tower. For five minutes of TV time, I got to dance like a spaz with Britney. But B had nothing on the Backstreet Boys, who gave a mini concert on the show when they drank from a magic bottle that Sabrina left behind to give her friends a boost at the school talent show. I remember Nick Carter's eighteenth birthday fell on a shoot day, and when he asked me to join him for some birthday fun, I offered him my eighteen-year-old sis Lizzie instead. (I already had James, re-member?) Three years later, Nick and I would end up in a lip-locking session in Sydney, Australia, while I was there producing a film; my sisters started uncontrollably screeching when they saw him kiss me good-bye in the elevator—so embarrassing.

Every day, Mom busted her ass with *Sabrina* business while try-ing to get other Hartbreak projects going on the side to expand our brand beyond the witch. We explored independent films, reality TV shows, and even a possible hair-care line, but the show was the most powerful force of all. Video games, a top-selling Scholastic book series, dolls, and even a Sabrina ice-cream pop kept the checks coming. In 1999, we also shot a cartoon series called *Sabrina: The Animated Series,* with my sister Emily as the voice of a young Sabrina, and me as both her aunts. Mom was incredibly hands-on and proved she was more than just a fluffy stage mom who got credit as producer per her kid's contract. She belonged at the helm of the show. Mom was the heart and soul of *Sabrina* and its franchises, and she protected the brand and character like her own children.

While shooting *Sabrina,* I passed on a lot of feature films, es-pecially those in the emerging horror genre, like *I Know What You Did Last Summer* and *Urban Legend.* Wearing a revealing shirt while screaming "What are you waiting for?!?!" to some man with a hook wasn't the meaty part I was after. So I held out, and during summer hiatuses, I went back to NYU for some credits. In 1998, my mom hinted to the network about how much I wanted to shoot a juicy *Roman Holiday*–themed movie on loca-tion, which somehow turned into me doing *Sabrina Goes to Rome.* This wasn't the film I had in mind, but I was loyal to *Sabrina* and to ABC, and I did relish the idea of living like a local in Italy for a few months. To sweeten the deal, ABC hired a lot of my friends and even my boyfriend, James, to act in the movie, and they brought along my closest crew, including Eryn for makeup, Kimi for wardrobe, and Colleen to do my hair. Some of the Salem puppets came, too, though the live one we got from an Italian wrangler was pretty scrappy; he looked like the sick, balding, scruffy alley cat cousin of our fluffy real thing. A year later, I got the travel bug again and it was off to Australia to shoot *Sabrina, Down Under*.

No travel memory, however, compares to when 'N Sync, who did a cameo on the show in 1999, asked me to join them in Turks and Caicos at the end of their 2001 summer tour. I knew JC Chasez and Justin Timberlake from when they worked on *The Mickey Mouse Club* in Florida, and Joey Fatone from when he worked as a performer at Universal Studios for the character Wolfie in *Beetlejuice's GraveYard Review*. But it was on *Sabrina* that I became buddies with the rest of the band. In the Caribbean, we had a great time sipping fruity drinks and partying with some other celebrities like Tori Spelling and Olympic medalist Tara Lipinski. The boys took off for the States on September 10, while the rest of us hung back to worship the sun a little longer. The next day, planes hijacked by terrorists struck the Pentagon and New York City's Twin Towers.

I was worried about being so far away from my family, since nobody was sure how the United States would react to the attack by the time I'd get back home. For five days, I manically searched the sky for a passenger plane, to see if the airspace had been cleared to fly home. I understood the phrase "island fever." After a lot of phone calls, Mom was able to send a private jet to get me and a friend, and though it was a seven-seater, nobody else wanted to hitch a ride, no matter how much I tried to convince them. They wanted to wait for a commercial plane, but I knew that with only me and my friend aboard this one, there wouldn't be any terrorists to sabotage our flight.

Once we touched down on U.S. soil, I kissed the ground, and in homage to my country and the victims of this tragedy, I wore red, white, and blue for at least one scene in every episode for the rest of *Sabrina*'s season. If you catch my USA necklace, flag belt buckle, or any other patriotic wardrobe choices in a show, you'll know it's a season six episode. Four months later, I'd present an American Music Award to 'N Sync, and it would be the first time I'd seen the boys since 9/11. When they stepped on the stage, before accepting the award, they quickly hugged me and asked if I was okay after all that had happened. They apologized for not taking me with them on the tenth, as if they could have known what would happen the next day.

I always try to see the good in a situation and give people the benefit of the doubt, but when it comes to work, I hope for the best but expect the worst. Hollywood can be so fickle. Each time *Sabrina* was renewed, I was ecstatic but also stunned, so when I heard our seventh season was our last, I handled it well. In March of 2003, our director called, "It's a wrap!" on our final show, and it was time to party. The cast, crew, and I took lots of pictures and shouted our favorite *Sabrina*-esque inside jokes so loudly that we scared the hell out of one of Cathy's trained cats. It clawed her arms and then scurried away, and she later found it cowering under a sofa. At the end of the night, my besties Eryn, Kimi, Maureen, our script supervisor, a few others, and I took a last tour of the stage. We thanked it for the memories and chose our souvenirs. I took a pine bookshelf and iron coatrack that we used on the kitchen set, which I still have, along with the papier-mâché bust of a woman that was in Sabrina's living room. It now sits on my dresser and holds my necklaces. As a parting gift to everyone, the crew wrote "Hart #1" on the back of my favorite jacket, a reliable gray fleece we called "Bear" that kept me warm on early and late-night shoots. They hung it from the rafters, illuminated by a single spotlight. It was hard not to look back.

Chapter 11

JUST SAY "WHY NOT?"

Los Angeles in the '90s—I can't think of a better place for the young, rich, and recognizable to stir up trouble, except maybe Seattle. (Then again, the Pacific Northwest is really into coffee and nature, and who needs to be that caffeinated to stare at trees?) So once I landed ABC's *Sabrina*, I really cut loose for the first time. I was in my twenties, free from the stifling expectations of my youth, and anxious to define life on my own terms. Which is to say, I was ready to party.

When in Hollywood, right?

My boyfriend James, who I met during my first semester at NYU, always knew how to have a good time. At my nineteenth birthday party, he earned a rep for rolling the best doobies, and when we moved to L.A., he graduated to the role of my perfect partner in crime. We got an apartment together in the Valley, not far from the house where Mom, Leslie, and my five siblings were living. When I told him one night while folding laundry that I hoped to make my twenty-first birthday one to remember, he was anxious to help me cut the cake and keep the shots flowing.

I decided I'd get completely hammered for the first time and—spoiler alert—keep going until I yacked. (Yep, I like being organized and in control so much that I even planned my first big drunken escapade.) I mentioned this idea to James, and he was on board. Since my own star was rising, I also wanted to celebrate this milestone the way that I'd read other celebs rang in their birthdays—in style. I rented a dark little bar on Sunset Boulevard that had pool tables, three bars inside and out, and a movie theater where we played only Quentin Tarantino movies all night.

After *People* magazine finished taking pictures and I'd cut the cake with James, I realized the party was almost over and I was barely buzzed. I bellied up to the bar and did a few double shots of tequila with the crew of *Sabrina,* then a shot of Jägermeister, then back to tequila . . . until two hours and eighteen shots later, my head was in the toilet. After I clogged it three times with my black Jäger-puke and the bar owner kicked me out, my friends and I piled into a limo. I urged the driver to take the freeway so I didn't upchuck even more from the infamous twists and turns of Laurel Canyon. I hung my head out the window like a Shih Tzu desperate for fresh air, and James held back my hair. I had alcohol poisoning for about two days after, even though James put me on a plane the next afternoon for Vancouver to shoot the NBC TV movie *Silencing Mary.* At least all that barfing gave me the dehydrated, gaunt, flat-belly look that so many actresses covet.

James and I began to build a glamorous life together—just call us "Jamelissa." First, I bought us an amazing house. It was a three-bedroom Spanish colonial with wrought-iron balconies, two fireplaces, a pool with a waterfall, a hot tub, and a fully stocked bar in the rec room downstairs. The house was on Wonder View Drive in the Hollywood Hills and every room overlooked the San Fernando Valley. (Three years later, I took *MTV Cribs* on a tour of my abode to show off the "Witch's Brew" sign that I stole from the *Sabrina* set and hung over my bar, a paper towel roll made from a Sabrina doll, Shirley Temple–autographed sheet music for "On the Good Ship Lollipop," and a movie poster for the classic Audrey Hepburn film *Sabrina*. The episode is still on YouTube, if you want to check it out.) By moving into my first major investment together, James and I now had a place to entertain our growing circle of West Coast buddies after premieres and star-studded events. We enjoyed being around our friends just as much as being alone, so we asked Parker, the PA from the *Sabrina* set, to live with us. We adopted a beautiful, pregnant Dalmatian, named her Pele, and kept one of her puppies, named Haleakala. I began collecting art— Rembrandt and Erte, mostly. James had encouraged me to get a car with real horsepower, so I leased a red convertible BMW. We spent a lot of time driving stick through the Hollywood Hills, and beating the speed limit once I got the hang of it. Thanks to *Sabrina*'s popularity, I was quickly becoming a Hollywood cliché, and I had all the sexy trappings to show for it.

To people who thrive on being scandalous, this time in my life will seem like a careful rebellion. But what can I say? I like to chase a buzz with a sensible amount of caution, and it rarely gets in the way of how much fun I have. I always tried to be around friends or family in case I got too wasted or freaked out on drugs, and I always made sure that I had a safe ride home. And while most party pals are only as good as their impaired judgment, mine always came through for me. One time, I tagged along on a surf trip to Tijuana with *Sabrina*'s camera loader, Todd, his girlfriend, and some of his buddies. By day, they caught waves; by night, they caught shit. When we hit a club called Papas and Beer, full of busty *putas* and rough *gallitos*, the bouncers tossed us out because some of the guys started a fight after someone ogled Todd's girlfriend. We got out alive, though we were banned from coming back in, and at this point, feeling invincible, ate some street meat and took a remote dirt road back to our villa. The car was going thirty miles per hour when Todd climbed out the window and decided to "surf" on the roof. Though I'd never even boogie-boarded, I decided to join him. Todd jumped on top of me and held me down until the car slowed to a stop, and we both bailed out before someone got seriously injured.

Putting myself in safe hands often involved being with James, who always made me feel protected, even if he was the one who introduced the precarious situation. As a skier and woodsy guy, James was into a lot of natural, recreational drugs, like pot and mushrooms, so I got into them too. I'd done shrooms with college buddies once on my own, when I was at our New Jersey home and my parents weren't around. Though he wasn't there at the time, I called James when I was tripping to talk about how cold the kitchen tiles felt, and how, if I laid down at the right angle, I could see straight down the grout line to the other end of the room . . . it was a playful high.

But when James and I took drugs together in Colorado, we nearly put our lives in danger. During a hiatus, we went with our roommate, Parker, and my *Sabrina* costar Nate, who played Harvey, to Parker's cabin in the Boulder woods and did shrooms. It was the most beautiful, magical walk dotted with neon green pine trees, mountains that appeared to move, and small mushroom villages that I swore were occupied by Smurfs. We also heard a pack of coyotes, which sounded like barking dogs. At nightfall, we walked to a rocky cliff to look at the constellation-packed sky, and the boys carried rifles and flashlights, and me, a knife, just in case the coyotes or Freddie Krueger attacked. At one point, Parker saw what looked like the glowing yellow eye of an animal, and then Nate saw it too. We put our backs together, forming a square and facing outward, and listened for the echo-y crunch-crunch of branches breaking underfoot. After ten minutes of total tripping, panicky, sweaty silence, our jittery instincts told us to make a run for it. We bolted for the house, falling over sticks and rocks, but made it there with only a few nicks and scrapes. The next day, we wondered if Nate and Parker hallucinated the whole thing, but when we went back to the clearing, we found proof that their sighting was legit—giant day-old animal droppings. To use a phrase from my dad's T-shirt, that night in the woods was no bullshit.

James wasn't the only rabble-rouser in my life. When eleven of my friends and I went to Cabo San Lucas to celebrate a group bachelorette party for my friends Eryn, Kimi, and Christine, they didn't exactly hold back on having fun. One night we ran into the famous, and famously handsome, boxer Oscar de la Hoya at a bar. We guzzled our yard-tall drinks and danced on tables, as he sent over shots. Each time, though, I noticed that there was a special one set aside for me, and it didn't taste like tequila. I didn't have the most sophisticated palate for spirits, but I suspected he was sending me shots of water. I get punchy when I'm under the influence, and I couldn't tell whether Oscar was helping me stay sober, punking me, or implying that I couldn't handle my liquor. No matter what, I didn't like it.

I stormed right up to Oscar's table, backed by my eleven-girl posse . . . and proceeded to hang out, have some laughs, and end up at his place. I'd fully intended to give him some sass, but his big brown eyes got the best of me. Back at his house, when Oscar suggested we pile into his hot tub, I noticed that there was no water in it. Fool me once, shame on you; fool me twice, I'm gonna think you're fucking with me. So when his bodyguard kindly brought me a tall glass of water to help me sober up, and Oscar simultaneously referred to me as "Sabrina," I decided it was a good idea to throw that water in his face. I didn't care that this big, strong man had defeated seventeen world champions or came from a long line of hard-core boxers; my tequila was liquid courage. It's weird because people called me Sabrina all the time, and still do, but I'd never reacted like that—nor have I since. Oscar's bodyguard immediately pulled me away to keep us both safe, and the girls and I left soon after that. It wasn't until the sober light of day that I realized I had soaked a man with lethal weapons for hands in a foreign country. It was a pretty stupid move, but at least when we left and walked past his car, I didn't puke into his sunroof like my friend did.

On that same trip, six of us girls decided to get tattoos. My friend Jenna, who played Libby on *Sabrina,* went with a sparrow on her ankle, Eryn got her soon-to-be-married initials on her lower back, and Danielle opted for a kiss mark on her upper butt cheek. (The tattoo artist had her kiss a piece of paper while wearing lipstick, and then traced those lips onto her, so she basically kissed her own ass.) I chose a Celtic cross that I'd found on set and was once a prop. I knew it would make the perfect tattoo, so I had kept it in my wallet for years, waiting for the right moment to have it grace the back of my neck. I felt like this epic trip with my closest friends was just the time to pull the trigger. My girls Tara and Lindsay sat with me while I dropped my head and let a man stick a sterile needle in my flesh. Though we were all sober when this went down, our celebratory dinner afterward was anything but.

Next stop: a burrito and a striptease. Beautiful, half-naked Latino men humped all the ladies and poured shots directly into our mouths. One zeroed in on me, took his belt off, and wrapped it around my neck. He pulled the leather back and forth across my raw, swollen new tat, and no matter how much alcohol I had in my system, it hurt like a bitch. I bit my bottom lip to keep from screaming, but not in a flirty *Fifty Shades of Grey* way.

We then went back to the bar El Squid Roe, where we'd met Oscar the night before. I have only fuzzy memories of this, but my friends say they lost me in the crowd, and the next thing they saw was me dancing in a cage, up above the dance floor, dry-humping professional dancers. When the girls dragged me down, they said I refused to get in the cab unless they promised we could party at Oscar's house before calling it a night. They agreed, lying to get me back to our hotel. Then I apparently tried to make out with all of them. The next morning, I saw the faded imprint of my tat stuck to my pillowcase and went nuts. I vaguely remembered getting the tattoo I'd wanted for years, but I had no idea what happened after that. The girls had to help piece it together for me, like in *The Hangover*.

A few months after I got back from Mexico, I found out that James was cheating, like my first boyfriend, Mike, had, five years earlier. Even the bimbos' names were the same. But instead of abruptly ending the relationship, I tried to move past it, though I no longer trusted him or anyone named Stacy. I broke up with James for good a year later. I drowned my sorrows in a lot of Patrón, but for all my inebriated nights, I never forgot to set the house alarm now that I was alone in my house for the first time. Thank God for ADT. I tested that system weekly, just like the pamphlets tell you to.

Not long after I ended things with James, in the fall of 1998, I began shooting the movie *Drive Me Crazy* with Adrian Grenier, or, as you may know him, Vinnie Chase from *Entourage*. It was a relaxed set with a young director named John Schultz. For the first three weeks, I was on hiatus from *Sabrina,* and then I finished the film by doing my show in L.A. during the week and flying to Utah on weekends. I missed at least one full night of sleep a week due to this schedule. I was also busting my bum at the gym and on a strict juice diet to keep up my shape. I felt harried and tired, but by now, burning the candle at both ends was second nature to me.

Adrian and I had a very close and intimate relationship from the first day we met, but not the romantic kind that everyone imagined we had. He and I admired and respected each other, and just truly enjoyed the other person's company. We had a similar work ethic and sense of humor, so the chemistry we were trying to create on-screen came pretty naturally to us. I did give him a sneak-attack smooch in his trailer, under the guise of rehearsing our kissing scene in the movie, but it meant nothing and we were mostly good friends. We were also falling for other people. Adrian began dating actress Ali Larter, who's also in the film, and I was really into Gabriel Carpenter, who played my crush in the movie, too. Gabriel and I liked to flirt and tease each other on and off the set. After the movie wrapped, we went on to have a hot and heavy love affair over the next year, whenever I wasn't searching for a serious relationship.

Our movie was originally titled *Next to You,* but the producers at Twentieth Century Fox changed it to *Drive Me Crazy* to cross-promote the film with Britney Spears's hit by the same name. A lot of the movie's PR involved Britney, so she and I did a few interviews together, bumped into each other at awards shows while waiting for the film to come out, and even dropped by each other's day jobs. I made an appearance in her music video for *Drive Me Crazy,* along with Adrian, and she was a guest star on *Sabrina*.

When Britney was on *Sabrina,* I was six years older than her and had been in the business longer, so I could sense that she was already under a lot of stress. I constantly asked her to grab lunch, which caused her to smile a wide, friendly grin as if it sounded like the best idea ever. But when she'd turn to her agents, publicist, assistant, and bodyguard for their okay, they'd remind her of the super-busy agenda they'd laid out for her that day and she'd turn me down. She didn't have time to grab a burrito on the Paramount lot? I guess not, when she was also shooting a Pepsi ad, recording an album, prepping for a tour, doing photo shoots and press, and hitting the gym every day. I felt a protective instinct come over me and decided to support her the best way I knew how. I devised a plan to sneak her out of her hotel and then take her dancing so she could chill with people closer to her age, if just for one night. Britney loved the idea.

At go-time, Britney ran out of her hotel lobby and into my car. Her enormously scary but sweet bodyguard called Big Rob jumped in front of the vehicle and asked where I was taking her. I lied and said we were going to my mom's house for homemade lasagna, so he let us leave. When we pulled up to Club Cherry, a raucous weekly dance party, L.A. club promoter Pantera Sarah met us around back to sneak Britney in and get us a booth. But once we were inside, Britney got absorbed by the crowd, and I lost her. After looking for her to no avail, I assumed she was fine and went off to dance with friends. At the end of the night, I found her in a private booth with dozens of people kissing her ass as she basked in the attention and down time she'd worked so hard for. She gave me the okay to leave without her since I had to work the next day, and Sarah promised to get her to the hotel safe. Since then, Britney's been snuck in and out of more back doors than I can count, but I shudder to think that I first showed her how it's done.

———————

In January 1999, I cohosted the American Music Awards along-
side the fabulous recording artist, actress, and producer Brandy.
It was a huge honor to be offered such a high-profile gig, and I
took the job very seriously. By the end of the night, my adrenaline was pumping. I'd never been at the center of a show like
this and surrounded by so many incredibly talented people who
I respected and adored. I heard that after the official after-party,
all the presenters and talent were going "upstairs at Dublin's." I
had no clue what this meant, so I hopped in my limo alone and
asked the driver to take me there. I met the door girls, was ush-
ered through a large crowd, and taken to my own table. Dublin's was a dark Irish bar with a dance floor in the middle, and it
teemed with A-listers like Fred Durst of Limp Bizkit, Rick Fox,
and Adam Duritz. I knew I had to become a regular. I began going on Mondays and rubbed elbows with young Hollywood.
After seeing the same faces over and over, a few of us began hitting a different bar every night of the week. Mondays was Dublin's, Tuesdays was Las Palmas, Wednesdays was La Poubelle,
Thursdays was Cherry. On weekends, we recovered from five
days of hangovers and went to house parties.

I've never been the type to opt for staying home, ordering
takeout, and plowing through my laser disc collection alone—
not when I can be out with friends. L.A.'s club and bar scene was
a perfect fix for what little free time I had. I also looked the best
I had in ages, thanks to all that juicing and gymming, so slipping
into tube dresses or leather pants was fun for once. Going out
also created a stronger bond with girlfriends like Soleil Moon
Frye and China Shavers, who played Dreama on *Sabrina*. We'd
grab sushi, have a gin and tonic, dance, and get home by 1 A.M.,
so I could still function at work the next day.

After two years of the same routine, though, I got bored and needed a change. I decided to open my own nightclub. I'd become close to one of the promoters, Dave Osokow, who knew I'd always fantasized about having my own bar and had the cash flow to back it. He asked me to invest in a small club that he and some other guys were opening on Sunset Boulevard called Trocadero Sunset Lounge. It was named after the first iconic Hollywood bar that was owned by *Hollywood Reporter* founder and nightclub legend Billy Wilkerson. (No relation to my future husband, but I did wonder if Mark's last name was a sign when I met him.) The original Trocadero was a black-tie supper club, now demolished, that in the 1930s was filled with movie producers and stars such as Fred Astaire, Bing Crosby, Cary Grant, Jean Harlow, and Lucille Ball. It was a hot spot for movie premiere parties. The Troc is still a small, intimate scene with a nice patio and French doors, and dark, old-school art deco décor inside. The bar was the perfect place for me to entertain friends and hold parties, take casual meetings, and hang out after we'd hit the louder clubs. Every time I directed an episode of *Sabrina*, I treated the crew to a Friday night there. I also made out with my longtime crush Josh Hopkins (Grayson Ellis on *Cougar Town*) in the women's bathroom on a drunken St. Patty's Day, hosted Soleil's twenty-fourth birthday, and later celebrated one of my bachelorette parties there before I got married. The Troc was officially my spot—literally.

Sometimes I feel bad for Hollywood's younger stars who are constantly stalked by paparazzi whose job is to get a high-paying shot of their cellulite, dark under-eye circles, or fashion faux pas. I'm so relieved that back when I was sowing my naughtier oats, there were no TMZ, Splash, or Flynet photographers to harass me as I left the latest club or piss me off until I felt tempted to chase them down. I could stash my most uninhibited moments and mistakes under wraps, unlike a lot of today's bigger names, who may just be bumping around their twenties like the rest of us did. I often suspect that the reason I'm able to maintain such an untarnished image isn't that I'm such a good girl, but simply because I've never been caught with my pants down, so to speak. Though one time I came dangerously close.

In the summer of 1999, I was invited to my first Midsummer Night's Dream Playboy Mansion Party. This is a tawdry annual event held on the first Saturday in August. I couldn't wait to drive through those famous iron gates, past the "Playmates at Play" street sign, and get a glimpse of what really goes on in the grotto. Since I was single, I asked my new crush Jonny Moseley, who'd won the Olympic Gold in freestyle skiing in 1998 in Nagano, Japan, to join me and a few mutual friends for the party; earlier that year we'd met at the X Games, where he took the silver. The Playboy bacchanalia's dress code called for sleep-wear, to put it modestly, so I spent days working with my *Sabrina* wardrobe team, choosing just the right set of bra and panties that would complement my curves and keep me from feeling too exposed and slutty. I chose a pair of vintage-inspired cream lace bikini bottoms, and a matching bra that was trimmed in red and printed with cherries. I paired them with a red silk robe and matching heels that had fluffy caribou feathers across the toes. I looked like a pinup from a 1930s issue of *Esquire*.

When our limo pulled up to the circular drive, the Playboy Mansion reminded me of an old Scottish castle. This was before *The Girls Next Door* was on E!, so I didn't know what to expect. I passed through a grand foyer to get to the tented backyard. If you've seen *Bridesmaids*, it's the same area where Kristen Wiig's character destroys the chocolate fountain. To the right was a pool and grotto area with beanbag chairs for hanging out, and to the left, a zoo with peacocks and monkeys. A nearby guest-house held a pool table, pinball machines, and private rooms for getting it on, though you could pretty much do that anywhere on the property without causing a stir. The Playmates working the party were sprayed to look like they were wearing bathing suits or lingerie, though they were actually nude and completely shaved. When I was talking to one of the waitresses, I didn't even realize her naughty bits were exposed and painted until she told me.

Not long after we got to the mansion, some friends and I decided to drop ecstasy. I'd used it before, but here I thought the elaborate décor, grounds, and sensual atmosphere would drive my touchy-feely senses into overdrive in a fascinating way. It made me feel sexier, more talkative, and gave me a little swagger around guests like James Woods and Vince Vaughn. After a few hours, I grabbed Jonny, and, on the limo ride home, me and another half-naked lady began putting on a show for our dates. I'm not sure if she was black, Hispanic, Asian, or maybe a combo of all three. I'd kissed some girlfriends in high school and college for shock value or to get in the "gay door" at a club, but this was the only time I'd really made out with a woman to this kind of lengthy degree. On X, my tongue tingled and my libido surged. Of course, after twenty minutes of this, I looked over and noticed that two of the guys we were with had passed out and the other was on his phone. All that hot girl-on-girl action did more for us than for the boys.

When the limo dropped me and Jonny off, I crashed, but wasn't asleep for thirty minutes before my car service arrived to take me to a shoot for *Maxim*. Earlier that year, I'd made *Maxim*'s "Hot 100" list, and they ran a photo of me in a long skirt and tight sweater, so I didn't realize their audience was horny men.

The magazine's readers wrote in a lot, asking to see me on the cover, so an editor called my people about it, and since I had an adult movie coming out (okay, PG-13), I was down. What I didn't realize was how long the X would last after the Playboy party, and that I'd still be high when I got to the studio.

Senses impaired, I knew I was there for a cover shoot but felt unfazed when I saw the wardrobe rack full of bras, panties, and nothing else. (I'm sure my publicist was there to protect me, but I was in no position to remember details.) I'd been at shoots before where they tried to get me to wear barely anything, but I would never consent to that. This time, however, after having just come from a party full of naked people, with me in my skivvies, and still coming down from rolling, I wasn't feeling like my more modest self.

I was in hair and makeup for nearly two hours and spent most of it asleep. Nobody said a word to me about the state I was in, and thank God the magazine had scheduled an interview on a different day, so I didn't need to be articulate. The shoot began with pics of me half-naked in bed—first, with a white sheet concealing just my breasts, which is the shot that made the cover, and then with my legs open to the camera but the private stuff covered. After lunch, the photographer wanted to try a picture from below and between my legs, but I had the good sense to at least say I'd need to approve a test shot first (this was before digital cameras came along). It was a terrible and trashy photo, so I tore it to pieces and turned to the side, which turned out to be my favorite picture from the day. I'm leaning forward, tits heaving, on a set of stairs. In the final photo, I was lying on a sofa, and I'm pretty sure I passed out a few times, because I remember the photographer yelling, "Wake up!" When it ran in the magazine, I can't guarantee that they didn't airbrush my eyeballs onto the image.

For publicity reasons, the story was timed to hit the stands with the release of *Drive Me Crazy*. During the after-party for the New York movie premiere at Planet Hollywood, I was sipping a martini when my concerned-looking lawyer pulled me aside, very seriously, and insisted that I avoid the press until further notice. Apparently, *Maxim* had just hit the stands and Archie Comics wanted to have me and my mom fired from the show for breach of contract since I was allegedly representing their character in a tawdry way. Hearing this, I felt like someone had punched me in the gut. I stepped outside to have a cigarette and called Mom. We were both really scared, and she was also pissed off at me, wondering what I'd done on this cover that was so damn sue-able. (Archie dropped it after my lawyer and I sent an apology letter.) Frankly, I wondered, too—I could hardly remember. All I could hope was that it'd be good press for *Drive Me Crazy,* and at the very least, show some range and sex appeal. That month I was also on the very first cover of *Cosmo Girl,* which targeted young teens—a very different demographic.

Sure enough, the Archie threat only made the press more interested in me, *Maxim,* and my first starring role in a major motion feature. My name and the movie's were mentioned almost every day in the media, including by Jay Leno, Regis and Kathie Lee, and in the *New York Post.* ("Melissa Joan Hart Sheds Teen Image: Sabrina, the Bare Witch Project"—*ba dum bum.*) Suddenly, everyone cared about whether the star of ABC's biggest Friday night family sitcom should be posing suggestively on the cover of a men's magazine. Good thing they didn't know I did it while coming down from a high. Mom publicly got my back by saying we were just showing people that I was a grown-up, which was true to a large extent. I mean, I was in my twenties, far from underage, and had already been in my panties for the cover of *Details* magazine a few years prior, which nobody seemed to bat an eyelash over. The real problem, I later learned, was that *Maxim*'s cover line said, "Sabrina: Your Favorite Witch Without a Stitch," and using Sabrina's name, near an undressed image, allegedly made it look like I was playing the character naked, which was against the contract. But I've never heard of an actor having any say over what a magazine writes on its cover, so to my mind, Archie should've tried taking *Maxim* to court, not me. I didn't do anything illegal; I was just promoting my film. Anyway, *Drive Me Crazy* opened to great numbers, thanks to all the scandalous press, and I took some friends and cast members to Cancun for a celebratory margarita to toast the fact that the movie grossed more than it cost to make.

As you can tell, I've always liked to take a risk, push my limits, and feel some kind of immediate gratification from it all. This is the main reason I got into racing cars. In 1997, the Toyota Grand Prix of Long Beach asked me to be in their competition and offered to send me to training camp to learn how to drive like a pro. I turned the invite down, since I was busy with *Sabrina,* but for the next twelve months, I regretted the decision every time I sat at a red light and wondered if I could take the car next to me. So on and off for the following five years, I jumped at their invites and raced a white Celica beside George Lucas, Alyson Hannigan, Donny Osmond, and Coolio. I did really well each time, but I never won. Also revving my engine: pro driver and NASCAR hottie Casey Mears, who I dated for a few months during this time.

While living in my house on Wonder View Drive after James and Parker had moved out, I constantly threw parties—it was the go-to spot for weekend BBQs or a dip in the hot tub or pool after a long night of dancing. A lot of chlorinated, wasted strangers came and went, often without an invitation. Most of the memories are an intoxicated blur to me. I do remember that twice I tried to kick Ashton Kutcher out, when he made smart-ass remarks to me after I asked him not to smoke in my house, but he never wanted to leave, and since I'm not burly enough to intimidate him into going, I eventually gave up. And another time, I went to soak in the hot tub and found Marlon and Shawn Wayans hanging out, though I'd never met them before. Others who came and went included Andy Dick, Geoff Stults, Wilmer Valderrama, and Ben Foster. They were usually drinking, smoking, and having a good laugh. During this party phase, I met another young actor—let's just call him "Weenie," since I later found out that's what my friends called him behind my back. He and his brother ran in similar circles, and I liked his charm, persistence, and intense features. It was also clear that he was a loose cannon. He had delusions of grandeur, acted like he was invincible, was occasionally paranoid, and got obsessive about a monthly interest, whether it was working out, art, or acting. Weenie's personality was dizzying, but since he held down a job on a TV show for teens, I figured, how messy could he be? We were a couple in no time.

After six months of dating, I began to find strange things lying around Weenie's place and mine, like broken lightbulbs. His apartment was really dark, because he'd screwed every bulb out of its fixtures except one. Then, while cleaning out his pockets on laundry day, I found the outer casing of a pen, with the ink cartridge removed. I called a friend in town, since I suspected drugs; I thought she might know better from being around Hollywood types longer than I'd been. I'd done some shrooms, ecstasy, and pot, but that was it; I didn't know much about anything harder. I've never snorted or shot anything into my body, and the one time I was offered coke, which happened to be by Paris

Hilton, I turned it down. (She asked to bum a Parliament Light, and, as she dipped the recessed filtered end into a baggie, asked if I wanted some. It pissed me off that she wasted my cigarette for that.)

My friend told me to touch the tip of the pen to my tongue to see if it was bitter. I did and it was. If Weenie was doing drugs, that could explain why he'd act so focused and upbeat one day and then tired, irritable, and depressed with me the next. I broke up with him after this, but we got back together and were on again/off again for the next few years. We went to counseling together, where he said things like, "I think you need therapy more than me." He told me he still got high before auditions to help him focus, and before shrink appointments, just to see if the doc could tell.

During one of our breakups, I went out of town for a few weeks and needed someone to watch my dogs, so I asked my friend, an actor named Angelo "Spizz" Spizzirri, to stay at my place. After I saw how Spizz lovingly cared for my home and animals while I was away, I asked him to be my roommate. Spizz was a faithful, protective sidekick when we went out, and it made me feel safe to have a man in the house when we got home. We liked to party but kept it under control most of the time, which was a refreshing change from Weenie's increasingly erratic behavior. When we went to Sundance to see a movie that Spizz was in, my boyfriend encouraged me to take the psychedelic drug mescaline, which he told me was like a pill form of shrooms. It's not. It can create an altered sense of time and self-awareness and made me think the girl across the room was speaking to me with her brain waves. I tried to take off running down the snowy street, and it was Spizz, not Weenie, who stopped me and calmed me down.

Spizz also appreciated my brassier side, which Weenie seemed to barely notice. Spizz once told me that one of his favorite moments from living together was when he brought some friends home late one night from partying to hang out in the hot tub. I was asleep because I had a big day on camera the next morning. I heard loud voices and a ruckus outside, since my room was just above the hot tub, so I ran to my balcony in delirious anger and screamed at the guys, "Shut the fuck up! *Some* of us have to work in the morning!" One of Spizz's best friends, a guy named Danny, the drummer for the hard rock band Tool, was there. He was shocked to learn that all women aren't like the eyelash-batting, doormat groupies he was used to. Spizz got a kick out of this for years.

Though I was respectful of people's schedules when we got our drink on, Weenie never seemed to care who had to work when he wanted to party. The night before *Sabrina*'s season six finale in the spring of 2002, in which Aunt Hilda marries her true love after meeting him at a mall in the Other Realm, I begged Weenie to come home around 10 P.M., so I could get a good night's sleep without hearing him rustle around. I was both acting in this episode and directing it, and because the show was a season finale and a wedding, it was an expensive, arduously produced, and heavily promoted stressor. Though I explained all of this to Weenie a million times, he still called at 9:59 P.M. to say he was staying out a little longer instead of coming home when he promised. After fighting on the phone and getting a restless night of irritated half-sleep, I heard him knock on my door at 3 A.M.

I let the guy in but told him to sleep on the couch, and then went to work an hour later. From the makeup chair, I furiously called my friend and assistant Kerry and asked her to pack up his stuff and make sure he was out of the house before I got home that day. Spizz helped, and for weeks after made sure Weenie stayed away, often while wielding a baseball bat. I was done for good—*finito, no mas*. I'd dealt with my boyfriend's selfish immaturity, narcissism, and instability for two years and realized I wouldn't have a future—hell, I couldn't even have a present—with a man like this. I couldn't trust him, rely on him, or be with him in a way that made me happy for more than a few days. The breakup also made me realize that Weenie wasn't the first guy I'd taken care of, and I was tired of that too. As the oldest child in my family, I had the protective nurturer thing down pat and went into autopilot with those who needed it. It was time to find someone who could take care of himself and—here's a novel idea—me, too, when I needed it. I've always been strong and self-sufficient, but carrying two people in a relationship wasn't working for me anymore. I was worn out.

A few years after I met my husband, Mark, who met all of these needs and then some, we faced an unspeakable tragedy. In 2007, my friend Spizz took his own life. I was in unbearable pain from it, and I still find myself praying that he feels at peace and always knew how much I loved him. Spizz's death also marked the end of an era for me, and the severity of his passing issued a reality check on my rowdier years. James was a free spirit, Weenie needed help, and Spizz had his own stuff to deal with. But me? For the most part, my antics were part of growing up and into myself. I liked staying out late with friends more than drinking and getting high; hell, I barely like to drink a lemonade in one sitting, much less chug a fifth of vodka. And when I did tiptoe on the wild side and experience the darker corners of Hollywood, I was still what they call a "normie" in AA. All things considered, I'd call it a compliment.

Chapter 12

THE ONE THAT NEVER GOT AWAY

I'm rarely a betting woman, and here's why. When I went to the Kentucky Derby in May 2002, I put money down on a few horses but swore I wouldn't get serious with any man I met there. By the end of the weekend, I lost about five hundred dollars at the races and fell for my future husband.

For the second year in a row, I was invited to the Mint Jubilee, a celebrity-packed gala held during the Derby to increase awareness and funding for cancer treatment. Since I was on a guy-atus, so to speak, I took my close friend and assistant Kerry as my date. We couldn't wait to feel spoiled and to hobnob with Southern gentility. And sure enough, when we got to Louisville, we had a full escort team ready to take us to fancy events, complete with a police car as our ride.

One of the stops along the party route was a local hostess's mansion. I'll never forget her massive and impeccably organized closet full of awesome designer shoes. Looking inside it was actually part of the official house tour. Once we were done gawking, we mingled. I talked about Louisville's famed food and music with upper-crust donors and even ran into my old classmate from PCS and NYU Jerry O'Connell, who was on NBC's *Crossing Jordan* at the time.

Jerry hardly showed me any attention when we were at school or bumping into each other around Manhattan, but that night, he followed me around like a puppy dog. I was flattered by his persistence, but I stopped myself from seeming too available. I bantered with Jerry, but I was being playful, not trying to initiate a hook-up. I'd broken up with Weenie only two months before, and I'd been cheated on twice and dated Weenie while he was courting an addiction, which is a different type of sneaking around but painful nonetheless. I wasn't anxious to trust or open myself up to anyone soon. If experience taught me anything, it's that charismatic flirts are rarely boyfriend material— and Jerry sure thought a lot of his own charms. I also wanted to give him a taste of his own standoffish medicine, since he pretended to barely notice me for four years even though we saw each other all the time.

By the next night, Jerry was out of my mind. Kerry and I got really dressed up to attend the actual Jubilee event, where an elaborate dinner and entertainment awaited. We made the most of an open bar with Howie D from the Backstreet Boys, actress Jamie-Lynn Sigler, and plenty of other recognizable faces. Halfway through the night, a man with a walkie-talkie asked if I'd mind introducing the next band. I said I'd be honored. I quickly ran backstage to learn what I needed to say about the Southern rockers from Alabama called Course of Nature.

I was studying the index card with my lines on it backstage. As the more outgoing members introduced themselves, the tall, broad-shouldered lead singer made his way to me more slowly. I kept my eyes on him as I shook hands with everyone else. Be-

THE ONE THAT NEVER GOT AWAY   167

fore we could say a proper hello, I was called to do my thing, and when I was done, I'd missed the chance to meet that mysterious hottie. I walked back to my table very carefully, standing up real straight to make sure my new crush didn't see me trip or slouch, all while making sure to suck in the belly.

Back at my table, I told Kerry about the head-turning front man and decided to ask my publicist to introduce me to him when the group was done with its set. She was already on it, thinking we'd make a cute couple. When the band finished and walked past our table to the bar, they didn't stop to say hi. I had to make a move first. So much for my break from chasing guys.

I told all five men—four band members and the tour manager—how much I liked their music. We took pictures together, and I learned that the lead singer's name was Mark and that he liked tequila. Bingo. Mark and I decided to do a shot, but when we got to the bar, they were out of the Devil's water. We didn't want to leave each other's side, so we did a shot of vodka instead. I've been told that when Russians drink vodka, it constitutes a very special ceremony. If I'd known this at the time, my inner romantic would've swooned about what this might foreshadow down the road. But I don't think it would've made the rocket fuel go down any easier.

After a few more drinks, Kerry and I walked the guys to their bus to say good-bye. Mark's mom, Jen, was touring with them at the time, so I briefly met her and then spent a few minutes smoking a cigarette and chatting with Mark. I don't even remember what we talked about, because I was so mesmerized by his gentle, puppy-dog blue eyes. He literally made my knees go weak, and I knew right then that he was the most handsome man I'd ever met. But he had to get back on the road. Mark's tour manager, Eric, gave me his business card and said to keep in touch.

Though my heart told me I'd met a game-changer, there was no telling if I'd ever see Mark again. He was a touring musician and I had a packed schedule as an actress. How would we even make things work if fate *was* on our side? On the one hand, I'd never let a little challenge, like a few thousand miles or a hectic career, stop me from pursuing true love at all costs. But I'm also realistic, and I know that instant chemistry doesn't always trump a logistical long shot. I tucked Mark's number in my purse for safekeeping and went on with my weekend. This included getting super drunk and running into Ashton Kutcher, who threw me for a loop when he told me my ex Weenie had moved in with another girl. The news made my head spin, as did the martinis I then began to chug at warp speed. Before I knew it, Jerry O'Connell and I were passing the time with our tongues in the corner of the VIP tent.

The next morning was rough. Kerry and I made our way to Churchill Downs, the Kentucky Derby's racetrack, where one disaster followed another. First we decided to wear vintage dresses to the event. I had on a white, lacy frock with a matching fluffy hat that was shaped like a deflated soufflé. I looked like I was about to reenact the horse-racing scene in *My Fair Lady,* but with less panache. Kerry had on a vintage green floral-print Doris Day getup with a beret. Again, not our best looks. We were also stumbling around with massive hangovers and nursing a mix of Alka-Seltzer and Bloody Marys, hairing the dog with an antacid. But what really bowled me over was that I saw Jerry gushing all over another woman in the center of the room, surrounded by all the Derby guests. Manwhore suspicions confirmed.

After a horse called War Emblem took home the trophy, and I won Mom three hundred and fifty dollars on a twenty-dollar bet she called in at the last minute (again, that woman with her killer instincts), Jubilee's people whisked all the celebrities off to a party at another local hot spot. With the other woman MIA, Jerry turned his attention back to me. Too bad I was on to his wandering eye, since I had just witnessed what happened when he spied fresh meat. He asked me if we could see each other when we got back to L.A. in a few days, and I said that I didn't think that was going to happen.

"What—why?"

"Because I think I met the man I am going to marry." I was not to be outdone.

"The band guy from last night that you were doing shots with?" he asked.

"Yup."

I wasn't sure if I'd see Mark again, but I gave Jerry a shit-eating grin anyway.

Back in L.A., I unpacked my stuff and put the tour manager's card on my bedside table. I called Eric's phone the day after I got home (I needed time to recover), made small talk about their gigs, and then asked if Mark was around. He was napping in his bunk, but Eric passed his cell to him anyway. Mark and I spent two hours on the phone that day, and after we reluctantly hung up, he called me right back and said he wanted me to have his cell number since I had called Eric's. Mark told me to reach him at any hour, day or night, since he slept with the phone by his head in case of an emergency. He had a two-year-old nephew, and he was always on alert in case his sister needed him. This alone told me Mark was a good guy. I later learned that he and his family speak all the time, track each other's flights when they travel, and call numerous times on road trips to check in on each other's safety. How sweet is that? He was also a rock star surrounded by groupies, and he'd just given *me* the go-ahead to track him down at any moment.

Mark and I spent the next two weeks on the phone, talking about everything from music (we both listened to '90s rock) to problems we'd had with our exes (lots of cheaters in our pasts) to our astrological signs (I'm an Aries and he's Virgo, which was good news since I'd had no luck with Capricorns and Pisces). We also laughed a lot, which was important to me. Mark and I had so much in common that we knew we needed to see each other again to find out if our chemistry was just as intense in person and if there was a future for us. I was nervous because I knew I gave good phone but wasn't sure if I'd be awkward when we were face-to-face again.

We decided to meet up in New York in the middle of the month, when Mark had five days off and I'd be back from traveling to Monaco and the Cannes Film Festival with my family and best friend from elementary school, Nicole. Mark and I planned to meet each other's families in New York, California, and Alabama. It would be the longest "date" I'd ever had.

Though I should have been soaking up the French Riviera, I spent most of my time there obsessing over Mark and driving my mom, stepdad, and Nicole crazy. At one point, Mom tried to get me to flirt and dance with some member of the royal family that we met at the dance club Jimmy'z Monte-Carlo. When she reminded me, "If you married this guy, you'd be a princess," I had other ideas. "I don't wanna be a princess," I insisted. "I want to be a rock star's wife."

As Caroline Rhea might say, I had serious verbal diarrhea about Mark. While we were apart, I also went to the hotel gyms so I'd look good naked, talked to Mark on very pricey international calls, and stared at a picture of him in orange leather pants on the back of his album cover. I hadn't been this smitten since I was fifteen and obsessed over Anthony Kiedis the same way.

When I flew into Long Island from France, I rushed back to Dad's house to freshen up, and then turned around to pick Mark up at the airport four hours later. I wasn't wasting any time to see him again. Our rapport was a little awkward at first as we drove the hour back to the house, but I knew we were in the clear during dinner at a local Sayville diner. Under the table, Mark smoothly put his hand on my thigh. Afterward, at a dark Irish pub called Portly Villager, which is my dad's favorite watering hole, Mark tried to kiss me but I backed away. I didn't want my first kiss with him to be in that scrappy bar, especially since Dad was there with his buddies and they might start ribbing us. So we waited until we got back to my dad's house, where we couldn't wait any longer and made out in my sister Liz's childhood twin bed. Not any less strange, I guess.

A few days later, I took Mark to New York City for two days, and though he'd been there before, I wanted to show him the city the way I always knew it. We made sure to stop by my favorite pizza place for a slice and hit a Mister Softee truck for ice-cream cones. He also met a bunch of my East Coast friends, including my ex-boyfriend Mike, who I'd become close to again after ending things with James. Everyone got along great, which made me very happy.

The next stop on our trip was Enterprise, Alabama, where Mark grew up. He introduced me to his two sisters, brother-in-law, nephew, and his dad, Walt, who stood quietly off to the side in an intimidating way. It was also nice to see his mom again and get to know her a little. I even started calling her Miss Jenny, since she was a dance teacher and that's what all the sweet and respectful girls in town did. She and Mark's sisters had lots of questions for me about my family and life in L.A. They were very easy to talk to, which made me feel really comfortable. However, I also sensed they were hesitant about their son dating an actress, since they thought all women in Hollywood were casual about commitment, marriage, and divorce. I did everything I could to assure them that if Mark was game, I was in this relationship for the long haul. Looking back, the experience reminds me of a hometown visit on *The Bachelor,* but without the cringe-worthy surprises like how Dad has a scary gun collection or Mom still cleans her son's bedroom.

I went with Mark and his band to a show in Tampa the next day; this was the first stop of a multi-city tour for them, and I was joining them for the next few. During the Florida concert, Mark made me stand where he could see me, right by the sound booth in the center of the crowd, and he dedicated the song "1000 Times" to me. He knew it was my favorite on his album. The lyrics are crushingly romantic—*I've felt so strong for you ever since/The day you caught my eyes and I/Can't help but wonder if my life/Is turning upside down this time.* I knew he didn't write them for me when we met, but I felt like he was singing them to me and that was more than enough. It was unbelievably hot to have the man I was quickly falling so hard for show me this much attention in front of thousands of people. I later found out that Mark actually wrote the song about the type of woman he'd hoped to spend his life with, which turned out to be my type after all.

After the show, I waited for Mark by his car. He came up behind me, dripping wet and spent, and wrapped his strong arms around my waist. He picked me up off the ground, and as I turned around to kiss him, I stopped to open myself up to him. I wasn't scared anymore.

"I think I'm falling in love with you," I said.

"I think I am, too," he said.

Sweaty PDA ensued.

The next day we flew from Tampa to San Francisco with the rest of the band, where they played two nights in the Bay Area, and then went to L.A., where Course of Nature opened for Nickelback at the Palladium. We went back to my house afterward. In L.A., Mark took a good look at my life and liked what he saw. He met the rest of my family, including my mom, Trisha, and little sisters Ali and Sam, and impressed them with his handsome looks and incredible talent. They were also taken by his rock star persona. Five-year-old Sammy gave Mark the nickname "Nine Hole Wilkerson" when she pointed to his piercings and exclaimed, "What are all those things in your face?!"

When it was time for Mark to leave the West Coast, we had a long, heartbreaking kiss good-bye. In just nine days, we'd met each other's families, shared our life stories, and visited each other's hometowns. We were inseparable. I called him at least three times a day, but I still felt gloomy without Mark by my side. Kerry knew how badly I was pining for him, so she called a week later to see if she should book me a flight leaving LAX in two hours to Houston, where Mark was making a tour stop. Of course she should! I was having lunch with my friend Kimi, but I jumped at the impromptu trip, stuck my pal with the check (she didn't care), and stayed on the road with Mark and Course of Nature until *Sabrina* needed me back on set to begin its seventh season.

I was on tour with Mark and the band for a month, during which time he just kept getting better and better. He had the piercings and shaved head of a badass, but I quickly learned that when the rest of his band was partying, he was the guy who stayed behind to vacuum the tour bus and write lyrics in the lounge. Though Mark fronted the band, he didn't care about being the center of attention; he just wanted to be the best artist he could be and make really good music. He wasn't the type to smash expensive equipment onstage to get a rise out of the audience. And if something wild did happen during a performance, he made it immediately clear how he felt about the situation. I found the transparency of his emotions refreshing. I liked watching his face startle if the bassist hit a wrong note or the equipment started to fail, and if he made a single mistake himself, he'd get visibly upset about it. But he could always come down from whatever he was feeling at a show to snuggle with me at night, sometimes in the back lounge of the tour bus. He was breaking his own rule of "no nookie on the bus," but we were too in love to care.

By the time I was back in L.A., it was understood that Mark and I were in a serious long-distance relationship. We each always kept a packed bag near the door, so he or I could go to Alabama, on the road, or to L.A. at a moment's notice. We didn't date in a traditional way, with weekly dinners and "Did I see him too often this weekend?" hand-wringing, but that may not have even worked as well for us. We preferred to passionately dive into the relationship and give it everything we had. Mark and I had similar values, interests, and a lot of love to give. Everyone around me could see that I was head over heels for this guy, even though some of my friends weren't sure what to make of how quiet he could be. Mark's like his dad that way. But I'd always hoped as a little girl that my knight in shining armor would give all of his attention to me and nobody else—coming from a big family, can you blame me?—and that's exactly what I got.

About two months into our relationship, Mark asked what my plans were for Christmas, even though it was still summer. I blew him off. I said it was too far away to discuss, that I never spend Christmas with boyfriends, and that we should each be home with our families.

"But this might be our last Christmas together without being married," he said. I couldn't tell if he was gauging my reaction to getting hitched or telling me what he thought I wanted to hear so I would agree to spend the holidays with him.

"All the more reason to spend it apart one last time, then," I said, hoping to change the subject.

Mark was visibly disturbed. I secretly thought it was adorable how adamant he was that we spend the holidays together, and especially how he basically just told me that he was already thinking marriage, but I wasn't ready to verbally commit to spending my life with him just yet. I had a strict rule about dating for at least a year before getting engaged, since I'd always wanted a short engagement and that meant I had to know someone for at least a year before it happened. I had noticed that the few people I knew who had long engagements took forever to pull the trigger or ended up not going through with it eventually. I didn't want that to happen to me.

Mark and I compromised. We'd spend Christmas with our own families, and then, together, have a snowy New Year's Eve in Lake Tahoe. We also agreed to spend Thanksgiving in Alabama. But on Turkey Day, I went to my first University of Alabama football game and had such a good time that I invited Mark's parents to join us on New Year's Eve with me and my family. I meant nothing more by this, but Miss Jenny knew her son had something up his sleeve. She kept telling Walt, whose work schedule conflicted with the trip, about what a terrific time they'd have.

"It's going to be a very special occasion," she insisted.

I thought that was a weird comment. Why would a boozy New Year's Eve in the snow mean so much to a grown woman who doesn't drink or ski?

Back on set, I told the story to my friends at *Sabrina* one day at lunch, and our director that week, Anson Williams, who famously played Potsie on *Happy Days,* had a theory.

"He's gonna show up on Christmas Day and propose!" he said.

I wasn't sure what to think about this.

Mark and I spent Christmas with our families, and his parents took me up on Tahoe. Mark was set to arrive on the twenty-sixth, and that afternoon, I went with a bunch of the *Sabrina* crew to watch the ponies run at one of our favorite hangouts, the Santa Anita racetrack. While we sipped Bloody Marys among our favorite thoroughbreds, I couldn't shake the feeling that something big might happen that night. My friend Eryn even drew a diamond on my left ring finger with a pen and singsonged, "You're getting engaged today!" I hoped everyone's instincts weren't taking me down the wrong path. What if I expected Mark to propose and . . . he didn't?

I was also concerned that if Mark did propose, I might jump at the chance to be a wife for the wrong reasons. This had nothing to do with Mark being the right or wrong guy. As a child of divorce, I worried that I might say yes just so I wouldn't end up alone. And also, years earlier, my costar Lisa Dean Ryan on *Silencing Mary* told me a story about how she'd accepted a proposal without thinking, because she got so swept up in the moment with a big, shiny rock staring back at her. She broke it off and then promptly bought herself a simple engagement ring, so she'd never let diamonds distract her again. This stuck with me. To guard myself from the same fate, I'd followed her lead and in 1998 bought myself a diamond ring from Tiffany. I called it my "Nobody Loves Me Like Me" ring. I was between James and Weenie at the time, so no boy could dispute it.

I tried to put all my fears and hesitations out of my head. I got ready to pick Mark up at the airport. I loved Mark with all my heart, and I had no real reason to be anxious, but I was about to make an epic memory, no matter how it turned out. I put on a dress, washed off Eryn's inked ring, and wore zero jewelry just in case. At the airport, I thought I'd pass out from the nervous anticipation of waiting for Mark to descend the escalator. When he was finally in front of me, he gave me a big hug and kiss, and we held hands walking to baggage claim.

That's it? I thought, as if I expected him to drop to one knee at the LAX escalator, in front of hundreds of strangers. I've always figured that the best way to keep from being disappointed by a situation is to try to control the outcome, but this one was out of my hands.

As we waited for Mark's bags, still in an embrace, I thought I felt a small box in his coat pocket. But when I checked his face for a reaction, he was a blank slate. We were headed back to my house when Mark told me he had to quickly stop at my mom's to talk to her, which piqued my interest. I excused myself to the bathroom so they could have a quick chat about whatever was on his mind.

When we got back to my place, we were anxious to open gifts by the tree. Mark gave me a scarf, and I gave him a tow hitch for his truck. He gave me a waffle maker, and I gave him tickets to the Super Bowl. He was so excited about the tickets that he began sending messages to his buddies on his SkyTel messaging pager (it was like the caveman version of texting). At that point, I wasn't sure what to think about the engagement. I'd given him the perfect moment to pop the question, and he didn't take it. I began to clean up the wrapping, and softly said, "Thanks for my gifts," when the lightbulb went on over his shaved head.

"Oh, wait! I have one more gift for you!" he said.

I smirked, sat back down, and Mark told me to close my eyes.

My ring finger began to twitch in anticipation of what I hoped would come next. When he said I could open my eyes, he presented me with a large princess-cut diamond, flanked by two smaller diamonds in a heart-patterned filigree platinum setting. I screamed and covered my face with my hands.

"Shut up!" I said. That was not the reaction either of us anticipated.

"Will you marry me?" he said, and laughed.

I was blown away, but one little thing was off. Mark and I were sitting on my red chaise. That's not how it was supposed to happen?

I asked Mark to get down on his knee and ask again. He did, God bless him, and then I accepted his proposal. After a kiss, we ran to the phone to call our families and share the good news. The next day, we drove eight hours to Lake Tahoe to meet up with them for New Year's Eve. Trisha came with us and kept popping out from the backseat, shouting, "Happy Fiancée Day!"

We set a date that week. By July 2003, we planned to get married in a destination wedding in Florence, Italy. Seven months of dating, plus seven months before marriage, equaled just over the year I'd always hoped for. *Sabrina* ended that March, which was sad and hard for me, but I was also ready for a fresh start. I'd begin my next chapter as Mrs. Wilkerson.

The only concern I had about marrying Mark was how well I'd fit in with his family for the long term. I could promise loyalty, but I couldn't change the fact that they'd always be a proper Southern family, and my upbringing was more laid-back, bordering on white trash. For instance, when Mark and I were first dating, he started tickling me during a snuggly post-coital moment, and I accidentally farted while sitting on his lap. He pretended to ignore the situation while I, red-faced as ever, made a joke of it by running to the shower laughing. I was mortified, and he never talked about the incident again, which was somehow worse than confronting it. Mark comes from a family that holds doors and controls bodily functions; the Harts are much looser with their manners and toots. After we got engaged, I made the mistake of telling Miss Jenny this story and insisting that I couldn't marry her son until I heard him pass gas and we leveled the playing field. Her response? "Wilkersons do *not* do that in public." I was horrified a second time, but to this day, I still won't sit her next to my dad at dinner, especially if we're eating Mexican.

The next few months were a whirlwind. If it weren't for Soleil knowing me and my tastes so well, they could have been pure hell. When Mark and I got back to L.A. from Tahoe, we started looking for a new home to start our life in right away. Mark didn't like the idea of staying in a house I'd bought with James and lived in with Weenie. Soleil said she knew the perfect one for us, and after checking it out, we jumped on the opportunity to buy it. Her husband, Jason, had started a production company with Ashton Kutcher called Katalyst, and Ashton's agent was the one moving out of this amazing ranch in Encino. It had a two-hundred-gallon fish tank that we couldn't stop staring at. Soleil then suggested an ideal villa for our wedding that she'd visited the year before called the Grand Hotel Villa Cora, so we added it to our list of places to see when we did our search in March. We were taken with the space the minute we saw it and booked it ASAP.

If you ever meet someone who says coordinating a wedding brought out the best in them or their families, smack them, because they're lying. Our families had some typical tugs of war, like where to have the rehearsal dinner, what religious traditions the service would follow, and whether to serve chicken or veal for dinner. They also have different customs they like to honor at weddings—my Catholic family wanted a statue of the Virgin Mary present, and his wanted to invite everyone he'd grown up with from their hometown. We met in the middle. My sister bought a small statue of Mary at the Vatican, and we had a seven-hundred-person engagement party in Alabama to celebrate with Mark's family and friends. There wasn't a dry eye in the place when he sang "Angel Eyes" to me. But through it all, Mark and I always tried to look at the big picture. He didn't want to be a demanding groom, and I didn't want to be a Bridezilla. (Mark did let me call it "my wedding" versus "our wedding," since I was doing most of the planning.) We'd found true love and were committing our lives to each other during a beautiful ceremony, surrounded by our closest friends and family in Italy. It was a fairy tale coming true.

When Mark and I announced our engagement in the press, MTV called us about doing a new reality show for them about Hollywood newlyweds. It was tempting, since they could help us pay for a dream wedding, but Mom passed on the opportunity because she thought it was a bad idea for the public to watch us figure out our first tough year of marriage. Reality shows were still a new format, and we weren't sure what to expect from this. (When we walked away, the network approached Jessica Simpson and Nick Lachey, and the result, *Newlyweds,* basically proved Mom's point.) So Mom proposed a similar show to ABC Family, since they already liked me and Mom, and we could expect a sweeter outcome. It was called *Tying the Knot* and

covered all the wedding prep, dress shopping, scouting of locations, our engagement party and Alabama tool party, my bachelorette in Jamaica, the week of activities leading up to our
nuptials, and our beautiful wedding night. ABC Family even
footed most of the bill, including hotel rooms for all eighty-five
guests and flights for our families and wedding party as part of
the show's budget.

In Florence, we had a breathtaking experience with family
and friends. We hosted dinner parties almost every evening,
took cooking classes during the day, went on museum tours,
and organized golf outings for the guys and brunch for the
girls. We even had late-night pool parties and an impromptu
bachelor/bachelorette party on the villa's rooftop, overlook-
ing the spectacular view of the Florentine skyline. I wore a
strapless Reem Acra dress and had Mark's tie cut from the same
fabric. I stashed a penny in each shoe, which is a Southern tradition for good luck—one from 1976 for my birth year and another
from 1977 for Mark's. I walked down the aisle to a song from
Nanny's music box that my little sister Ali, who was nine at the
time, played on the piano. We said "I do" in an elaborately gilded
hall draped with white roses, and during the reception, we dined
at one long table lit by hanging lanterns. Mark and I did a shot of
vodka when the reception was winding down, in homage to the
first night we met.

From the start, I knew Mark was the man for me. He had
strong values and put family above all else. He wanted kids, but
didn't care when that happened as long as it was with the right
person. He was disciplined and passionate about his work,
health, and career. He also felt very strongly, as his lyrics attest,
that trust is paramount in a relationship, which meant the world
to me. And like me, Mark had a bit of a wild side that was
matched by his affinity for planning and thinking of the future.

He's still all these things, and every day he surprises me by peeling back another layer of who he is and wants to become. Ten years later, I want him as badly as I did that night at the Derby and his eyes still make me weak in the knees. I don't think that will ever change.

Between setups on location at the Piazza di Spagna in Rome for *Sabrina Goes to Rome*, with Tara Charendoff Strong, 1998

Lindsay Sloane, Nate Richert, and me in our best rock star gear for "The Band Episode," 1998

Three peas in a pod: me, Tara Charendoff Strong, and Lindsay Sloane (with Keri Russell in the background to my right)

One of the highlights of my life, meeting the incomparable Shirley Temple Black

Having a laugh with Britney, 1999

I would've made a great waitress—on the set of Britney's "Drive Me Crazy" video, 1999

Showing off my bedroom eyes—
and a few other things—for
Maxim in 1999

MICHAEL ZEPPETELLO

With Ashton Kutcher
and January Jones
at my twenty-third
birthday dinner

Eryn, Kimi, Christine—my
gang of girls—and me
doing one of our many craft
projects in the mini yard
outside my *Sabrina* trailer

Doing a little kick-ball-change with the legendary Dick Van Dyke, one of the incredible guest stars on *Sabrina*

Joan Rivers gave my look a thumbs-up at the 2002 Cannes Film Festival, with my childhood friend Nicole

My longtime girlfriend Soleil Moon Frye and me stirring up trouble, as usual

May 2002, the night I met the love of my life, Mark, at the Mint Jubilee event at the Kentucky Derby. I love that his fist is closed on my shoulder—awkward!

Partying at the 2002 Kentucky Derby with Jerry O'Connell and my girlfriend Kerry, the morning after I met my now-husband, Mark. Good thing he didn't see this ridiculous outfit then.

My first University of Alabama football game. Note to self: never again dress like the mascot.

Minutes before Mark proposed!

July 19, 2003: the day we said "I do!" at the Villa Cora, Florence, Italy

With partner Mark Ballas,
just before dancing
my favorite routine,
the Charleston, on
Dancing with the Stars

With one of my closest friends,
Kellie Martin, at a 2009 charity
event

My hero: Mom

I debuted my favorite dress—with the patriotic eagle decal—on *The Tonight Show* and have worn it every July 4th since

Two childhood pals, me and Joey Lawrence, playing make-believe on *Melissa & Joey* in 2011

My beautiful boys! Me and Mark with Mason, Brady, and Tucker in 2013

Chapter 13

OUR TRAVELING FAMILY CIRCUS

After we finished honeymooning all over the UK and Ireland, Mark swept me into his arms and carried me over the threshold of our new house. Then he practically tripped over the two long extension cords that crossed the foyer and led to our beloved two-hundred-gallon fish tank. Before we left for our Italian wedding, we stocked the container with twenty-five exotic and expensive saltwater swimmers and decorated it with an artificial coral reef to make them feel at home. We even named our babies. Tinker Bell, a yellow cow fish, and Big Al, a red star fish, were among our favorites.

But now that we were back, something was up. A harried call to my assistant revealed that while we were gone, our power went out and the fuse that kept the tank's filter going had blown. The result was a smelly fish soup. She would have called, but she didn't want to upset us on our honeymoon, knowing how attached we were to our little aquatic pets. The aquarium store had cleaned it up and replaced the innocent casualties, before we could say good-bye. I hoped it wasn't an omen of things to come. Would our first few years of marriage go belly-up, too?

Life felt unusually calm as we settled in as husband and wife. Mark's tour had ended, and *Sabrina* was over. And as mushy newlyweds, neither of us was in a rush to line up new gigs. Before we got hitched, we spent all our time hurrying to each other's side, sad that we'd soon need to leave again. But under the same roof, we did everything together. We ate breakfast, lunch, and dinner together. We chose furniture and paint colors together. We played tennis on our courts, hung out by the pool, and spent a lot of time at our in-home movie theater. It was the size of a two-car garage, with 35mm projectors and a remote control that closed the drapes, dropped the curtains, and started the film—all with the press of one button. We snuggled up to watch movies in the evenings, had football parties, and hosted weekly movie nights that screened every film from the American Film Institute's "100 Years . . . 100 Movies" list, starting with *Citizen Kane*. Well, okay, only I did that. Mark wasn't too interested in vintage celluloid.

We also locked in our best couple friends during those first few months—Kellie Martin, who I'd met in my *Clarissa* days, and her lawyer husband, Keith, who looks just like Jimmy Stewart. We'd bumped into them at a charity event before we got married and made a double date for after the wedding. Over Greek tapas, we got so into our conversation that the restaurant had to kick us out at closing time, and we loitered on the curb for another hour. Mark and I even did an analytical postmortem of the entire evening driving home, wondering if they liked us as much as we liked them. We fantasized about doing brunch and going for long walks on the beach. The feeling was mutual.

Though I liked the change of pace, so much inseparable nest-ing with Mark began to make me itch for a new adventure. A few weeks into this, my agent called to say I had been offered the part of Sally Albright in a West End stage show of *When Harry Met Sally* at the Theatre Royal in London. I loved spending time with Mark and our new terri-poo, Copper, but nonstop domestic bliss also made me feel disconnected from the one thing that had kept me consistently fulfilled for the last quarter century—my job. Plus, the script was winning, London in the fall is hard to beat, and Sally is a lively character any actress would die to play. I also knew I'd hit that orgasm scene out of the park, since I'd faked a few climaxes in my day. Relax, pervs. I'm talking about when I was in *The Vagina Monologues* back in 1998. I know what you were thinking.

I told my agent I'd take the part, but weeks before I was meant to leave, the theater's grand chandelier (that hung over a seven-hundred-person audience) slipped from its bearings, causing chunks of the plaster ceiling to fall on the audience below. The fixture and its two thousand lead crystals swung from a safety rope above and chaos broke out. Fifteen people were injured and fewer fans attended the show. Ticket sales never fully recovered, and the play closed. On the day I was supposed to have gone to London, my girlfriend Kimi tried to cheer me up. We spent the afternoon boozing at a local British pub in L.A., stuffing our faces with bangers and mash and sporting tank tops she'd bought us that said "Bollocks."

At twenty-seven years old, I was married and unemployed, which basically made me . . . just a housewife? I'm a careful investor and frugal by nature, so thanks to what we'd put away, we didn't worry about money. My sanity was another question. I knew I had to meaningfully fill my time or go bananas. I live to be busy, and if my calendar shows even a minute of downtime, I fill it with three different events and squeeze it all in. I wasn't content watching soaps or sitting by the pool with a book for too long. I'm a doer, and I needed to do. Big time.

I got involved with some great charities and found new hobbies. I worked closely with Friends of the Family, Lupus LA, and March of Dimes, to name a few that I really cared about. I rounded up auction items, called companies asking for sponsorships, sold tables to people with deep pockets, you name it. If someone were to ask me to mop floors to raise money for these causes, I'd have probably done that, too—I was so eager to be industrious. I also began running five miles, twice a week, with Kellie. She started training for marathons and I tried to keep up, but my knees couldn't carry me past ten miles a day. I attempted to run a 10K with her, or a little over six miles, but even then I slowed her down. We began hiking the canyons around L.A. together instead. All this exercise made me hungry, so I then signed up for cooking classes. I roped Kellie and my sister Trisha into joining, but once again, Kellie the Wunderkind excelled and is now one teaspoon shy of being a gourmet chef on Food Network. The only thing that stuck with me were recipes for mashed cauliflower and chicken stuffed with goat cheese. I made these every week—just because I had the hours of a housewife doesn't mean I could sauté like one—until Mark stepped up to the stove and whipped out his family's Southern specialties.

Though Mark was always kind about my culinary hits and misses, we bickered a lot as newlyweds, as most do. Whenever I fought with guys I dated before him, I got them to behave by threatening to break up with them. But being Mark's wife took that choice off the table. In fact, he often reminded me that divorce will never be an option with us—big surprise, considering his mama once told me in her thick Wiregrass accent, "Wilkersons marry for liiiife." As comforting as that was, it didn't help me communicate how I felt sometimes. So

Mark and I had to learn how to fight fair, and a lot of times, that included choosing our battles. And by battles, I mean nit-picky quarrels about nothing momentous. Even today, we're always at constant odds about nonsense. But in a strange way, all that squabbling reminds us that we're passionate people, and let's face it—making up is way more fun when you're hot and bothered.

One of the biggest newlywed fights we ever had was about ketchup. Yes, I just said that. Mark wanted to store it in the pantry, I wanted it in the fridge, and we kept moving the container back and forth after we each used it. The issue came to a head when I was stocking bulk-size Heinz bottles for a BBQ, and Mark saw me put one in the fridge. He'd had enough of eating his favorite condiment cold, and he couldn't let it slide anymore. Not in his house.

"Show me where it says that ketchup must be refrigerated! Show me!" he exploded, adding that at restaurants, the ketchup is left on tables all day long. Right? Right? I hadn't thought of this, but I told him I didn't care what the bottle said, or who kept it out where, because for me, it was about taste. I liked my ketchup cold, especially when I dipped my eggs in it.

"I didn't realize that when I took your last name I had to take on your condiment preferences too," I said, matching his height-ened tone. Then I chucked a full plastic bottle of ketchup at him, hoping that all those years as a wide receiver would pay off and he'd catch it. We were each serious about winning the argu-ment, but we were admittedly having a little fun with it too. Mark caught the bottle, but then picked me up and carried me outside, plopped me on the roof of the car like Mitt Romney's Irish Setter, and locked me out of the house. I ran around to the doggy door, crawled through it, and went back to putting ketchup in our fridge.

Eventually we calmed down and resolved to keep one bottle cold and one in the pantry. We still do, although I occasionally catch Mark using the cold ketchup now. I guess I should just be glad that Mark doesn't put his warm ketchup on his pasta. That would be unforgivable.

Though Mark and I never argued about it outright, a more serious sticking point that first year was my mom's relationship with Mark. Although Mom got along with my three previous long-term relationships, plus a handful of decent boyfriends, she turned green with envy when she met Mark. She must have sensed how serious our relationship was early on, because she always seemed uncomfortable around him, and then once we got engaged, she began to act out. Whenever we talked, she took on a needy tone, and she also began picking ridiculous fights with me, like about whether my arms were too fat to wear tank tops on *Sabrina* (I said no, but she insisted—this, while I was eating spaghetti with garlic bread that she'd made me). I think she feared that Mark would take her place in my life. Meeting The One meant she'd no longer be my plus-one for parties, award shows, premieres, and trips. In fact, after we got engaged and the initial novelty of being Mother of the Bride wore off, her response was, "Looks like I've lost my travel partner." It seemed a small price to pay for her daughter to gain a husband, but to be fair to Mom, *Sabrina* ended around the same time, and my sister was getting married that same year, so she may have felt overwhelmed by so much change.

What I wish she'd realized was that building a family meant we'd include her in our lives in different, though no less special, ways. Our Encino house was closer to hers, so we never missed birthdays or Sunday night dinners. After a few years, particularly after our first son was born, all that tension dissipated, and she became our strongest support. Their major turning point happened when Mom's brother died and Mark reached out on his own and offered to help her clean out his apartment. Mom and Mark now have a terrific relationship with mutual under-standing and respect that puts my heart at ease.

Almost two years into being a Mrs., it was time to seriously get my post-*Sabrina* career on track. I decided to produce and direct next—I wanted to show the world my vision, and my ability to tell a story on the big screen. In January 2005, I began working on a short film called *Mute* that my agent and good friend Elena helped me set up and get running. I produced and financed it with my friend Steve Fischer, who I knew from my partying days. I met him through Soleil, and we spent a lot of time drink-ing by his pool, going to spin class, and hanging out at bars; he was a Wall Street guy who I basically convinced to get into the business. I helped cast a bride played by Emily Deschanel, who'd just signed on to shoot *Bones* for Fox, and my buddy Patrick Dempsey as her groom (we met on a private jet to the Indy 500), though *Grey's Anatomy* caused scheduling conflicts, so I replaced him with Dylan Neal, the love interest from *Sabrina's* last sea-son. Even director Garry Marshall made a cameo as the priest who married this pair. Casting the lead, a deaf-mute who tells the story with very little dialogue and mostly voice-overs, was much tougher. I needed someone with expressive eyes, and the only person I could think to pull it off was my sister Emily. She had to seem both believable and likable, despite her hurt soul, all while trying to sabotage her sister's wedding to the man she loved. Because the character was deaf, all of that had to come across on Emily's face. Although she was initially nervous that she couldn't do it justice, she agreed to do the part.

As if I weren't busy enough, Mark and I also decided around

the same time to move, after two years in our Encino ranch. We wanted to find a place that was a little less sexy and also smaller, since it was just the two of us and all the extra rooms in the house were inviting squatters—my sister, her boyfriend, my brother, and Mark's vagabond band members among them. We'd also been itching to find property in our favorite vacation spot in the world, Lake Tahoe, and by selling our giant Encino house, we could use the profit to make that dream come true. We found an unfinished construction in Sherman Oaks, one town over from Encino, which excited us since we could add our own touches to it.

While unpacking boxes and simultaneously polishing and prepping for *Mute* that spring, I shot a pilot for Fox called *Dirtbags* with Laura Bell Bundy, a regular on *Guiding Light*, and Balthazar Getty, best known for his roles in *Lord of the Flies* and *Brothers & Sisters*. *Dirtbags* was an acting job for me, not directing or producing, but it felt good to exercise multiple skills on several projects at once. The script was originally written as a small workshop play to test its small-screen potential. I'd done it the previous summer as a favor to the show's creator, and Fox thought it would make a great series. It was about a group of twenty-something friends who lived in a blue-collar suburb outside Boston and were stuck in their high school glory days.

The weekend after we wrapped the pilot, I became pregnant with my first son, Mason, and I began to worry about how I'd hide my bump on the show if it got picked up. Turns out, I had no reason to sweat it. Five weeks later while I was dancing with Bill Murray at a party held after his annual Caddyshack Charity Golf Tournament in Florida, my agent called to say *Dirtbags* wasn't on the fall schedule. I was disappointed and really wanted to see this show fly, but with our little one coming, I knew I had something even bigger on the horizon. I blurted out our baby news to

Bill—I'd golfed in the event for two years running, so we were friends—and he was the first outside the family to know!

Life began to move again at the pace I liked. I returned to shooting *Mute* in June for six days at Mom's house, with a crew that was basically paid in lobster: I had Dad overnight us a generous lunch to thank my team for working for so little. My belly grew. We worked on the house, but now with a baby on the way, it began to feel unsuitable for a child, given its steep driveway, busy nearby road, and many stairs. After living there for only six months, we sold the place to comedian Wayne Brady, who I knew from his days as a "pizza delivery boy" guest star on *Clarissa*, and moved to a Mexican-style ranch around the corner. I was nine months pregnant. Come hell or high water, I'd make a home for our new family yet.

Work and family grew in tandem. *Mute* premiered at the Palm Springs International Festival of Short Films, which was a big deal for me and Steve. On January 11, 2006, I gave birth to our first beautiful son, Mason Walter, at a whopping nine pounds. He had big blue eyes and an infectious smile, which made my twenty-four hours of arduous labor feel worth it. I spent that first month recovering in bed from the natural delivery, with help from my family and Mark's. I may have been home with a newborn, but that didn't stop me from submitting *Mute* to every prestigious film festival around. Once I was up for it, I dragged the little man to showings all over the country, including the Tribeca Film Festival, Vail Film Festival, and Sonoma International Film Festival. Mommy's groove was back.

When the festival frenzy died down, I couldn't help but think, *If I could turn a dream into a project for me, why not do it for my husband too?* I was so proud of my little short film. I thought it turned out fantastically for a low-budget, limited-location film, and it was a passion project that I made happen from beginning

to end. As for Mark, he needed a new label, since Lava, his previous one, had dropped him, and he was having major complica-
tions with his asshole manager. This meant he had thirty newly
written songs but no label to release his record and no manager
to find him a new one.

Once Mason was old enough for my sister Ali to babysit him,
I set off to take music business classes at UCLA. Mark's a talented musician but hates the business side of his job, so as his
best cheerleader with an enterprising spirit, I thought I'd start a
label for him—complete with distribution, radio play, and an
iTunes connection, which was a new technology at the time.
Mark found a great producer, put together a band, and went to
New Jersey to record an album. I stayed home with Mason and
took care of business. Once the record was complete, we realized the process was costing us too much money and marital
stress, so we passed his tunes on to a smaller label to take over.
While all this was happening, unbeknownst to us, one of Mark's
demos made its way to Clive Davis, who liked it for his new
American Idol rocker Chris Daughtry. In the midst of putting out
his own album, Mark was nominated for a Grammy for Daughtry's song "It's Not Over." We were all bummed when he lost to
Bruce Springsteen's "Girls in Their Summer Clothes."

The day after Mason celebrated his first birthday, I went back to
work. I'd landed the part for the ABC Family Christmas movie
Holiday in Handcuffs, which was shooting in Calgary, Canada,
for five weeks. I took Mason and my brother Brian, so he could
watch my son, as I didn't have a nanny. In the movie, I play
Trudie, who gets dumped by her boyfriend on Christmas Eve
and kidnaps a new guy, played by Mario Lopez, at gunpoint so
she isn't humiliated in front of her family. I worked twelve-hour

days, and on weekends, Brian, Mason, and I went to Banff National Park so Brian could get some snowboarding time, and I
could practice ice-skating for a big scene in the movie (we traded
off babysitting duty). It wasn't a conventional arrangement, but
growing up, our family always combined business with pleasure
and family time, so I knew how to make it work for us. My job
brings me to such interesting locations that I really like to make
the most of my downtime, take in the sights, and share this
privilege with my family as often as I can.

Being on set again made me realize how incomplete I felt
without working for the year I stayed home with Mason. This
was confusing to me, since I always thought motherhood would
be an entirely satisfying job that would trump all others. But I
realized in Calgary that my own need-to-be-needed feelings
seem to be more fulfilled on set than at home, and the smell of
newly painted props and a collaborative creative process were
much more satisfying to me than Gymboree and backyard picnics. Don't get me wrong—there's nothing I love more than
spending time with my children, but I like to feel useful and
satisfied in more creative and immediately gratifying ways. The
last time I checked, I was also good at what I did, and I didn't
want to ignore how satisfied I felt after I completed a job well
done. From then on, I decided I had to work but I'd take my
family with me as often as I could, because they were also my
world. I'd do my best to "have it all"—work long days, be there
for my kids, and still find the energy to get it on with my husband at night, as often as I could see him. Career and family always intersected in my own mom's life, and she seemed to handle
it just fine. I could do the same! When the ratings for *Holiday in
Handcuffs* came out, they told me my instincts were guiding me
in the right direction. The movie was, and still is, the most
watched telecast in ABC Family history.

That said, Mark and I also wanted to have a second child, and I knew I wouldn't be able to get back on set right away after that little one was born. So in the spring of 2007, I was anxious to knock a goal off my professional bucket list: to guest star on Mark's and my favorite show, *Law & Order: Special Victims Unit*. Nearly every talented actor I knew had done this, and I was desperate to join the club. I met with the casting director and asked my agents to annoy the hell out of them, but we didn't hear anything for months. Then, as luck would have it, Kellie Martin and I went to a charity tea in Beverly Hills and Mariska Hargitay was there (that's Detective Olivia Benson to you). Kellie knew Mariska, since she'd been a guest star on the show already, and introduced me with the side note that it was one of my dreams to be on her show. Shortly after, my agent called and said I'd been offered a role. Mark, Mason, and I were going to New York.

Shooting *SVU* wasn't the joyride I'd hoped it would be. No, it was intense for me. I was out of practice with dramatic acting, and I didn't know the set or crew. I was nervous all the time and felt out of my element, but I tried to channel this discomfort into my performance. My character was a schoolteacher accused of rape by a young boy, though the whole time she swears that he raped her. Every day, the director called for more overwrought emotion than the day before, so I did everything I could to muster a raw performance. I wrote suicide letters in my dressing room, listened to songs that upset me, and watched the rape scene from *The Accused* on a loop. Even still, I came off as emotionally timid and the director was unimpressed. It didn't help that I've never been a great "crier" on camera, or off, for that matter. I can never produce the pretty, single tear down my cheek the way Claire Danes and Demi Moore do. They seem to just turn on a tiny faucet the second the director calls action. I, however, get a red, blotchy face and build up a lot of snot before my ducts give way. I've had sound guys remove my microphone, because my heart beats too loud to hear the dialogue. Even at my own wedding, Mark was the one who needed the vintage hanky I'd shoved in my cleavage, not me.

For two weeks, I tried everything to give a poignant performance. I took the opposite approach of being a downer and kept my spirits light, I worked my way into character an hour before my scenes . . . nothing worked. I was lost. Having given up for the most part, I decided on the last day to pop into character as the camera rolled with help from the makeup girls blowing menthol crystals into my eyeballs, which is a trick used to help actors cry. After a little vapor action with no real emotion from me, I finally shed the tears they wanted. The director and crew effusively congratulated me on "really getting there." I'll never kill myself over making real tears again, especially when there's help nearby (unless Jerry Bruckheimer or Martin Scorsese insists).

Don't get me wrong, I got a lot out of shooting *SVU*. I became close to the brilliant and hilarious Diane Neal, who played Assistant DA Casey Novak, and had the honor of working with the vivacious Annie Potts. My agents also liked that I now had a weighty piece of tape on my demo reel. But during those two weeks in the city, I almost rethought the career that I couldn't wait to supposedly balance with being a mom. It was so hard on me that I didn't work for a while, until I was pregnant with my second son, Brady. Maybe morning sickness got me back on track.

Soon after I got knocked up a second time, I was offered the lead in Lifetime's *Whispers and Lies*, a horror flick about two cousins who visit a seemingly perfect island with dark secrets—a place where nobody seems to die (*dun dun DUN*). Though I swore up and down that I'd never do a scary movie when I left *Sabrina*, the genre was a profitable one, and as a working mom,

who was I to pooh-pooh that? I was also about five months pregnant, but I failed to mention my growing bump for fear that
producers would discriminate against me. I took the part, and
once the directors saw me in Vancouver, they realized camera
angles and wardrobe would need to be carefully thought out.
Though my growing uterus popped while shooting toward the
end of my second trimester, I had a lot of energy and maintained
an average weight, and I did everything they needed. Okay, so
maybe I ran a little slower when the zombies began to hoof it,
but the movie was a bust anyway, and I'm fairly confident that it
had nothing to do with the bun in my oven.

My son Braydon Hart Wilkerson was born on March 12, 2008.
With my second child, I felt more confident and relaxed as a
mother, so I went back to work sooner than I did with Mason—
only this time, I took the whole family with me, since Mark had
just finished touring. When Brady was about four months old,
Mark, the kids, and I flew down to Baton Rouge, Louisiana, to
shoot Hartbreak's first feature film, called *Nine Dead*. This movie
was my mom's passion project after years of busting her hump
and trying every avenue to make the flick happen. It was yet
another thriller, but we used a special RED digital camera. At
the time, this was a newfangled technology that let us keep the
scene rolling without worrying about having to cut with every
actor's tiniest stutter. We also didn't need to wait hours for the
camera to reload film or rehearse like crazy to perfect a scene
because we were putting it on expensive film. We could essentially "rehearse" while the cameras were rolling, or play around
with the dialogue and blocking because the machine caught
every bit, and we could play it back. It felt like we were filming a
play, because we shot the script from beginning to end in real
time, with only a few retakes here and there. Usually a movie or
TV show is shot out of order—sometimes with the biggest scenes

first, like a make-out scene or important climax (probably to get it out of the way before the actors feel burned out or get on each other's nerves and the chemistry is unfixable). But with the RED, we shot the whole thing, start to finish, in twenty-one days.

As a new mom, working on *Nine Dead* was a dream come true. I was surrounded by supportive family, so I had my pick of childcare if I wanted it. There was only one major wardrobe change, which meant I could spend more time breast-feeding and playing with my boys, instead of running between scenes to my trailer for hair, makeup, and clothing tweaks. Finally, my character was handcuffed to a pole in a small room, so I didn't need to coordinate blocking with our director, our rhythm was never interrupted with prop and set changes, and I could really focus on my performance. Oh, if I could only be handcuffed to a pole in all my projects.

Mark and I had a lot of friends in California, but we always knew we'd eventually want to be part of a community that's close-knit, safe, and entertaining for kids. In L.A., locals drive like erratic pricks, even if you're pushing a stroller down a street that doesn't have sidewalks. We rarely met our neighbors, which meant never waving at friendly faces or borrowing that proverbial cup of sugar. Public schools are underfunded and private schools are ridiculously expensive. Then there's the traffic, which is a time-suck at all hours of the day. Mark and I made a pact that before Mason began kindergarten, we'd find somewhere else to raise our family. Since we were both East Coasters at heart, we began to brainstorm spots on the East Coast to lay down some roots.

In the summer following *Nine Dead*, I auditioned for the role of the murderess Roxie Hart in the Broadway production of *Chicago*. I know I'd sworn off musicals, but a few nonprofessional singers had starred in this role, so I thought I could too. I didn't get the part, but it put us in a good place to start our house hunt out east. We began by listing all the areas we wanted to see, then called the local realtors and asked family and friends in those areas to join us. We brought our new nanny with us, and leaned on family for babysitting.

Our exhaustive search would have bankrupted HGTV. We started in Nashville, which was Mark's first choice, since he's from the South and so many music execs live and work there. We had fun at a Titans game, but when we toured those oversize homes, they were spread too far apart to shout to a neighbor during an emergency. I also couldn't walk to a store or Starbucks, which felt isolating. We moved on to my old stomping grounds on Long Island—albeit the more upscale sections of the North and South Shores that my family could never afford when I was a kid. But like Nashville, the best homes were far from town and inconvenient for errand running and play dates. By the time we reached Connecticut, which was next on our list, we felt defeated. We thought we'd hit a few places in Fairfield County, and if that turned out to be a bust, we'd consider North Carolina and Atlanta. Nonetheless, I cried all the way to the Constitution State. I wasn't hopeful.

We explored three towns in Connecticut, just outside Manhattan. The first was Stamford, but the people we met all felt a little older than us, and we needed our contemporaries. Next up was Darien, which has a pretty center of town, good restaurants, and beautiful homes, but none of the houses really fit our needs. Finally, we drove up the coast to Westport, which had an old Americana feel but with newer businesses and younger energy. It boasted a great school system, a private beach, a bustling downtown, and amazing farm-to-table restaurants—not to mention a regional country playhouse whose co-artistic director, until recently, was talented actress Joanne Woodward, Paul Newman's widow. I was impressed that this theater transferred a lot of hit shows to Broadway. We had family in New York and even our good friends and Mason's godparents, Michele and David, who worked with me on *Clarissa,* nearby. When I saw a group of kids pile off a school bus and run into the arms of their fit and fashionable moms, I knew we'd found our town.

Mark and I visited a handful of houses, and we found one new-construction home that I thought about every day after we returned to L.A. from our search. It was surrounded by woods, which made it feel very private, and we even saw some wild turkeys crossing the road, which was quaint. The backyard hill was sloped perfectly for sledding, and the nearby Long Island Sound smelled like my childhood. But we didn't make a move, because the housing market was in free fall, and we wanted to unload our place first. I prayed every night that our L.A. home would sell before that house in Westport did.

The best way I could think to get my head out of housing woes was—you guessed it—to get another job. In October 2008, I took Mark, the kids, and our nanny to Atlanta while I shot *My Fake Fiancé.* Mom and I were given a rom-com script that we loved about two strangers in dire financial straits who stage a fake engagement and wedding, just to collect the gifts. We optioned the story for Hartbreak and sold it to ABC Family, since they'd already shown us so much love already with our wedding show, *Tying the Knot,* our movie *Holiday in Handcuffs,* and years of *Sabrina* reruns.

My old pal Joey Lawrence and I costarred in it, which was a good time since we usually only saw each other in passing at events. Joey had just killed it on ABC's *Dancing with the Stars,* so the network was on board with our suggestion—that is, until Joey arrived in Atlanta with a shaved head, which they feared wouldn't go over well with their young audience. Just as they were about to ring my old on-screen flame James Van Der Beek to replace him, Mom put her foot down and insisted that Joey and I would have terrific on-screen chemistry. ABC Family conceded, the movie premiered with big numbers, and it led to a pseudo-spinoff, our current sitcom, *Melissa & Joey.*

On the set of *My Fake Fiancé,* where I was surrounded by my family and yet another loveable cast and crew, my work/life balance hit its stride. When I wasn't shooting, I took the boys to listen to a trumpet player on the corner, stuff our faces with fried chicken and tomato pie at Mary Mac's Tea Room, and visit the Georgia Aquarium at least once a week. At the age of three, Mason was obsessed with sea creatures, so I arranged to dive into the shark tank, full of whale sharks, hammerheads, and groupers. Diane Neal, who played my sister in the movie, carried Mason on her shoulders and followed me around the outside of the glass tank, so he could see his daredevil mommy in action. Mark was also able to take advantage of the travel perks. He spent time with his family and saw a few SEC college football games.

Almost exactly one year after our initial trip to Connecticut, we sold our L.A. home and loaded our bags and dogs onto a plane. The Westport house had waited for us. We knocked on our neighbors' doors and began making friends with other parents who happened to live within a seven-mile radius. We put Mason in school, just as we'd planned, and formed a community around like-minded transplants. When I wasn't working, I rowed crew on the Saugatuck River, went spinning with girlfriends, had coffee dates, formed a book club, and organized a dinner group that still meets every Monday night, so our husbands could bond too. We even bought a fish tank, though it's a twist on what we had in Encino. We scaled down from two hundred gallons to ten, and it's home to a hearty turtle we found in our backyard. The boys named him Dusty.

Chapter 14

IT'S ALL ABOUT THE
CANAPÉS, BABY

Whether you take entertaining cues from Lisa Vanderpump, Rachael Ray, or P. Diddy, God is in the details—the Pandora playlist or poolside DJ, cocktails-'n'-nibbles or a flashy prix fixe, a cozy private venue or the VIP room of a club. A theme can tie it all together, and for me, it has to be clever. But no matter how you play hostess, the point of gathering friends and family is to make memories you can cherish forever. Well, that, and to give everyone a reason to say nice things about you later.

I've been honing my entertaining skills for a while now— come to think of it, ever since I hosted my twenty-first birthday bash that landed in *People* magazine and bought my first home in L.A. Back then, the recipe for a good time included a well-stocked bar, a who's-who guest list, and ashtrays on every possible corner of the deck, poolside, and hot tub. And while Hollywood parties can be an epic statement of flash and ego, mine were mostly a way to spoil my closest friends and family. I wanted everyone to enjoy my little paradise.

When I lived in L.A., most of my friends happened to be crafty and creative, so I liked throwing parties that spoke to those instincts. Plain paper streamers and latex balloons were for other people. One of the best soirees I ever cohosted was for my friend Kimi. Eight of our girlfriends spent months organizing a Barbie-themed surprise party for her birthday, since Kimi is a girly-girl who lives for fashion and has a well-dressed Barbie collection to show for it. We decided to make the event a "progressive" party, meaning we'd move from place to place as the night went on. I rented a 1950s limo and driver for a pop of Hollywood glam, and we dressed like our favorite Barbie dolls or ones we made up. I looked like a Princess Barbie with a silky pink floor-length skirt and colorful halter top, which was the polar opposite of our friend Christine's Native American Barbie look. We surprised the clueless Kimi at her house and helped the birthday girl with her costume—a corset from her wedding she'd dyed bright red, a flouncy tulle skirt, and lots of gold, silver, and pearl necklaces. She was *Moulin Rouge* Barbie, based on our clique's favorite movie at the time.

The girls and I piled into the limo to begin our fun-filled odyssey. My house was the first stop, where my three-year-old sister Sammy's life-size Barbie propped the door open and welcomed us with stiff, plastic arms. I draped pictures, chairs, mantels, and the staircase in Pepto Bismol–pink boas and ribbon, and hired a bartender to serve pink cosmos. I had filled every frame in the house with shots of Kimi from different ages and events, and positioned various Barbie and Ken dolls around the plates of appetizers. After some serious noshing, we went to Mom's house for homemade lasagna. We ate dinner on her good china, in her formal dining room, as if it were a Barbie Dreamhouse, all while Mom served us dressed in her brilliant costume as "The Barbie Nobody Wanted." She wobbled around on one high-heeled shoe and wore a cockeyed crown, with messy hair and grass stains on her gown. We all wore shorts under our skirts, so after dinner, we stripped down and jumped on the trampoline out back. We ended our night at Eryn's house, where we opened gifts and dug into a Barbie cake—the kind where the doll's head and torso sits on top of an edible skirt. Most of us stayed over for a slumber party. We were like our twelve-year-old selves again, but with boobs and weed.

The Barbie party was such a hit that the following year, I threw a *Gilligan's Island* theme party for Eryn. The girls and I started by sending Eryn on a multi-destination scavenger hunt to help her collect pieces of her costume—first to our friend Ralph's house where she found a red wig and fake birthmark waiting, then to the produce section of the grocery store to discover a pink boa and a note telling her to go to my house. At Chez Hart, a life-saver pool toy hung on the door with the words "SS Minnow" Sharpie'd on it. We decorated the entire inside with almost a hundred straw skirts, hammocks, and a few blown-up palm trees. A bartender whipped up piña coladas and mai tais. Instead of singing "Happy Birthday," we tweaked the *Gilligan's Island* theme song with lyrics about Eryn's life and bludgeoned a hula girl piñata for what seemed like hours, until we got the last Kit Kat to fall out.

Remember how popular spa parties were toward the end of the '90s? When my friend Christine mentioned that if she could afford it she'd get a professional rubdown every week, I suddenly knew what my Christmas present to my friends would be that year. I invited eleven of my closest girls to my house, hired three massage therapists, three manicurists, a harp player, and a bartender (of course) for a Saturday night spa party. I lit candles, set up massage tables near the fireplace, and ordered personalized stockings for each girl and filled them with candy and inside-joke gifts. I also gave each girl her own bottle of champagne to make sure we were all loose as a goose. We had such a blast that massage-themed holiday parties became an annual tradition for the next nine years that I was in L.A., with surprise additions each time like a DIY facial station for mud masks, paraffin hand treatments, and a reflexologist for foot rubs.

Though I've been told I missed my calling as a party planner, sometimes I had to bring in the pros to pull off my bigger ideas. For my twenty-fourth birthday, I hired an expert named Jackson to help me throw a "Greek Orgy" bash for seventy-five guests. I was inspired by the mythological god and goddess paintings I always stared at on the walls of the spa when getting my seaweed body wraps. Jackson hung white drapes that billowed in the wind and arranged wine bottles, goblets, and grapes all over the pool deck. We hired masseuses to massage the guests' feet as ripped, toga-clad boys fanned us with large palms. It wasn't exactly Greek-inspired, but Jackson also threw in a few belly dancers and fire throwers for when the sun went down. Anything to up the debauchery ante.

I think my most inspired party of parties, however, was a New Year's Eve celebration I threw in 2001. I'd had a fine time in Miami at a Y2K bash, but the night wasn't as memorable as Prince's "1999" said it would be. Where was the purple sky? The lions in people's pockets? When I got back to L.A. on January 2, I began planning my own extravaganza in Mom's grand, marble-columned home, with the elaborate theme of an Italian Renaissance–inspired masquerade ball. Jackson and my assistant Kerry helped tremendously, as did my unlimited budget. It took us almost the entire year to nail down every detail. The invite went out to three hundred people and included suggestions on where to rent formal costumes and masks. I'd also arranged dance lessons with a choreographer for any guests who wanted to participate in a reenactment of the waltz scene from *Shakespeare in Love*, and included a schedule of those as well. *Sabrina's* wardrobe department worked for months on my four-thousand-dollar Renaissance gown. I hired a string quintet, a fleet of bartenders, and top-notch caterers who presented an elaborate meat-carving station in a massive red velvet tent we had set up in Mom's backyard. We ran limos like a taxi service all night, which picked up guests at their homes and drove them back when they were good and sloshed. At midnight, guests removed their masks and the DJ kicked it up a notch. The best part of the event, though, was sharing the Hart family's lentil soup with guests just after the clock struck twelve. Every year, Mom makes this traditional Hungarian dish to bring us good luck in the future. Legend has it that legumes are symbolic of money, and so far, this custom hadn't let me down. All our guests sampled the soup from a giant bowl, with individual golden spoons. I know it sounds like an extravagant night, but I considered it an investment in lifelong memories. Plus, my ta-tas looked really amazing in that overpriced corset.

I didn't know it at the time, but my fabulous New Year's Eve ball doubled as a last hoorah to hosting impressive parties for a while. I soon met and married Mark, who doesn't like celebrating his birthday, New Year's Eve, or any event that symbolizes the passing of time. He's always found these milestones depressing, and no matter how perky or encouraging I am, there's no forcing fun on my husband. He'll sulk, play sick to avoid hanging out, or if I throw a party without his blessing, he'll find a nice cozy corner and stay there all night. I, on the other hand, think creating a night to remember is what makes the aging process a worthwhile and digestible experience. Tomato, to-mah-to.

Early in our marriage, whenever Mark and I had people over in L.A., I tamed our guest list, budget, and attention to detail. What I loved most about entertaining was making guests happy anyway, so I focused on that during low-key dinner parties, movie nights, book clubs, and holidays. I found that intimate groups invited memorable conversation, "Bring a dish!" made neighbors feel useful, and easy décor meant simple cleanup. As a young adult, the only morning-after regrets I had were not giving away more leftovers and running out of vodka by 11 P.M.

There was one teeny problem with feeling like I should entertain like a mature adult, though: nobody really taught me how. I was never the little girl in a frilly nightgown, peering over a mahogany staircase to watch my parents clink glasses from afar. They hosted the random murder mystery or Halloween party growing up, but with five kids, they didn't have a lot of free time or money to do this with any regularity. So I gathered entertaining tips and tools wherever I could find them—in Colin Cowie's party books, in collaborations with my more experienced friends, and from studying reruns of *The Martha Stewart Show*. I could keep my book club ladies in Pinot Grigio or groan and cheer with the best of 'em at my annual Super Bowl parties, but any gathering that required a bit more sophisticated flair had the potential to turn into a hot mess.

One of my bigger entertaining catastrophes occurred when I invited both my family and Mark's to spend our very first married Christmas Eve at our house. Six members from Mark's immediate family had flown in from Alabama, plus five of my siblings, Mom, and Leslie. I really wanted to prove that I could create a warm, wonderful, and special holiday, especially for the kids. My old Sayville friend Joe and his wife were living in L.A. and dropping by as well, so I convinced Joe to dress up as Santa and run through the backyard as we watched from inside the house. My parents did this when I was young, and it was always a thrill. It's also why I believed in Santa for many years longer than I should have.

I wanted to keep our meal simple, so I decided that given my limited culinary skills, there was a good chance I could handle making Mom's legendary lasagna. Sauce, noodles, cheese, repeat. How could that go wrong? I scheduled our night around our big dinner. My plan seemed seamless. I'd go to church with Mark's Baptist family at 5, we'd eat dinner at 7, Santa would make his appearance around dessert, and then Mark and I would join my Catholic family at their 11 P.M. service. Done! What I didn't realize was that the church for Mark's family was almost an hour away, so by the time we got home, my family was sitting in their cars, in our driveway, in the rain, no less, beyond starving for dinner. I hadn't even boiled the noodles.

I'd also never cooked for more than four people, and now I had to feed twenty-four at warp speed. I panicked. I stressed. So much for posturing as a competent wife and hostess. My mom and Mark's helped make the lasagna, get it in the oven, and set the table with our new wedding china and crystal. We didn't end up eating until about 9 P.M. The moms also slipped snide comments to each other, fueled by lingering tension from our wedding, and I felt terrible for causing a mess when my intention was to do the opposite. And just when I thought Joe-as-Santa would save the day, he ran through the backyard and scared the shit out of the kids. He bolted past the back glass doors, inches from where they were peeking out for a glimpse of Sneaky Saint Nick. After everyone calmed down, Mark and I sped to our second church service, this time to appease my family. I've never prayed so hard for peace on earth and goodwill toward men—especially me.

Christmas mayhem was just a hint of things to come. In future years, I'd make Nanny's French silk pie for Thanksgiving, which looked like poop soup in a soggy crust. Then there was Mason's first birthday, with invites that said it was a "green-themed" party. This caused PC moms to call me in an eco-savvy panic about what the appropriate gifts and attire should be. No plastic toys? Organic cotton only? Good thing I meant for the day to revolve around my son's favorite color, not environmental consciousness. I'll also never forget the first of many summer lobster bakes in the backyard of our house. I didn't think to store the live crustaceans out of the children's reach, so after pulling a few from their boxes, they drove them around in bicycle baskets and sent them down the slide with their claws bound. My dog got hold of one and had her own feast. When it was time to cook the buggers, I was missing so many lobsters that we had to do a search-and-rescue mission in the nearby woods to hunt down a few of the escapees.

My Amelia Bedelia–like entertaining prowess all culminated in a dinner party that I like to blame on my son's preschool fundraiser auction in Connecticut. I passionately bid on, and won, a day of pheasant hunting with a local Italian chef named Chef Pietro. The prize? After we killed the birds together, he'd then help turn them into a fancy dinner. This seemed like a great idea, since I'm always up for trying something new and I'd get help with the hard cooking part.

I took my friend Lisa out with me on that gloomy New En-

gland morning. We skulked around the woods with two hunting dogs, a reputable chef, and loaded rifles. Lisa and I had never
shot a rifle outside of a firing range, and after some powerful
practice rounds, we surrounded our first bird and began reck-
lessly shooting into the air before realizing we'd better take turns
or risk blowing the other person's cute hunting hat off. Lisa
made the first kill when the bird flew overhead, and she fear-
lessly stuffed it into the large pocket of her fluorescent orange
vest. I shot mine as it scurried across a muddy path in front of
me. I didn't want to touch it, so Pietro shoved its bloody body
into my jacket, inspiring both sadness and awe in me. Is this
how the intrepid Katniss of *The Hunger Games* felt when she fired
her arrow into the eyes of squirrels? Though it was brutal stuff,
I did like learning to stalk and prepare a meal in a primitive way,
should I ever need to feed my family if, I don't know, there's a
zombie apocalypse or something.

Lisa and I killed five pheasants between us, and with Pietro's
help, I turned them into a feast that night for our friends. I mari-
nated the gamey-tasting birds in veal stock and served them
with vegetables. While the sides came out great, guests spent
half the night picking feathers and buckshot out of their teeth.
They told me the meal was impressive, but I think they were
just being nice since I could now shoot a gun. I haven't hosted a
real dinner party since. In fact, when I invite the gang over for
pizza and board games, I swear I can hear a collective sigh of
relief.

As I get older and our family grows, that spitfire twenty-
something who organized massage parties and scavenger hunts
feels farther and farther away. The thought of just hiding the
million tiny toys and shoes usually thrown around the house by
my kids is a chore I can do without. When I entertain now, I

give guests plenty of time to book a sitter, not pull together a cheeky costume, and as long as there are drinks and food to go around, people are grateful to dirty someone else's dishes for three hours. Now I save my biggest bashes for a few nights a year, so I can put more energy into making those parties memorable for everyone. I'm best known for having a New England–style lobster bake in the summer (I keep a better eye on the kids and crustaceans now) and an annual Tacky Sweater Christmas Party come winter. I still splurge on a trusty bartender but have added a housekeeper to help with cleanup. I'm no good at removing red wine stains from the rug or getting that lobster smell out of the kitchen when everyone's gone.

Once in a while, though, I still have my splash-out moments. My siblings and I recently threw Dad a surprise sixtieth birthday party, and for the first time in years, I unleashed my classic "go big or go home" party-planning instincts. The major difference is that I did a lot of delegating and divvying up of responsibility. We invited one hundred people, including high school friends Dad hadn't seen in twenty-five years. We put up a large white tent with tables and chairs in my uncle Charlie's backyard and hired a local BBQ joint to cater most of the food. Dad's buddy who owns an oyster farm set up an oyster bar, too. My brother Brian bought a shot luge—a huge ice carving that lets you pour liquor at the top and catch it in your mouth at the bottom. A lot of Dad's female friends pitched in (he's rather newly divorced), which I appreciated since I was extremely pregnant with my third son, Tucker, and needed the extra hands. Each woman had a different job—one decorated the tables, another kept us in beer. My sister Lizzie ordered an amazing cake that looked like a case of Budweiser, Dad's brewski of choice, with foaming cans made of fondant balancing on top. We even saddled up the

Naked Cowboy, a New York City icon who serenades pedestrians wearing only boots, a hat, and tighty-whiteys. He sang "Happy Birthday" to Dad, who was tipsy on Bud and touched by all our efforts.

Chapter 15

ARE YOU READY FOR SOME FOOTBALL?

I'd heard the term "football widow" thrown around before, but I never thought much of it. When I Googled the phrase, I half expected to find support groups devoted to women whose husbands were killed by flying pigskins. Instead, the first thing that popped up was an Urban Dictionary definition that went like this: "Football widow: A woman who must cope with the temporary death of her relationship during football games." *Holy moly,* I thought. *That's me.*

Growing up deep on Long Island, I was rarely exposed to the game. First of all, Dad was hardly the athletic type and always preferred to work or go fishing instead of watching "the big game." I'd only been to one football game in my life, an Army vs. Navy game where I didn't understand what was happening, but did make lots of "tight end" jokes while drooling over all those uniformed cadets. There were no nearby professional teams to root for, since both of New York's played at a stadium in New Jersey, and this felt as far away to me as the Alps. And while our small-town high school had a team, it was nothing like the legendary one on *Friday Night Lights,* so I had no interest in learning the game's complicated rules just to watch a bunch of local jocks chase a ball. When I enrolled in college, which is when most girls begin to take an interest in football (if just to score a broad-shouldered make-out partner at frat parties), I went to NYU. We were only good at tennis and basketball, and if we had a football team, I didn't know about it.

It's easy to see how one of America's most popular sports evaded me until I was twenty-six years old and fell for my husband. During one of our very first conversations, he asked me a question whose answer, he said, "might be a deal-breaker" for our relationship.

"What do you do for fun on a Saturday in the fall?" he asked.

It seemed like a simple enough question, and while I knew he was getting at something, I had no clue what. I proceeded with caution. I told him if it was September, his birthday month, we could do whatever he wanted! He said that was a good answer, but not the right one. The only other thing I knew guys cared about doing on Saturdays was watching men "throw the rock all over the yard" (another Urban Dictionary ref). Once I figured out he was talking about football, and he figured out that I had no interest in football, we both let out an exasperated sigh.

I racked my brain for "opposites attract" success stories with an athletic bent. In *Fever Pitch,* Drew Barrymore has a good relationship with Jimmy Fallon's baseball-fanatic character, and they shared a happy ending. But then in real life, I also had friends whose husbands never made plans on weekend afternoons, because they'd rather watch some ridiculous time-sucking sport. I always found it so silly to stare at other people doing amazing things on a tiny screen, instead of getting out there and doing something amazing in real life. But since I was just getting to know Mark, and I thought he was really hot, I decided that I wasn't going to get all crazy on him about his passions versus mine. At least, not yet. I figured I could roll with him being occasionally distracted, since it was a small price to pay for being with Mr. Right. In fact, I'd do him one better. I'd be the best football-fan girlfriend he'd ever known.

When Mark invited me to my first University of Alabama football game while we were dating and living in L.A., I strategically packed my bag for the trip to Tuscaloosa. I knew this was going to be a particularly big game because it was against Alabama's most rivaled team, the Auburn Tigers. I wanted to do it up right. Mark's U of A team is called the Alabama Crimson Tide, which means the team color is mostly a deep red, with hints of white and gray. Sometimes those colors are paired with a black-and-white houndstooth pattern in honor of its beloved legendary coach Paul "Bear" Bryant, who used to wear the design on his hat while making calls from the sidelines. With this in mind, I realized that I might not know much about the game, but I could at least dress the part and hope it proved my devotion to Mark and the Crimson Tide.

For my first real football game, I wore what I thought was both appropriate and enthusiastic gear that I bought at a team store in Alabama. It was also practical clothing. I'd been to a few sporting events before, and it was always a priority to be comfortable, prepared for beer spills, and dressed for walking to and from the tailgates. For me, all this boiled down to a team T-shirt with jeans, a team hair scrunchie, earrings with the team's rally chant, "Roll Tide!" printed on them, sneakers, and a team hoodie tied around my waist in case it got chilly at night, even though it was humid and hot outside. I also painted the words "Roll Tide!" on my cheeks. At the time, the stadium held ninety thousand screaming fans that I was told never sat down

and always shook their red, white, and gray pom-poms franti-
cally. I, too, bought pom-poms that'd give me an excuse to
scream my head off for my man's team and show him what a
good sport I could be.

Once we arrived at the tailgate parties at one of the sorority
houses on campus, I realized how inappropriately I was dressed
for a proper Southern football game. All the girls, including my
in-laws who came, were wearing nicely pressed skirts and pants
that were in team colors but in no way bought at the fan shop.
Some had on pearl necklaces, and each one of them looked more
prepared for a job interview at a law office than to pound beer in
a parking lot. When the girls asked me, "Could I have my picture made with you?" in their dainty Southern accents, I realized it was less about taking pictures with a celebrity and more
that I looked like the team mascot. But I was used to standing
out in a crowd, sometimes for the wrong reasons (see: Kentucky Derby). I went with it. I also yelled at Mark for not warn-
ing me about how foolish I'd look next to all those genteel girls
when he saw me getting ready earlier that day.

"I thought you looked cute," he replied. I could've died.

In the South, football devotion comes second only to the Bible—
and unfortunately, the worshipping of both happens on Sundays.
Even the pastors are aware of the game schedule, because they
know full well that if their sermon goes over by even a minute,
the congregation will start sneaking out the back to see the start
of the game. In Alabama, more people stick around, since the
state doesn't have its own NFL team and they love college football, which is played on Saturdays. It took me years to realize
this and then learn the differences between college NCAA and
the NFL.

Mark's family hails from Tuscaloosa as far back as they can trace, which isn't very far. When I first met Mark and asked where he was from, he told me "America." I rephrased the question and asked his heritage. "American," he said. But where were his ancestors from? "America!" He doesn't have a clue or care about his bloodline, but the one thing he will point out is that they're from the home of Alabama's Bryant-Denny Stadium and his beloved Crimson Tide.

You'd think that a guy who lives and breathes a college football team must have learned to love the sport from years of university pride and homecomings, but no. In the South, and especially in Alabama, college football affiliations are born, not raised. As I said, Alabama has its two major football teams, Alabama and Auburn. They're the biggies, the old staples, the stuff of legends and legacies. There are also smaller teams like Troy and University of Alabama at Birmingham, or UAB, but they're small potatoes. So you're either born into one "family" or the other. In Mark's case, his father and sister are both Alabama alums, and while Mark himself went to rival Auburn for a short time, he hates them as much as a Yankees fan loathes the Red Sox.

Following your team's adversaries is almost as important as caring about the team itself. Knowing who rivaled whom was hard for me to follow in the beginning. I could never understand why Mark had to watch every Auburn game. If you like Alabama, just worry about Alabama. When I asked Mark why he did this if he hated Auburn so much, he slowly turned his big head and widened eyes toward me and carefully said, "Because I need to make sure they lose." It's the same annoyed look he now uses on our kids when they ask "Are we there yet?" during a car ride. To this day, I still don't get why my day has to be ruined just so Mark can see a team weep. Couldn't we catch the highlights on SportsCenter that night? He's going to have it on anyway to watch recaps as I drift off to sleep dreaming of nachos and Peyton Manning.

Though I was still intent on being an über-girlfriend after that first outfit fail, dealing with Mark's devotion to his team and their contenders became challenging when I realized how much of my weekend was disappearing in front of a TV. For those who don't know, games last three hours minimum, so just two games in one day sucked up six hours of my time. Saturdays and Sundays used to be filled with adventurous excursions, race car driving, and Sunday brunches. But with Mark, they became a time to dutifully sit by my guy's side, while catching up on cheese-dip eating and tabloid reading, neither of which is good for the waistline.

I remember asking my friend Kimi, another sports widow, for tips, and her best one was, "When watching football with your man, just look up once in a while and ask, 'Now who did he used to play for?' He'll talk for at least fifteen minutes, you'll seem like you care, and then you can go back to your *InStyle* or whatever." Let me tell you, that worked. It still does. I even used Kimi's idea while writing this book. It was the only way to get time to myself while having Mark think I'm showing an interest in his sport, which means an interest in him and our relationship.

As you can see, not much has changed now that we're married, but there are random moments when I actually enjoy the game and wonder, *Who have I become?* Like when I've spent weekends alone while shooting on location and scream at the hotel TV while wearing my lucky Roll Tide T-shirt. I started watching so I'd know the final score if it came up with Mark at home, or worse, to see if a loss might cause him to be in a lousy mood all week. But now I tune in out of habitual interest. I recently realized how far I've come when I pretended to breast-feed our third son, Tucker, so Mark would put the other boys to bed and I could catch the end of a Giants game. Or when I occasionally call a foul before the refs or commentators do. It makes me feel so satisfied and informed, and I always look over at Mark to see if he's impressed by me too. He hardly notices.

The biggest thing Mark and I have in common is that we wear our hearts on our sleeve; for Mark, this goes for his football affair too. To prep for each season, he studies press reports and Internet stats, and has endless conversations all summer long with anyone who knows anything about the Crimson Tide or NCAA football. By fall, when his team takes the field, Mark has a precise knowledge of who the players are, what their strengths are, and where their weaknesses might lie. He has such a vast knowledge of the game, calling every play and complicated rule, that I really believe he missed out on being an ESPN reporter. We'll watch a game with about one hundred college kids on each team, with changes to its roster every year, and Mark will announce every player's first and last name, jersey number, and which high school he came from. Screw ESPN; Mark needs a job recruiting for the NCAA. As for me? It took a year to even learn what a "line of scrimmage" is. (It's the line they form when they're about to snap the ball. See, aren't you wowed?)

Most impressive is Mark's enthusiasm for the young brutes chasing a tiny triangle-shaped ball, maybe because he was one of them. The man was built for the game and worked hard to be the best receiver on his high school team, the Enterprise Wildcats. He took his sport so seriously that I believe it's what kept him out of trouble as a kid and teenager. He rarely partied like his friends did, because a hangover could affect his game. He spent most of his spare time training in some form or another, either at the gym, at speed camp, or by watching film of his plays.

These days, Mark paces the room during a game and demonstrates his ardor not with his broad shoulders or strong quads but with his amazing vocal cords. Remember that my husband is a rock singer, so he has the ability to make his voice incredibly loud and intimidating. Imagine naively reclining on the sofa on a rainy fall afternoon, catching up on the latest celebrity adoptions, when out of the blue this deep, dark, and extremely powerful voice screams, "HOLDING!!!" It's enough to give me the hiccups for weeks. When I was pregnant, the baby would literally jump inside me from shock. I've become so accustomed to Mark's shouting at the players that I encourage him to get tickets and head South to the games, because I know he won't have a voice for at least three days. That's when I take my cat naps on the couch.

When Mark and I first met, I thought it was healthy for him to have a hobby, even if it involved men wrestling around in the dirt over a ball. We'd snuggle on the sofa, snack on chips and salsa, and I'd think, *This could be a nice change of pace and a great way to spend time together.* I didn't mind his T-shirts with the team logo and mascot, because they were a warm shade of red. And when he bought me Alabama pajamas and hair accessories, I may have secretly preferred a La Perla nightie and diamonds, but I appreciated the team gear as a sign that Mark cared.

But the more I allowed this and possibly egged him on by acting grateful and interested, the more Alabama football began to tackle our lives. For every holiday or birthday, Mark's family would give us large, illustrated prints of his favorite team plays, and we'd hang them on our walls. He bought signed footballs that took over our bookshelves. Once Mason was born, the house was filled with Bama onesies, baby-size jerseys, and bottles and pacifiers stamped with huge red "A"s from all his Alabama family and friends. He even hung a mobile in the nursery that played a twinkly rendition of the school's fight song and dangled with elephants that had tiny "A"s stamped on their sides. Eventually we bought a giant SUV Yukon XL Denali, in crimson, of course, that now has championship stickers stuck all over the rear window. This is not good news for tinier cars on the highway, since the collage creates a major blind spot.

When we lived in Encino, I thought I'd show my husband how much I loved him by throwing a Super Bowl party in our impressive home theater. I ordered three kegs of beer, put cheese dip and pretzels all around the house in bowls shaped like footballs, and had Hooters send over their famous wings and a few big-breasted girls to kick the party up a notch. My friends Eryn and Kimi brought me my own Hooters shirt to drive home a theme, as usual. This was the year Janet Jackson had her wardrobe malfunction, which we replayed over and over on that really big screen, thanks to a new invention called the DVR.

But once halftime was done, our party went south and so did Mark's patience. He told me he didn't like entertaining and chatter during Super Bowl Sunday, since it distracted him from the game itself. He went in the other room to try out those chicken wings, but they turned out to be undercooked and gave everyone stomach issues. He slid his arm around a blonde wearing my coat, and realized he wasn't snuggling me but a chilly Hooters girl who'd borrowed my jacket. Though I had a great time surrounded by friends and comfort food, Mark sarcastically thanked me at the night's end for "trashing up his sport." I didn't realize that when dealing with a true sports fan, even Hooters girls are a bad diversion. I was angling for Wife of the Year, but

I'd have been better off leaving him a seven-layer dip and taking off for the mall.

When we bought the house in Connecticut, I was so thrilled with our move that I went along with Mark's most obsessed fan idea yet. There's a room right off our home's entrance that was meant to be a formal living room, but I agreed to make this a "Bama Room" in homage to Mark's love for the Crimson Tide. So when you walk into our wide-open foyer, the Bama Room is the first thing you see when you look to the left. It has a crimson pool table and crimson walls covered in football prints and memorabilia. Black-and-white houndstooth shades adorn the windows. We hung prints capturing the best moments in team history, including pictures of the coaches on the sidelines. We have a lot of signed gear, including Coach Nick Saban's football and Mark Ingram's helmet, since he was the first player to ever win the Heisman. (I surprised Mark with tickets to the Heisman trophy presentation in 2009.) Hanging off the mantel are Mardi Gras beads with elephants and "A"s on them from the 2011 New Orleans championship game, when Alabama won its fourteenth national title. And then there's the table lamp with a cartoonish elephant cooking up a tiger in a pot, to symbolize Alabama's desire to make Auburn stew.

Some of the Bama Room's best touches are personal to me and Mark. One of its focal points is a photograph from 1963 that I found in a Vegas gallery and gave to Mark as a Christmas gift. It's a simple shot of a very young Joe Namath, before his Jets days, standing on the sidelines in his vintage football uniform. Coach Bear Bryant is looking off in the distance, wearing a houndstooth fedora. Above the fireplace, I hung an illustration of a play that bowled us over. It shows the time Tyrone Prothro caught the football behind a defender's head with both hands, while wrapping the other player in his arms. The two somersaulted into the end zone for an incredible Alabama touchdown. Total Cirque du Soleil moment.

Outside the house, we're a hard Connecticut family to miss. If Mason's soccer game falls on a Saturday, we pile out of our giant crimson car, dressed in crimson T-shirts, and push our crimson stroller across the grass to where we set up our crimson "A" chairs. Once during a game, a guy pulled over on the side of the road after seeing us, a large red blur from afar, and got Mark's attention. He said he'd been looking for "the Alabama family," ever since his daughter told him a boy at school wears Alabama T-shirts. He's a Crimson Tide football fan, too.

And so we carry on the Wilkerson family tradition. During big games, Mark chats with almost every one of his family members via phone or FaceTime at least every quarter. When we head to Alabama for Thanksgiving every other year, we spend the weekend watching all the college games with the family, and when Alabama plays, even Gama (Mark's ninety-one-year-old grandma) comes over to cheer in her crimson logoed gear. Cars and fridge magnets show off their favorite team colors. Mark's sister Sally, who's only fifteen months older than him, has made football a hobby and in a way I never thought a girl could. (For years, I suspected that chicks who went to sports bars in oversize jerseys, guzzling beer from the bottle and screaming "That ref is blind!" were just trying to put in their time so their guys would take them to the ballet.) Sally owns every piece of logo gear and encouraged the clothing label she works for to design cute college-colored women's dresses and tops. Thanks to Sally, I'm all set with my crimson one-shoulder dress with houndstooth shoulder swag. I plan to wear it to the Iron Bowl game against Auburn this fall.

Even most of the Harts have gotten into football, now that Mark's part of our family. My siblings sometimes hang out on weekends to watch Alabama games, and they own their share of team apparel too. My brother Brian's girlfriend wears crimson colors on Saturdays, and Trisha won't watch a big game against a skilled rival because she thinks it's bad luck for the Tide. We are probably the only family in the northeast United States that refuses to wear orange in the fall because that's one of Auburn's colors. My mom's had a harder time with Mark's passion. She gets it, but has trouble when Mark calls Thanksgiving "a big football holiday" or watches the game on Christmas. Those days were always reserved for movie classics like *It's a Wonderful Life, Meet Me in St. Louis,* and *Elf.* With Mark in our lives, we've had to add at least nine hours of football to the holiday must-watch list.

Though one would imagine I'd be used to Mark's ways by now, I'm constantly surprised by the extent of his and his family's loyalty. After my baby shower, my MIL suggested the ladies have a cup of tea before going back to my house, since she thought the guys there needed time to wind down after Alabama lost. Mark has insisted we leave a friend's wedding early to catch a game—after cocktail hour and before dinner—and I felt compelled to lie to the bride about my son being sick when he wasn't. He also teased me that he wouldn't be at our first son's birth if it coincided with the Rose Bowl, so I got him tickets for the game for his birthday, so I wouldn't have to wonder whether he meant it (thankfully, Mason was born seven days after the game). And when I learned I was due to give birth to our third son, Tucker, in the month of September, Mark immediately planned a trip to the first Alabama game of the season in case he couldn't make another game all fall. I went into labor on a Monday, and we listened to the Falcons take the Broncos as I was busy doing my HypnoBirthing relaxation techniques.

Mark's habits aren't lost on our three sons either. I like to joke that we're making our own "Manning legacy." (If you don't know what that means, I'm jealous.) Mark has supported their interest from the age of four, even if being in the stands for live games included a ton of trips to get ice cream and toys from the gift shop. When we first taught Brady to spell his name, he'd spell it "B-A-M-A!" since he heard this cheered a few thousand times before. Then again, all the boys know the fastest way to Daddy's heart and getting away with murder is to call out one of Alabama's cheers, play its fight song on the iPhone, or turn up in a jersey and helmet. If they're mad at Mark or throwing a tantrum, they scream Auburn's battle cry, "War eagle!"

Though I like to complain that football's been forced on my life like a bad case of lice, there are upshots to all this. For one, it's easy to get Mark a gift. On RollTide.com, I have my pick of A-bearing items like barbecue covers, table lamps, and lawn gnomes. I can count on spooning after a big win. The crimson SUV is a pretty color, and I can always find it in a packed parking lot. I don't have to wonder where to scatter Mark's ashes, since he was impressed with my idea to sprinkle them on Alabama's field when nobody was looking. And while we're all still here, a common love of the sport creates a strong bond between my boys and their father. I know that football will become an even bigger part of their lives as they start to play on teams. I'll be part of that, too.

Despite all my best attempts to be the finest football widow—er, wife—ever, nothing's helped earn me street cred with my husband and his family the way Twitter has. By logging on a few thousand times a day, I keep up with Mark's favorite players, which gives us stuff to talk about and helps me keep him in awe of how much I know about their personal lives. It's even made the games more interesting for me. If I like a player's tweets, I'll root for him that weekend.

The ultimate Twitter touchdown happened around the National Championship game in New Orleans in January 2012. I was following a former Alabama player, Javier Arenas, who now plays in the NFL for the Kansas City Chiefs. I tweeted something about Bama football with my usual Saturday trend hashtag, #RollTideRoll. Later that day, Arenas then tweeted me, saying that he thought I was an incredible person and brought laughter to his life with *Melissa & Joey*. So I hit him back, asking if he was going to the championship game in Nawlins, and when he said yes, I asked if he'd want to meet up for dinner one night.

We booked a private room at a restaurant called Antoine's in the French Quarter for me and Mark, Mark's family, and some of Arenas's friends—maybe twenty people total. Mark and his family were beyond excited and appreciative. It felt good to be able to introduce my husband to someone he admires, and okay, okay, I liked meeting someone so extremely talented and skilled at his job, too. The famous cornerback and I keep in touch and are setting up a play date for our kids.

Chapter 16

FOUR THINGS I NEVER LEARNED TO DO FOR MYSELF

Having a steady, successful entertainment career from a young age gave me tons of advantages. I was mature and responsible early on, had my pick of smart, talented role models, and I rarely worried about money when I was ready to live on my own. But being on two hit TV shows during my formative years also meant that I never learned some basic skills that seem to be second nature to other women. Putting on makeup in the school bathroom, spending hours on your hair, going to the mall to buy clothes, making ramen noodles on a hot plate in college . . . Apparently these are all tasks that turn girls into well-groomed and gastronomically talented adults, and I managed to miss out. I'm all thumbs when it comes to:

Putting On My Face

I spent so many hours on set in a makeup artist's chair that it's no wonder I'm still close to the women who made me look like a million bucks. As I've mentioned, my friend Eryn did my makeup on *Sabrina,* and we're still as thick as five-year-old mascara. When I'd arrive on set at 6 A.M., we'd either commiserate about how early it was or I'd fall asleep in her chair. Eryn got very good at doing my eyes with my lids closed/mouth open. I can still list the order in which she applied my makeup, as if the final pie piece in a game of Trivial Pursuit depended on it. Foundation, concealer, powder, blush, eyeliner, eye shadow, mascara, lipstick or gloss! I just don't know how to use any of it. Why learn how to do myself up, when I'd always have Eryn?

If I had plans after work, Eryn touched me up with a quick new eye or lip color, and off I'd go, into the night. But on weekends, I was entirely on my own. I always liked the idea of "a natural look"; it seemed like such a fresh and foolproof way to look pretty. As anyone who worships at Bobbi Brown's altar knows, it takes good instincts and a lot of beige to make it look like you're naturally beautiful and not wearing any makeup at all. When I did try to use blush or eye shadow, I'd always worry that it was too dark and then scrub it off. This actually left me with the look I was going for—a smudged black line around my eyes, flushed natural cheeks, and a dewy lip. But the effect didn't last, so I'd go back to the drawing board. Since I couldn't judge how much foundation, concealer, powder, blush, eyeliner, eye shadow, mascara, and lipstick or gloss was too much, I'd trick myself into wearing more by getting ready in the dark. I'd turn on one lonely lamp across the room, attack my face, and pray. I'd hoped I wouldn't look like Tammy

Faye Bakker, who it's safe to assume put her makeup on in the dark for years.

The how-much-is-enough issue confused me most on and around the eyes. Then one day I had an idea. Maybe I could avoid shadows and liners if I learned to perfect my lashes. A lot of people think they're the finishing touch to the face, but I have nice eyes—or, as Bill Murray's brother Andy says, "eyes second only to Elizabeth Taylor." Eryn experimented with highlighting my lashes more times than Lady Gaga changes wigs. We tried natural mascara, tinting, curling, hot curling (yes, they make tiny curling irons for lashes), and even used Rosebud Lip Salve without anything else. I have naturally dark, thick, and long lashes, so the salve was the best way to give me the shimmer and holding power we liked. My lashes became my face's focal point.

This only worked because Mom gave me the good advice to avoid mascara for as long as possible to keep my lashes thick and luxurious. She didn't let me wear it on *Clarissa,* and I didn't use it until I started *Sabrina* and wanted to look more put together, although I only wore it when I was working. Even so, just a touch of the oil, wax, and water formula thinned my lashes. Ten years later, I'm compelled to wield a wand all the time. On camera, we even have to use fake ones since the Kardashians made it a thing to look like you have tarantulas glued to your lids. And when I take them off, they yank out at least three real lashes with them. I hope I'm not eye-bald by fifty-five.

It goes without saying that the natural look is at its best when you have great skin. In my twenties, this was simple. My skin was already tight, supple, and easy to maintain. The adults on *Clarissa* used to talk about how soft my hands were or how they wished they'd used eye cream at my age. They insisted I immediately start making every effort to preserve my youth. I began to take preventive measures that ensured I'd always look and feel like I was thirteen again.

I created a nightly beauty routine that took me an hour to finish, though I was barely old enough to shave my legs. Before bed, I put on a mask that I made from egg whites. I let the sticky mixture soak into my skin as I moisturized my whole body and then feet, with special lotions for each part. I cringed at the thought of dry, cracked heels—or even worse, wrinkly elbows. (I always loved when Patricia Heaton put moisturizer on her elbows before climbing into bed on *Everybody Loves Raymond*.) I used a toner and lotion on my face and was careful not to pull the skin around the eyes, causing it to crepe like amateur origami. I applied a slick layer of Vaseline to my feet and hands, and then slept in cotton gloves and socks. I also snoozed without a pillow to avoid back and neck issues and slept on my back to avoid wrinkling my chest and face.

This routine lasted fifteen years, until I had my first baby and finding time to brush my teeth became an epic quest. Now with three young boys in the house, putting eggs on my face or Vaseline on my bunions would be a monumental feat when trying to feed them, bathe them, and coax them to sleep. I'm usually passed out in their beds before they are anyway—with or without a pillow, face- and chest-down, rooms away from an anti-aging cream that's never been opened.

Doing My Own Hair

Because I've worked with some of the industry's best hair stylists, like José Eber and Laurent D, I never experimented or "played" with tools or hair products on my own. I rarely touched a can of hairspray, and when I did, I'd lacquer my head into a rat's nest rather than mist it for a light hold. As with my face, my full and shiny mane turned dull and lifeless when I didn't have pros to help.

This is clear when I look at paparazzi and red carpet photos of myself shortly after *Sabrina* ended and before *Melissa & Joey* began. I was on and off jobs, so I didn't have regular guidance. In my glamorous days on *Sabrina*, I'd ask my stylist to give me a different look for every event, and I'd rarely repeat a style, even on the show. When we ran out of ideas, we dyed my hair red and tried different hair accessories. If I did my own hair, I wore it in a tight high ponytail or used a pair of sunglasses as a headband. The rest might be straight in some areas, slightly wavy in others, and always flat to my head. I let my stringy bangs flop to the side.

As I get older, my biggest hair issue is volume. Much like my relationship with makeup, I'm terrified to use too much product, so I never get the height or density the way I want it. And when I see stylists for a trim or blowout, they make me look like a Texas housewife with a poufy mane. I feel like they'll go to any effort to curl, shape, and zhush my hair into something other than what God gave me. I still try to preserve the look as long as I can, but it usually doesn't hold for more than a few days, so I've started ripping out magazine photos of hairstyles and copying those. My friends give me rave reviews when I do, which goes to show how sad my hair looks when bobby pins are an improvement. I'm glad I don't have a daughter who'd go through a braid phase. She'd ask for a fishtail, and I'd give her a crooked banana-clip ponytail instead.

Because on-set stylists have used so much product and heat to manage my mane, I've gone on a deliberate hiatus from hair care to replenish its natural oils. When I was traveling in Italy in the mid-nineties, I spent three weeks adding oils to my hair and kept it wrapped in a bun. I used ylang-ylang and lavender oils mostly, which gave off a potent scent, especially mixed with the aromatic garlic and tomato sauces already in the air. During *Sabrina*'s second season, my costar Beth Broderick spooked me with a story about her hair falling out from being too dry and brittle, so I insisted my stylist Colleen use Evian spray instead of hairspray to tame flyaways for one whole season. You heard me right. I asked for bottled water instead of tap for my hair.

Getting Dressed By Myself

I was never down for wearing restrictive clothes and heels for sixteen hours on set, and then changing into something fab for the car ride home. After a long day, I dressed for comfort. One of the best days of my unfashionable life was when Juicy Couture launched its velour tracksuit. Suddenly, I could be "in" for work, flights, the gym, and lounging at home. Dress it up, dress it down—J. Lo did! When I needed an upgrade, I turned to our wardrobe closet at work. On *Sabrina*, my lawyer negotiated a nice-size clothing budget into my contract so I could take home clothes and go shopping for events and appearances. It took me nine years after the show ended to donate most of the looks. I didn't want to admit that midriff tops and low-cut jeans weren't flattering on a thirty-something mom of three. I also didn't have the fashion IQ to realize they weren't stylish anymore.

Without stylists at my beck and call after I left *Sabrina,* dressing to impress became less of a priority, and it showed. For the Leukemia & Lymphoma Society's Inaugural Celebrity Rock 'N Bowl, I wore a velour hoodie, T-shirt tucked into jeans, white belt, and Nikes. For an upscale Elizabeth Glaser Pediatric AIDS Foundation event, I wore gray cargos and a T-shirt. I was pregnant for a Power Women Hollywood luncheon, so I threw on the only thing that fit: a green-striped sweater poncho. The sweater wasn't bad in person, but it made me photograph like a circus tent.

Luckily for me, my friends Michele and Kimi both worked in wardrobe with me and still care enough to save me from myself. Once a year these girls, or my trendy sister-in-law Sally, help me do a closet purge. Kimi especially despises my red cotton dress with a large eagle decal on the front. I found it in Melbourne, Australia, in 2000 and initially bought it for when Mom and I went to the Persian Gulf on a USO tour to meet and entertain our troops. On July Fourth, I signed autographs at the U.S. base for the families stationed there, three of which had cats named Salem. I also wore it on *The Tonight Show* not long after 9/11, to further underscore my patriotic spirit. But Kimi said that pairing it with white patent-leather heels, which is how I styled it, was a major fail for late-night TV. Thanks to her frequent and sarcastic jabs, I've retired the eagle dress to my Lake Tahoe closet, where I show it off on the beach every Fourth of July and send a pic to Kimi for sport. I even managed to squeeze into it when I was seven months pregnant with Tucker. I liked how the bird stretched and soared over my swollen belly. I can't believe the seams didn't burst.

One reason I hold on to things long past their expiration date is because I hate shopping. The way I see it, there's no point in wasting an afternoon at Bloomingdale's if repeating an outfit or handbag gets me on E!'s *Fashion Police* for the wrong reasons. What's more, when I'm working, I spend hours in fittings and doing various wardrobe changes. By the time I get home, I don't want to try on anything but a terrycloth robe after a long, hot bubble bath (this never happens, by the way). So I borrow clothes from work if I need them, or ask the ladies who shop in wardrobe to grab me an extra pair of cowboy boots or jeans in a size that we know fits. Even then, nothing's too formal. Why wear Manolos to chase a toddler or a silk shirt when I'm leaking breast milk? Even V-necks seem wrong when they make your sons yell, "Mom, I can see your boobies!"

I was raised to think I could do anything I put my mind to, but dressing well for my husband doesn't seem to be one of them. Mark's known this from the start. When we were first married, I went shopping with his sisters and tried to run in to Abercrombie & Fitch for new cargo pants, but his sisters blocked me at the cash register. Mark gave them specific instructions to do this. Apparently, he was on a mission to replace my usual black, gray, and army green wardrobe with jewel tones like emerald greens, turquoise, blues, and of course, Alabama crimson.

Like father, like sons. My boys are very conscientious about their fashion choices. Brady only wants to wear Hulk sneakers and Mason will only wear shirts with sea creatures on them. They both love to accessorize with hats and ties, which I find dashing. I'll never forget when the kids saw me in that blue-and-white-striped Betsey Johnson tulle dress with fluffy bright pink pumps, a candy necklace, and a Ring Pop for the opening of my candy store, SweetHarts, in L.A. When I emerged from my bedroom dressed like the Sugarplum Fairy, Mason literally gasped.

"You look *perfect*," he said.

Making Food

Craft services, catering crews, and studio commissaries prepared most of my meals and snacks for eleven influential years of my life. Oatmeal, breakfast burritos, burgers, chili, salmon—all good, none made by me. On my days off, I ate out with friends, spread peanut butter on bread, or reheated the previous night's doggie bag. I also dined on English muffin pizzas with jarred Ragú sauce and mozzarella cheese. When Mark and I got engaged, my sister Trisha bought us a nice toaster oven so I could keep my husband happy with the only dish I knew how to make.

Clearly I never really learned how to cook, and I'm not sure I ever will. On set, the men and women in aprons made it seem so simple. The caterers kept busy in their little truck, making everything from chicken Marsala to silky custard flan. At home, I hate dealing with the massive cleanup, but before I even get there, I despise the prep work. It takes planning to find a recipe, shop for it, and drive off without leaving the bag on the roof of your car. I'm so indecisive. What if I go through all that trouble only to realize I don't want filet mignon with risotto for dinner, and I'm more in the mood for sea bass with polenta? Not that I've ever made either of those dishes with much success. Maybe I could hire a food truck to back up to the house at meal times.

You'd think I'd learn to cook, given how much I appreciate a delicious meal. Mark and I are foodies and could eat our way across the United States. We have our favorite spots in certain cities and airports, and get excited about visiting each one. On our next trip to Alabama, we plan to fly into the Atlanta airport and drive across the state line so we can hit up Mary Mac's Tea Room for some cheese grits and cornbread dressing. We look forward to nights out in New York City when we can eat ourselves into a food coma at our favorite steak houses and Mexican restaurants. We are also not above driving forty-five minutes to have breakfast at the nearest Cracker Barrel.

Eating out with the kids is also easier for me than feeding them at home. Our boys, especially Brady, are picky eaters and expert mess-makers, so it's nice to give them a range of choices and sneak away from the milk and pasta sauce they always spill on restaurant floors. I think eating out has also developed their young palates. Mason was already a better cook at five than I was at thirty-five. He's like Mark, who never lets a morning go by without whipping up ricotta pancakes, chicken sausage, cheese grits, bacon biscuits, or chocolate-chip waffles. Even when it's a recipe that comes from a box or the freezer section of our grocery store, I still clap and thank Mark when he channels Bobby Flay because, frankly, it means I don't have to.

I'm in no way complaining. Right after I had Brady, I tried using Jessica Seinfeld's cookbook to sneak veggies into my children's favorite dishes. I put a pot of water on the stove to boil, but got so involved in slicing and dicing that I let the water evaporate and the pot burned. Who burns water? I tried again, this time remembering to add the macaroni to the H_2O, but I didn't realize the noodles would expand. I used the wrong size pot too, so the macaroni tumbled onto the floor and what was on the bottom burned. I gave up and made English muffin pizzas.

Chapter 17

WHEN MOMMY'S WORLDS COLLIDE

Until we bought our home in Connecticut, Mark and I had only moved to other cities for our careers. But Westport was entirely our choice and was intended to benefit our growing family and life together. Such a freeing decision, coupled with the fact that our town is straight out of a Norman Rockwell painting, made every experience feel heavenly. We immediately invited couples to dinner, said "You bet!" to every play date for the boys, became regulars at the restaurants, and made friends with our neighbors. We were your average suburban family and loving every minute.

But in the fall of 2009, just three weeks after we moved, I was called back to L.A. to compete on the ninth season of ABC's *Dancing with the Stars*. In the past, I might have taken Mark and the kids on a job with me, but now I wanted them to have consistency and community. My sons, especially, needed to sleep in their own beds, stay in school, and make friends since we were new in town. For the first time in my babies' lives, I had to pick up and temporarily leave them, but not without first bawling my eyes out in the parking lot after dropping them off at school. (Parents I'd never met gave me awkward, comforting hugs. But I took what solace I could get.) The good news was that Mark's job gave him the flexibility to let me travel for work, and he was good at being Mr. Mom. Mark's amazing with the kids and an awesome disciplinarian. Though I'm the oldest of eight, and Mark's the youngest of three, my parenting instincts don't guide our family. I'm just the sucker who gives in to every sob and chance to spoil the kids with toys and sweet treats. Anyway, Mark also knew *Dancing with the Stars* was something I'd wanted to do since the show asked me to participate in their first season, although being pregnant with Mason at the time made it impossible. Mark would do what he had to do to cheer me on.

Despite the show's demanding rehearsals, I jumped in with both feet. I went to L.A. for five days to meet my partner, Mark Ballas, and begin practicing, and then he came home with me for five weeks where we rehearsed every day in a ballroom at our local YMCA. I was no fly girl, but I felt good about the progress I'd made. I also think watching me work so hard at home made it easier for the kids to see me leave again to shoot the show in L.A. for ten weeks. I promised the boys and myself that if I was going away for so long, I'd give every performance my all. I was ready to work hard, deal with sore muscles, and use plenty of cornstarch to prevent quarter-size blisters. And because I always wanted to be a dancer when I was young, I was curious to see if I still had what it took. I knew the judges would be critical, but I planned to handle their analysis with grace and aplomb. I couldn't be any worse than Cloris Leachman or Jerry Springer, right?

My bubble popped pretty fast. I loved the billowy, twinkling costumes, but that's where the joy ended for me. I've never experienced pressure and stress like what I felt from fans and myself during that time, especially since I was on live television. The slightest misstep could end up on mean-spirited blogs and in tweets as soon as it happened. I wasn't sure I had the head to stay positive and focus on learning complicated moves at the same time.

When I first heard that British man's voice announce "Dancing the Viennese waltz, Melissa Joan Hart and her partner, Mark Ballas," I thought I'd vomit all over my flowing white gown. But I kept it together during my first ninety-second dance to David Cook's "The Time of My Life." Throughout the song, I felt like I was gliding on air, and I was so proud that I didn't miss a one-two-three step. I felt amazing about my performance, my heart pumping with adrenaline.

I gave Mark an emotionally charged victory hug and cascaded over to the judge's desk. I couldn't wait to hear if the judges thought I was the elegant swan I imagined in my head. Um, they didn't. Bruno Tonioli said I was "prim," "proper," and that my dance "lacked a little bit of magic"; Carrie Ann Inaba called my moves "choppy"; and good ol' Len Goodman said I had "poor footwork." To be fair, these comments were padded with generic compliments on either end, but all I heard were the insults. I felt like I'd been punched in the gut, seconds after one of the biggest highs of my life.

Week after week, I found it harder to hang in there, as the judges began to favor certain dancers who weren't me. My partner, Mark, had already given up on us and began to spend more time playing and composing music, his other hobby, which cut into our rehearsal time. I became frustrated and upset very quickly, and so did my fans, who were starting to prefer other contestants too. I couldn't hide my disappointment in the weekly on-camera interviews, which only worked against me since voting viewers at home liked watching their favorite celebrities have upbeat, positive attitudes no matter what. The kicker was that when I got booted in week six, the next morning my boys were supposed to fly in to spend a week with me and watch me dance the quickstep to Mason's favorite song, "Bear Necessities" from *The Jungle Book*. I was relieved to be done with *DWTS* but bummed that I never got a chance to perform for my boys.

Olympic swimmer Natalie Coughlin, another contestant that season, perfectly summed up our feelings about being eliminated. She said it's like someone gave us a guitar and taught us how to play it, and then took it away and never let us play the instrument again. And though I was no Ginger to his Fred, Mark and I have stayed friends. At least I'll always have the Charleston. It was the only dance that earned us two nines and a ten (from Bruno!), and I think I nailed it because the dance allowed me to get into the character of an animated 1920s flapper, much like I would if I were acting in a movie. I even fixed a wardrobe malfunction mid-squat, when my fishnets stuck to a sequin near my crotch and nearly tore my tights off.

The week after I waltzed my way off *Dancing with the Stars*, I shot a pilot for ABC Family's *Melissa & Joey*. It was inspired by our movie *My Fake Fiancé*, which had aired earlier that year. We did this in front of a live audience, and I was so spooked from my live *DWTS* experience that I forgot my very first line. Joey messed up on his during the second take, so I didn't feel as bad. But I had to remind myself, *I've got this*, and that I act for a living, not dance in flouncy costumes in front of experts and perfectionists. After that, I coasted through the filming, and in spring 2010, we started production on the first season of the show. In L.A.

For the next forty-five weeks, this working mom spent a lot of time away from her family, though I never went longer than two weeks without seeing my boys. Mark and the kids came to California once a month, and every fifth week, I got a week hiatus to go back to Connecticut. Though plenty of travel stressed me out when I was on *Clarissa,* so much back-and-forth was even more emotionally trying with a family. I felt guilty and sad about missing out on the kids' daily lives and not spending quality time with Mark. We spoke a few times a day and tried video chatting with the kids, but they didn't like talking to a computer screen, and Mark got frazzled trying to get them to sit still for long. Instead Mark sent me short videos and photos of the boys going about their lives without me, like testing for their latest belt in karate. I watched them over and over when I was alone in my three-bedroom rental apartment just outside the studio's gate.

While Mark was forced to be a single parent in my absence, I filled my spare time with business meetings, sushi dinners, and Thai massages—minus the happy ending. I felt blue a lot but tried to distract myself as best I could. I was only mildly successful, made obvious by the fact that I gained ten pounds and developed adult-onset acne. I actually didn't realize how depressed I was until we shot our final episode of the season, I flew back to Connecticut, and was beyond elated to see my family. My face cleared right up and I lost the extra pounds without even trying.

When the producers called to say season two would start shooting in August 2011, I panicked about having to deal with these feelings all over again. I was so grateful for the work because I loved the show and my character—Mel is actually my favorite role to play to date—but that didn't mitigate the fact that I felt alone and lonely in L.A. And even though our company, Hartbreak, produces *Melissa & Joey*, which means I worked with my mom every day, life felt incomplete without Mark, Mason, and Brady. But I also suspected that my absence was much harder on me than it was on everyone else, so I convinced myself that I had to make this sacrifice work for our family's benefit. Better that I quietly suffer than uproot the whole gang every few months to follow me around for a TV show or film shoot.

I knew that if I was going to stick this show out, I had to tweak the work/life juggle so I could spend more time with my loved ones. I was determined to find another way, even if it was logistically trying. I decided that during season two, I'd fly home on weekends. Almost every Friday night, after we finished shooting the live show from 5 to 10 P.M., I drove like a bat out of hell to LAX airport and boarded an 11:30 P.M. red-eye back to New York's JFK airport. Once I landed, I'd jump in a car service for the seventy-five-minute drive to Westport and get into town around 9 A.M., just in time for my driver to drop me off at Mason's soccer game so I could give him a quick hug before he took the field. I'd snuggle with Brady while watching the game, go for lunch with the family after, and doze off on the couch while Mark watched football and the boys played nearby. Sunday after lunch, I'd head back to L.A. and work all week, or if I needed more time with my babies, I'd fly into L.A. very early on Monday morning, arriving just in time for a table read of the week's script. Most of the time, spending thirty-one hours with my family felt like a triumph. But no matter what our schedules entailed, one ritual was consistent. While waiting to board my plane at JFK, I'd call Mark in tears and say, "As soon as we pay off the mortgage, I'm done with this."

I tried to find comfort in the fact that I was "doing it all" like I'd always hoped—that is, being a good mom, wife, and successful career woman. But the harrowing "commute" and long stretches of time away from the family were taking their toll on me. I began to envy other working moms that I knew in town. Their schedules were grueling, but unlike them, I couldn't ask Mark to adjust the kids' naptime so they could see me before bed, and if I got home late, I couldn't peek in on the sleeping angels after a long day. The upside, I told myself, is that I could focus on my job at work, and when I was home, I went into overdrive to be there for the kids. I shuttled them to play dates, doctor's appointments, practices, and went to parent/teacher conferences with Mark. On weekends, I took the kids to a nearby farm to tap a maple tree for syrup and treated them to blue ice cream with gummy bears and rainbow sprinkles. When I was on hiatus, I picked them up from school, where they ran into my arms for a giant hug and kiss. Would it have been healthier or more fun to work part time, get my nails done after a lunch with girlfriends, and spoil the boys with froyo on a regular basis? Clearly. But that's not the situation Mark and I had fallen into, so I had to appreciate the time we did have and work my ass off in between.

After spending a full fourteen months with the kids in 2011 and 2012 when *Melissa & Joey* was between seasons, I couldn't imagine keeping this schedule in season three. I'd also just given birth to our third son, Tucker McFadden Wilkerson, on September 18, and couldn't justify splitting up the family as we'd been doing. Mark and I decided to rent a house in L.A. together, and moved the boys to new schools for the four months we were shooting, at the start of 2013. We packed up the kids and dogs, and shipped my red Mini Cooper to L.A. so we wouldn't have to drive the Dodge Ram pickup truck with snow tires that I'd brought down from Lake Tahoe. Let's just say I got turned away from a lot of valets with that monster.

Having the whole family in L.A. made me feel normal again.

I got the kids out the door to school, hit the gym, headed to work, and made the most of family dinners, weekends, and field trips. Even though we adore our life in Connecticut and still consider it home, this was the best arrangement and it came in the nick of time. I'd told myself I could make anything work, but I had to be realistic and cry uncle before my schedule caused real damage to our family or my head.

With a life like mine, I can't pretend that Mark and I do it alone, nor would we want to. My Hooter Hider nursing cover goes off to any mom who can balance kids, marriage, home, trips to the vet, laundry, carpooling—and still have time to make a hot meal (microwaves and toaster ovens count), take a quick bath, and catch an episode of *Revenge*. I have a fantastic housekeeper who makes my bathroom sparkle and mops my messy kitchen, and landscapers who take care of my yard every week.

Also, since Brady was born, we've always had a nanny to act like a second mother to my boys. We had one wonderful nanny named Canyon who we all loved. She made sure the whole family ate healthy meals, took vitamins, and drank plenty of water. I also liked having another woman around to give me clothing advice for auditions, meetings, and red carpet events. But sometimes Canyon was so good at her job that it made me a little jealous. The boys listened to her more than me, and out of confusion they occasionally slipped and called her "Mommy" and me "Canyon." She was also a better disciplinarian. If the kids misbehaved, I'd quickly lose my temper and get so frustrated until Canyon calmly stepped in, steered the boys gently by the shoulders to the time-out chair, and had a levelheaded talk with them about what they'd done wrong and how to be better next time. But on the whole, Canyon was patient, fun, and fabulous, and we all loved having her around. Sadly, the voice that crooned my children's lullabies ultimately caused her to leave us and pursue a singing career. We had such a great experience with our first nanny that it made us feel comfortable with hiring other great girls to help us out.

I'm not sure why I'm not the Super Mom that other women in my family, like my mom and sister Liz, seem to be. If anything, I'm proof that intuitive parenting skills aren't inherited traits. Mom and Liz are nurturing, know how to manage their time, and are good at outsmarting their wily little ones. (Liz convinced her kids that frozen peas are a dessert food.) As a working-mom role model, Mom's always been able to balance her enormous family while running our careers and TV shows at the same time. Maybe managing temperamental networks and 150 employees on set isn't so different from running our wild family? Regardless, she always made it look simpler than it must have been. Then there's my sister Liz, whose mothering savvy really shone when she came to visit us in L.A. when Mom had her brain surgery. With her son Jonny in tow, Liz was an emotional rock for me and my siblings, and even found the time and wisdom to get Mason, who was two and a half, to stop using his pacifier in less than an hour. This was a task I did not have the imagination or energy for.

One mixed blessing that came with being a mom for me was how much more attention I got as a celebrity after having kids. The media suddenly cared about what parks I visited, what stroller I used, and whether our bottles were BPA-free—all welcome PR. But they were also obsessed with my pregnancy weight, which was hard on me. I never minded staying trim for work-related reasons before. I'd always kept in shape, though never obsessively. If given the choice between eating a Snickers or slimming down to host *America's Got Talent,* the candy bar won out. But after having a child, feeling pressure to immediately battle the bulge felt like an unfair fight.

Back in 2009, a year after I had Brady, I remember we were sitting down to a Chick-fil-A dinner in Alabama when my publicist called to say *People* was interested in covering me in a standard "body after baby" story. I wasn't ready for this photo op but liked having the motivation to lose some weight. I dropped my chicken strip in its secret sauce, agreed to do the shoot, and sucked on mustard packets for the rest of the meal. For the next six weeks I did everything I could to lose weight on the advice of my nutritionist and a trainer. I shed ten pounds in that time and went from 24 percent body fat to 17.5. This was a huge accomplishment for me, and I was all too excited to share it with a reporter. Frustratingly, though, when the magazine printed how much weight I'd lost, they included my peak weight when I was carrying my child, and right next to the main, flattering pic of me in a purple bikini was a smaller, humiliating shot of me shoving chips in my mouth just one month after giving birth. The cover line read, "How I lost 42 pounds!" It's not like I'd deliberately let myself go as a new mom . . .

Another surprise: regular people care how celebrity moms like Tori Spelling, Jessica Alba, and Heidi Klum clothe, diaper, and feed their kids. These women are just a few famous ladies who've turned being a mom into a second career, and when Mason was born, the phones rang for me too. I struggled with wanting to both share my life with fans and protect my kids from the prying spotlight. But I also needed to help provide for my family, and I had to be practical. I decided I'd use my celebrity, then, to only endorse products that I really believed in.

One of these items was Pull-Ups, a diaper intended to help with potty training. In 2008, I agreed to a lucrative deal that also kept me in years of free diapers for my kids. Since my oldest son, Mason, was two and a half at the time, I agreed to blog and speak to the press about potty training him with their product. Potty training seemed like a daunting task to me, as it does for a lot of moms, so I was also excited for the expert advice that came with the gig.

The problem was, Mason wasn't really ready to be potty trained. For weeks, I lured him to the bowl with every possible bribe from stickers to Hot Wheels toys, though he refused to do number one or number two on command. I even tried a few tips from the Pull-Ups people, like using different types of potties and taking him to the bathroom every half hour after loading him up on juice and salty snacks, but my son wouldn't have it. He just didn't seem to care that I had a job to do!

After six months of this, I was anxious to be done with diapers and nervous that Pull-Ups might call BS on my parenting skills. Between all the backaches and self-doubt, I realized that something had to give. So I resorted to a dirty trick I'd read about online: I cut a hole in Mason's diaper. The thinking here was that he'd sit on the potty, his feces would fall out, and Mason would think the poop was too strong for his diaper. (I read that kids have a psychological attachment to their stool and like to keep it close to them.) Until now, when the kid had to go, he'd just hang out around the potty with his Pull-Ups on, but never really sit on it to finish the task. It was so frustrating because he was inches away from the money shot.

With a hole in his pants, Mason didn't act any differently when his belly began to rumble. He felt the urge to poop, ran to the bathroom for some privacy, lingered near the loo . . . and then encountered the game changer. He let it rip, but the hole in his diaper made the turds fall through the opening and all over the bathroom floor. This was not what usually happened, and it seriously weirded Mason out. In a desperate effort to see what was happening behind him, he ran in circles like a dog chasing its tail. He was so confused and startled, screaming and stepping in his own feces, that it broke my heart. I won't lie—it also made me giggle to myself and wonder if I should record the fiasco to show future girlfriends. Once I calmed Mason down and cleaned him up, I explained that his poop was, in fact, too strong for the diaper. He never used one again, though maybe for the wrong reasons: I literally scared the shit out of him. This tidbit never made my official blog. I didn't feel like the model celebrity mom that Pull-Ups thought they'd hired.

No matter how much help or fame I have, I continue to be miles away from perfect. For every proud moment I have where my kids clean their plate during a peaceful dinner, there are twice as many times that I seem to bomb as a parent. Like when I met actor Jesse Tyler Ferguson from *Modern Family* and his fiancé, Justin, for sushi. My sons were in town, so they joined us, but the twerps whined, hid behind menus, and played with their edamame the whole time. On our way out of the restaurant, we ran into Neil Patrick Harris and his partner, neither of whom I'd met before. I was so smitten with Neil and so exhausted from the kids that I missed it when they ran out the door and into the parking lot. I reluctantly had to end my grown-up conversation.

My all-time favorite moments are when our family has a public meltdown for everyone to see. Just before Thanksgiving in 2012, Mark and I took the kids to the season opening of *Elf* on Broadway. Tucker was only eight weeks old at the time, but we drove all three boys ninety minutes into Manhattan for a night that we'd hoped would be memorable (the good kind). Tucker had been great about sleeping in his car seat, even at the movies, and the boys were big fans of the Will Ferrell flick. What could possibly go wrong?

The answer: everything. We hit a mess of traffic, the kids fell asleep in the car and woke up cranky, they refused to eat their BBQ dinner in Times Square, Tucker pooped up the back of his diaper without a change of clothes . . . and by the time we hit the play's red carpet, we were a mess. In one publicity shot taken at the backdrop known as the step-and-repeat, Mason's literally pulling my hair. When the curtain went up, Tucker cried as soon as the loud music played, and I spent seventy-five minutes rocking and breast-feeding him in the bathroom. This felt mildly inappropriate, but not nearly as pioneering as breast-feeding while getting a pedicure or on the Finding Nemo ride at Disneyland, as I'd done in the past. We left at intermission covered in doody, breast milk, and clingy kids.

Though it can feel awkward to open myself up to parenting criticism from the public, it can feel significantly worse coming from women I like to call "Mommiacs"—those horrible ladies who'd dictate your child's delivery, diet, naptimes, means of discipline, and TV schedule if they could. They're also fiercely competitive about how perfect they and their children are. I've found that there are a lot more Mommiacs in L.A. than there are in suburban Connecticut, which says a lot considering I live in a town that Martha Stewart put on the map. On the left coast, having a conversation in a preschool parking lot felt a lot like being at an audition, with everyone artfully discussing their kids in a way that made them sound so very special and blessed, if they humbly say so themselves. L.A. Mommiacs also took pride in their homemade baby food, no-TV rules, and their progeny's ability to count to ten in Mandarin by the time they were two.

When we lived in L.A. with our first son, I'll admit that I drank the Kool-Aid (organic substitute, that is). I was also a first-time mother and wanted to do everything "right." Imagine my embarrassment, then, when I suddenly realized in our weekly Gymboree class that Mason was the only kid who didn't know his colors. Convinced he'd flunk out of college, I made him spend the rest of the week watching Preschool Prep DVDs and naming every color that crossed our path. You'd better believe that by the time he got back to Gymboree, he knew every color from navy blue to azure. When my son Brady was born, I was less interested in proving how fabulously talented, smart, and good-looking my kids were and more concerned about holding together my marriage, family, and career. I stuck close to old friends like Kellie and Kimi, and was drawn to women I met at preschool and Gymboree who were always late and frazzled too.

In Connecticut, however, finding these like-minded mommies was much easier. I still gravitate toward women who are open and honest about parenting struggles. These ladies admit when they forget to pick up their kids from school, don't mind asking for a play date when they feel overwhelmed, and call each other up to meet for a meal when nobody has the energy to cook. We are a group of mommy misfits, and there are more of us out there than I suspected. It feels good knowing that we can vent about our universal shortcomings over a glass of wine.

There is one area of parenting where regular moms *and* Mommiacs are wont to outdo themselves: birthday parties. Just like on a sports team where every child gets a trophy, when it comes to birthday parties, the whole class gets an invite these days. And not only do the kids attend at least one party a week, but they're incredibly over-the-top affairs. When I was young, my friends and I threw parties in our backyards and refinished basements. We put on a dress, played pin the tail on the donkey, ate homemade cake. On a good year, there was a tiara or piñata.

Nowadays birthday parties, especially for a first or only child, are as involved as a quinceañera or small wedding—complete with formal invites, giant cakes, and the best face painters and balloon animal artists around. Don't forget the hand-delivered thank-you notes and gift bags! Backyard events might include a small petting zoo, if the local planetarium is already rented out. Parents also like to book the nearest American Girl store, mostly in major cities, the way our moms reserved bowling alleys and the Ground Round for all-you-can-eat popcorn. This may sound excessive, but I admit I get swept up in the scene. I'll take any excuse to host a theme party.

I also like to snap a lot of photos, and when I'm looking at them, I can tell how much energy I had while planning the parties. Mason's birthday is in the beginning of January, so I coordinate his events when I'm on an entertaining roll. But by the time we get to March for Brady's big day, I'm so completely spent and partied out that I lean on simpler (okay, lazier) concepts. Mason gets real fire truck rides, aquarium tours, and a private party on the USS *Intrepid* aircraft carrier in New York City, but for two years in a row, Brady went to an indoor gymnasium with inflatable jumpy toys—our town's equivalent of a Chuck E. Cheese. I felt so bad about doing this that on Brady's fifth birthday, I sprung for a group of his friends and their entire families to see a hockey game. After the game, we dug into cake in a private suite upstairs and got high-fives from all the players. Brady felt like the coolest kid in town. Take that, Mommiacs.

Chapter 18

ABNORMALLY NORMAL

Once I hit my thirties, everyone from Kathie Lee to my Jet-Blue flight attendant became intent on asking me the same burning question: "How did you end up so normal?" Translation: "I can't believe you're not totally messed up, like those other '90s sitcom stars."

Yet of all the titles I've worked hard for—actor, director, producer, mom, wife—"normal" is the least surprising to me. I get why people think this, since I pick up my own dry cleaning and leave the house without makeup. It's like, *Here's a star that really is just like us.* But now you know my secrets. I am from a sane family, was raised to appreciate hard work and be responsible with money, looked up to grounded role models, and married a guy with strong values. It didn't hurt either that I grew up in New York instead of Los Angeles, and my career grew at a steady pace without ever reaching Angelina-level fame. Is it really so surprising that I've never cooked meth or made out with my dogs? I'm a focused, hardworking wife and mom who's seen every opportunity she's had as a real gift—an ordinary person with extraordinary moments.

But like anyone who's proud of her achievements, and I am, there've been a few times where I've thought, *Maybe I'm a little more than normal. Maybe people think I'm incredible!* But then I get a reality check. This comes mostly from high-brow, A-list, super-trendy crowds who, no matter what you do for a living, can make you somehow feel inadequate. It's like when my sister and I and some friends tried to skip the incredibly long line at a New York City club by dropping my name to the bouncer, and it actually made him send us to the *end* of the line. Because of incidents like this one, I shy away from using my own name to get special treatment, though I don't exactly stop others from pretending they're my agent or publicist to see what happens. We usually do this while waiting for a table at The Cheesecake Factory or the local barbecue joint that has my head shot hanging on their wall. (I signed it "Nice rack!") Yes, I know these are low-stakes gambles. I'd really love to throw around my name to get into a Mario Batali restaurant opening or go backstage at the VMAs to meet Linkin Park. Or hey, what about getting into the first-class lounge at the airport when I'm flying coach? That's some big pimpin' right there.

A quick word about flying coach. It's more of a frugal measure than an effort to appear modest. When our whole family travels somewhere, we don't see the point in spending money on a seat that's two inches wider, a shorter bathroom line, and a flight attendant who'll kiss our bums with free champagne. We put that kind of cash into the boys' 529 plan. Plus, the kids are already so spoiled with a big, beautiful home, a vacation house, and a playroom full of toys that I want to make sure I try to keep them real in other ways. A curtain that literally divides the classes on a plane could hurt my goal. Of course, there are downsides to traveling in steerage. Like that the airline usually seats large families like ours in the ass of the plane, so while I'm sleeping with my mouth open, fans and others who are standing in line for the bathroom snap pics of me on their iPhones.

There are some places I refuse to go unless I'm treated as television royalty, like Disneyland. My name might not be able to put us at the front of a line at a New York City nightclub, but during a forty-five-minute wait for the Dumbo ride? I'm VIP all the way. We also get our own tour guide and front-row tickets to any parade, fireworks, or dinner theater in the park. Special rules also come in handy when patrons wearing Mickey Mouse ears and carrying lit-up Tinker Bell wands think I'm a big deal. As soon as one person recognizes me, another will, then another, and before you know it the line to take a picture with me is as long as Goofy's.

Because the characters I've played over the years are girl-next-door types, people also feel they've known me their whole lives, like I'm their best friend. I'm constantly hugged, high-fived, and tapped on my head while hearing, "You're so short." That's a lot of sweaty handshakes and smelly armpits rubbing against my shoulder as we pose for photos. Once in a while if I am at a mall, zoo, or grocery store and stop to take a picture with a fan, it can turn into a good twenty-minute project. This is why I'll never go on a cruise. Can you imagine being trapped in a tiny cabin for a week with people wanting autographs? Or having someone Instagram a photo of you passed out on a deck chair? I'd rather float on a noodle in the middle of Lake Tahoe alone.

Seeming normal does have its upsides as an adult. For one, I rarely worry about being followed by anxious fans outside of amusement parks. I'm easily creeped out. The first time I was recognized for being on *Clarissa,* a teenage girl asked me for my autograph, and it made me uneasy. It felt weird that she "knew" me, yet I'd never met her until she started following me down the street. As the show became more popular and this happened more often, people began to stare and whisper. Were they trying to place where they'd seen my face, or were they making fun of my jeans? Maybe both. I didn't mind if a fan said she liked my show or thought I was funny, but anything more felt off to me. When I was on *Sabrina,* all the whispering escalated to loud conversations near and around me, as if I couldn't hear them because I was still stuck inside their TV screens. This still happens, and on a bad day, I may grumble, "Do they think I'm deaf?"

Since *Melissa & Joey* is higher up when you channel surf, some people who stop me now remember me as a twinkle in the eye of their youth. They might remember *Clarissa* for the clothes or *Sabrina* for the special effects, but that could be the extent of it. As a result, people approach me tentatively. Almost every day someone will say to me, "Do you know who you look like?" This is the worst possible question someone could ask a celebrity. For years I played along and answered, "No, who?" only to hear "That girl on the witch show!" There really is no reply for this. My choices are limited to sounding like a pompous jackass by saying, "I think you mean *Sabrina,* and yeah, I did play her. Would you like my autograph?" Or I could give a relaxed "Oh, thanks" and walk away. I usually go with the latter since that lets me get on with running errands or corralling my boys to the car. Any time I've made the mistake of definitively announcing, "That's me!" the conversation plays out like a Three Stooges sketch.

"No way . . ." they'll say.

"Okay, I'm not," I'll tell them.

"Wait, are you?"

"Yes!"

"No way."

"Okay, I have to run . . ."

"Prove it. Show me your ID."

I laugh about this, but it's less amusing when I'm balancing an armful of mail and the kids are fleeing the post office without me. So mostly I say, "I get that all the time," which covers all the bases and gives no real answer. If I'm feeling tipsy during a girls' night out and a guy asks, "Are you Melissa Joan Hart?" I'll have some fun with him and say, "Are you buying?" Or I'll tell him I'm Sarah Michelle Gellar, which usually gets me two drinks.

One of my favorite misidentifications happened in an airport when my sister Trisha and I were traveling together. We were waiting to board at the gate when we overheard a group of teenage boys arguing about whether Sabrina was in their midst. As one of the boys was pushed toward us, Trisha and I sighed about what might happen next. When the guy came over, he knelt down by Trisha's chair and quietly asked, "Are you that Sabrina girl?" My sister's vinegary tongue shot him a *no*, and the boy went back to his friends. "I told you it wasn't her!" he shouted. Trisha and I just looked at each other and cracked up. The boy didn't even look at me.

I've wondered what might happen to my career if I tried to get recognized by causing a hullabaloo in the press. Would I land sexier movie roles? Get comped courtside seats at a Lakers game? Look what happened when Kim Kardashian "got caught" making a sex tape; she's the highest-paid reality star on TV. Or when Charlie Sheen went berserk and mouthed off to his boss and network head; he became a Twitter phenom with a Comedy Central roast and a new show. Sometimes I think about checking myself into rehab for exhaustion just to see what happens. I could use a nap . . .

I got a little excited when I thought life handed me the opportunity to make a scene once as I was going through security
at LAX. I was shooting the second season of *Melissa & Joey* but
headed home for Valentine's Day weekend, and my gift to Mark
was a sex toy I'd bought at the Pleasure Chest in West Hollywood. It was a tiny pink silicone butterfly. The woman in the
store said that when the battery-operated antennae and wings
vibrated, it . . . well . . . use your imagination. I only packed a
carry-on bag, and though I thought the bullet shape might raise
some red flags with the TSA officials if they saw it, I wasn't too
concerned. If things got hairy, I could tell them it was a bath toy
for my kids.

A young security guy, no older than twenty-five, took one
look at my bag going slo-mo through the X-ray monitor and
asked if he could search it. I watched him root through my personal belongings. He pulled out my sweater, then my tooth-
brush, and finally the small black satin sack that I thought would
somehow shield my magic butterfly from prying eyes. Before he
could ask me what it was, I nearly fed him his line with a spoon.

"Is that what set it off?" I asked.

"No, why? What is it?"

I blushed as crimson as one of Mark's Alabama T-shirts.
What would Lindsay do?

"It's my vibrator!" I told him, maybe a little too loudly.

I decided to own it, rather than make a scene. I wasn't wearing lipstick or fake lashes, and I didn't want my only Radar Online scandal to be about a frazzled-looking mug shot. I looked
the TSA guy square in the eyes, as if to proudly say, *You bet that's
my vibrator. Now if you'll excuse me, I'm going to take that puppy
home and have mind-blowing sex with my rock star husband.*

The man dropped the black bag as if it were a hot potato and
explained that it was not my vibrator that had caused a buzz but

actually a box of business cards buried under my pajamas. *Womp womp.* If I'd played this right, the interaction could have ended up on TMZ or in the *New York Post.* It might have revamped my Pollyanna image, led to an offbeat new sitcom, and then, Mario Batali openings, here I come. But the man didn't even try to make a quick buck by telling this story to *The National Enquirer.* I'd like to think he was a closet *Sabrina* fan trying to protect me from the ruthless tabloids, but I suspect he just didn't care enough to call the reporters.

My own kids barely demonstrate an interest in what I do or who I am, besides being their mother—and yes, I know this is supposed to be a good thing. But I've shown them episodes of *Sabrina,* coaxing them to watch by offering up magic and a talking cat, and they only lasted six minutes and never turned it on again. Mason did pick up a line he found funny—"Mr. Pool is so annoying"—but it stopped being cute after the 135th time he said it. I try not to take it personally since the boys see their friends and plenty of non-actors making iPhone videos and posting them on YouTube the way I used to put stickers in a book. And I know they know what I do, because when we were walking down the beach in Lake Tahoe, a couple stopped me to say, "You know you look just like Sabrina?" I didn't want to pause for an awkward song-and-dance, so I said, "I hear it every day." A moment later, they whispered, "She does look like Melissa Joan Hart." That's when Mason surprised us all. "She *is* Melissa Joan Hart!" he shouted. I'd never used my professional name in front of him, and I thought he assumed that we all shared Mark's last name.

The next spring, Mason graduated kindergarten and had just learned about what it meant to pursue a dream. He told me I was lucky to live mine of being an actor. I thought this was sweet, but confessed that at his age, my fantasy was to become a trapeze artist. I wanted Mason to learn that dreams change, and it's okay to change with them. Since then, he's randomly surprised me with questions like, "Mommy, what's it like to be you?" I was tempted to tell him how it felt to be stressed by a demanding job, scrutinized by the press, and deemed a failure in the kitchen. But I didn't. "I feel very loved," I said and then kissed him and his brothers. I was talking about being a mom.

Truth be told, I've worked my whole life in the entertainment world, but it was never about being famous. I simply want to leave behind a legacy, if just for my family to talk about when I'm gone. Otherwise, I'm happy wearing lots of hats. I get to be a celebrity and everyday Jane, working woman and busy mom, cosmopolitan gal and suburbanite, wife and friend. Here's hoping my best attempts to juggle workouts, picnics, script readings, Bible studies, press opportunities, baseball practice, movie premieres, and Saturday football games gives me and my family the balance we need to thrive. I obviously like when people know my name and recognize my face, but I'm just as happy being known as a PTA mom with clever fund-raising ideas.

When Mark's on the computer, the kids are in bed, and I'm left alone with my thoughts and a bowl of Pop Chips, I realize how grateful I am for the attention I get when I tell a funny story or throw over-the-top parties. I don't need to strut down a red carpet with flashbulbs popping in my face only to hear Joan Rivers tear apart a dress that once made me feel so special. I'd much rather host a bake sale and ignore those who think you have to be messed up to succeed in this world. To them I say, have a cookie.

ACKNOWLEDGMENTS

There are some very special people that I need to thank for guiding my life, my values, my career, and this book.

To Mark: I could not have dreamed up a better partner for life. You are all that I could want and more than I ever knew was possible. Mason, Brady, and Tuck, you are my little angels! I treasure each of you more than you will ever know.

To my mother, Paula, who has shaped the person I have become and always stood by my side. My father, Billy, who may not have been around as much as we both would've liked when I was young, but who has become a great friend. Trisha, my best friend from the beginning and throughout this life—my "frozen" twin! Liz, who is always full of surprises and has given our family two beautiful boys, Chris and Jonny, who bring joy to all our lives. Brian, my favorite brother! I am so proud of the man you have become. Emily, my sweet and sassy baby sis who likes to keep things interesting. You have a special place in my Hart. Ali, Sammy, and Mackenzie—I've taken great pride in watching you grow into women. My family-in-love, Jen, Walt, Sally, Holly, Girod, Hayes, and Pierson. Thank you for opening your arms to me and being a source of love in my life. Aunt Susan and Uncle Mark, I miss the joy you both brought to my life. Nanny and Papa, who gave me the travel bug and taught me so much—from how to juice an orange to the proper gift-wrapping technique. I will never forget you, and I will always make sure there is French silk pie at holiday meals. Grandma Hart, while I didn't get to know you very well, you are a big part of my strength. I promise to always represent our family in the best way possible.

To my dear friend Spizz, I have never missed anyone the way I miss having you in my life. Just being near you made me feel at home, safe, and always kept me laughing. "I have everything!!!"

Thank you to my sweet, dear, and forever friends: Elena and Kellie, who are always there with sensible advice to help me pick a direction when the road forks. Kimi, Eryn, Kerry, Nicole, and Jessie, who have helped make my laugh lines a little deeper. Soleil, for leading me down many great paths and being such a big part of my life through our twenties. Michele, you have been like the big sister I could only dream of having, from your weekly check-ins to taking my kids for sleepovers when I need a break—you are a treasure. Thank you to you and David for always looking out for me and being the best role models a girl could ask for. To my cult jammers Amie, Line, Marlo, Mackenzie, Lisa, and Lisa, who all suffered through lunches and workouts without me as I whittled away at this book.

To Kristina Grish, for all your hard work and endless hours to make this book a success. From cookies to Deuteronomy, and all the conversations in between, thank you! To my lit agents, Alyssa Reuben and Laura Nolan, for helping make this project a reality and making great use of my time during my third pregnancy. And to my editor, Michelle Richter, and the St. Martin's

Press PR team, for believing in this book from the start and guiding me along the way.

To team MJH: My former agent/current lawyer, David Tenzer, for two decades of fighting on my behalf. My agents, Chris Schmidt, Jim Dempsey, Kathleen Trinh, Debbee Klein, and everyone at Paradigm, for guiding my career. My manager, Gordon Gilbertson, I look forward to a busy future. To Evan Bell, Liza Deleon, Melissa Pagano, and everyone at Bell and Company, for protecting my investments and steering me away from bad decisions. To my publicist, Marla Farrell, for helping me learn how to say no when appropriate.

I also want to thank the most inspiring people in this industry who I have had the pleasure of knowing: Garry Marshall, Delia and Nora Ephron, Bill Murray, Michael Strahan, Gary Sinise, Calista Flockhart, Connie Britton, Paul Lee, Nicky Weinstock, Gerry Labourne, Herb Scannell, Paul Mason, Perry Simon, and a small handful of others. Your talent is immeasurable and your kindness radiates. Also, Mrs. Shirley Temple Black, you inspired my life from a very young age, and I thank you for being a role model that a little girl could proudly look up to.

Thank you also to the teachers who helped shape my life and my passions—especially Mrs. Tresham, Mr. Demas, Chuck Yeager, Roz Secor, and Miss Diane.

Thank you to every lovely person I have had the good fortune to work beside. I'm grateful for your support, compassion, creativity, guidance, and mostly the fact that you laugh at my silly jokes.

To all my fans who have grown up with me and stood by me during my many career phases, I thank you for giving me a platform, a voice, and a bright future.

And finally, I would like to thank God our Father for all the blessings and guidance He's given me in my life.

After putting together the pieces of my life in this book, I realize that there is one running theme: I've always chosen to surround myself with good people—strong, honest, and beautiful souls. Thank you to every one of you who has helped shape a piece of my life, be it small or large, good or bad, then or now. Thank you for the journey.

INDEX